JOHN HANSON WALKER

JOHN HANSON WALKER

THE LIFE AND TIMES OF A VICTORIAN ARTIST

BELINDA MORSE

ALAN SUTTON
1987

Alan Sutton Publishing
Brunswick Road Gloucester

First published 1987

British Library Cataloguing in Publication Data

Morse, Belinda
John Hanson Walker.
1. Walker, John Hanson — Criticism and interpretation
I. Title
759.2 ND497.W2/

ISBN 0-86299-354-7

FI/115/1140-1008/R/230387/1030

Cover Plate: The Bubble Company: Reproduced by courtesy of Dai-Ichi Securities Limited, Tokyo.

Typesetting and origination by
Alan Sutton Publishing Limited
Printed in Great Britain

CONTENTS

LIST OF ILLUSTRATIONS

COLOUR PLATES

BLACK AND WHITE

Dedicated to my husband
Jeremy, for his help
and loving support, and to his
cousin, Mary Whiteley,
who taught me the ropes
and corrected the
manuscript.

FOREWORD

The great tradition of academic art has been carried on from generation to generation largely through the atelier or studio system. Ingres, Gerome, Bougereau, in France, were the product of the system by which students worked beside the master learning stage by stage the techniques and confidence which would enable their imaginations to range freely when they matured.

In England the system never worked as comprehensively as it did in France. Sir Joshua Reynolds certainly gathered about him a school of followers, but in the nineteenth century one looks in vain for the sophisticated organisations of the atelier world. If there is one artist of whom it might have been expected, it would be Frederic Leighton. He represents in British artistic history the acme of idealised classical art. Yet, though he taught in the Academy schools, Leighton can only really be said to have had one pupil; John Hanson Walker.

Leighton recognised in Walker the enthusiasm of the dedicated artist. Even when it was necessary to remind the young painter of his limitations, Leighton advised him with warmth and affection. The bond between the two artists was strong. In this one recognises Leighton's singular nobility and kindness.

A study of Walker's life is a valuable addition to our knowledge of the nineteenth-century art world. It casts light on greater figures like Leighton, but reminds one also of the teeming vitality of the studios in London a century ago: when painting was still the primary means of visual communication barriers were erected annually in front of the picture of the year at the Academy show. The catalogues of the Summer Exhibitions attest the number of lesser painters who added to the vast output of Victorian art. Walker, as the pupil and friend of Leighton, has a special importance among these artists.

Belinda Morse's study ranges widely over the artistic and biographical background of Walker's world. His American exploit shows the determination and originality which first recommended him to Leighton. Even when in later years his own career as a painter faltered he was firm in his principles: writing to Mrs. Barrington, Leighton's biographer, disparaging the modern school of slipshod painters, who in his view had never learned their craft. He shared with his old master a love of children, and the image of him in his last years, bearded like a prophet, painting for the children of his neighbours oil sketches of the gifts of fruit and flowers they brought him, is a happy one. While not perhaps an eminent Victorian, he clearly allied in his personality many of the qualities that make the age so fascinating and distinguished for us today.

STEPHEN JONES
Curator of Leighton House

INTRODUCTION

As a child I lived with portraits by John Hanson Walker hanging on our walls and never knew much about them, or about my great-grandfather who had painted them, except that he had been much helped by Leighton. When my father died he left me the portrait Walker had painted of him and his brother Jack as young boys in frilly shirts and blue velvet trousers. When our third son grew to be the same age he was so like the uncle we had never known, that I realised great-grandfather must have had an exceptional facility for catching a likeness!

My curiosity was awakened and, because it had always been said that great-grandfather had made money painting in America, a country I was fortunate enough to visit from time to time, I decided to find out what he had painted there. It soon became obvious that I must find out first, however, what work he had done in England! The search started with my knowing the whereabouts of a handful of his portraits, but now, as a result of much delving, about a third of his works have been traced. The hunt has been full of adventure, and luck has often been on my side in the most fortunate and enthralling way.

The deepest thanks are due to Mary Whiteley; knowing that I was a complete beginner she took me to the Courtauld Institute and showed me how to begin, and has continued to help ever since. I would also like to thank Stephen Jones, Curator of Leighton House, for the time he has generously given me. To my amazement on my first visit there he told me that by coincidence his mother had lived next door to Walker as a small girl, and that he himself now owned a small painting of apples that great-grandfather had given her! It was at Leighton House that I first read Mrs. Russell Barrington's biography of Leighton in which she quotes from many letters that Leighton wrote to Walker. I would like to thank my cousins Pamela Smith and James Stansfeld who now own these letters for allowing me to see and use them. Leonée and Richard Ormond, whose biography of Leighton has been constantly at my side have been generous with help, as has also Robert Stewart of the National Portrait Gallery in Washington, who suggested that I write a biography rather than just catalogue the work. I would like to thank many people in America, who went to untold trouble on my behalf, and wrote wonderful letters full of help. I would like particularly to express my gratitude to Carrie Rebora, of the National Academy of Design, New York, without whose help I should have discovered very little in the United States: she gave her time in research quite freely, despite the fact that I was a total stranger.

Libraries have been much used, and I would like to say a very heartfelt thank you to all the librarians – especially to those in my own local library in the Old Brompton Road branch of the Chelsea and Kensington library, who have supplied books with the greatest care and courtesy. Miss Sarah Wimbush, of the National Portrait Gallery library was particularly helpful and encouraging, and her support was especially welcome to an amateur. I would also like to thank Christie's for courteously allowing me to use their Muniment Room.

Friends and family have been immensely kind in delving into attics for paintings and into their minds for facts, and an especial thank you is due to all who brought their paintings to Leighton House to be seen and photographed. In this context I should like to extend my most sincere thanks to John Rogers, the Borough Photographer, who took superb photographs while surrounded by a crowd of people who tended to jump on the floorboards just as he was about to take the shots!

Finally I would like to thank my children for putting up with an abstracted mother, and my husband who did much of the work on the family history and who encouraged and supported me throughout in a wonderful way, and never complained when writing took priority over cooking! I hope this short work will encourage others to write about talented members of their own families while their memory is still alive.

Belinda Morse.

CHAPTER ONE

THE FORMATIVE YEARS

Queen Victoria had been on the throne for seven years when John Hanson Walker was born to two of her humbler subjects. John's parents, Robert Walker and Sarah Hanson were married at St. Dunstan's, the parish church of Stepney, in the east end of London, on December 1st 1843. Neither set of parents were present; the only relative to sign the register in the large medieval church was a Mary Walker. At the time of the wedding Robert was twenty-five, and Sarah thirty. Robert had come up to London for the ceremony from the small riverside village of Sunbury-on-Thames, where he was employed as a servant. His family lived on the Isle of Wight, where he had been born the second son of James Walker, sailor of Shorwell, and his wife, Jane Jolliffe of neighbouring Brighstone. Any education or refinement Robert possessed probably came from his mother's side of the family, for the numerous Jolliffes on the island had been there since 1415, and were descended from the 'Golaffres' family, who had originally come to England in the train of William the Conqueror. A family legend believed James Walker to have been (like so many on the island) a privateer, and Jane a well-born and rich Jolliffe whom he had charmed away from her family: an apocryphal tale attributed to George du Maurier, later re-told by his grand-daughter Daphne du Maurier in her book *Frenchman's Creek.* In reality Jane Jolliffe's family lived in an attractive small yeoman farmhouse, 'Willes', which is in Brighstone, a large village near the coast on the far side of the island.

Sarah's employment at the time of her marriage is not known: perhaps she, too, was in domestic service. Her father was the village baker and innkeeper in the small mining village of Oakthorpe, perched on a hill in what was then Derbyshire (now Leicestershire). Sarah's father William had married her mother, Ann Ison, when she was a widow living at neighbouring Ashby-de-la-Zouch, and Sarah and her sister Ann had both been baptized on the same day, September 24th, 1813. There was a belief, strongly held by John Hanson Walker, that his mother Sarah was really the daughter of the Duke of Devonshire, substituted at birth for a boy smuggled into the Devonshire household in order to secure the title. However, the Duke of Devonshire of

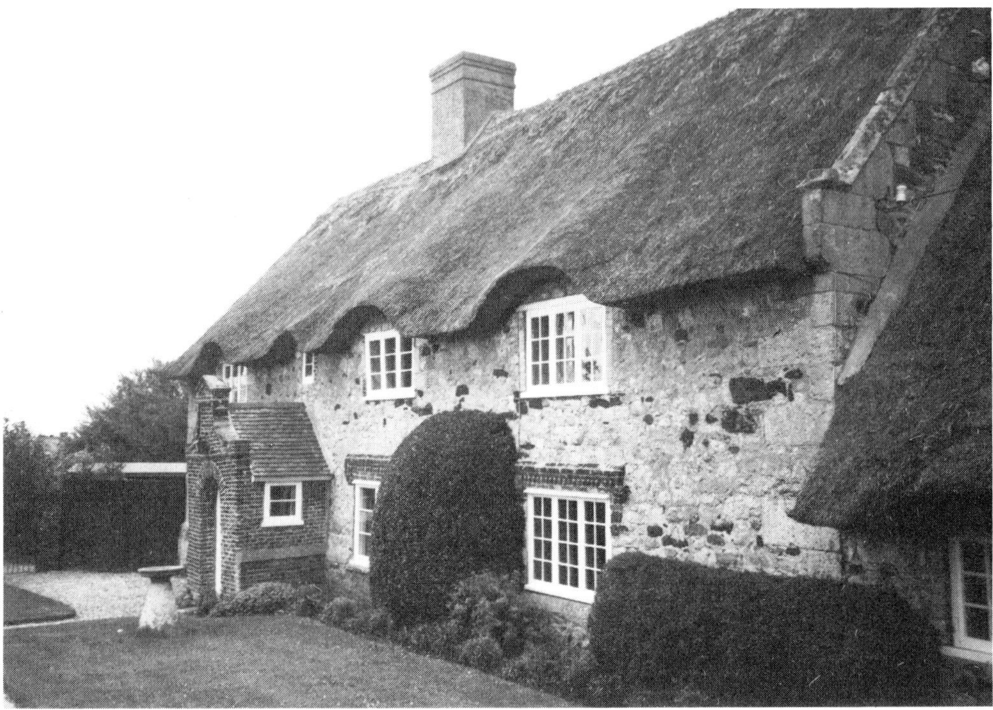

'Willes', Brighstone, Isle of Wight: the small yeoman farmhouse shared by the Jolliffes and the Walkers.

the day was a bachelor and the story may well be pure Victorian romanticism, although Walker's belief in it extended to passing it on in strictest confidence to each of his children on their coming of age.

Two months to the day after Robert and Sarah's marriage, their first son, John Hanson, was baptized at St. John's church in the neighbouring village of Donisthorpe. He may have been named after his mother's twenty-five year old brother, the John Hanson who was later wealthy enough to have a gravestone erected to the memory of his parents, William and Ann Hanson, although they themselves had died in poverty.

No trace can be found of Sarah and Robert Walker for six years after John's birth. There are clues indicating that they may have been employed at Ammerdown House, near Radstock, Bath by Colonel John Twyford Jolliffe, a bachelor. Ammerdown, built by Wyatt in 1789 and situated in a park commanding beautiful views over the Mendips, may have given Robert the incentive to paint, for he became a good landscape painter in the Dutch eighteenth century style, and with the knowledge of antiques which he was later to display. The Walkers appear in the 1851 Street Directory and Census

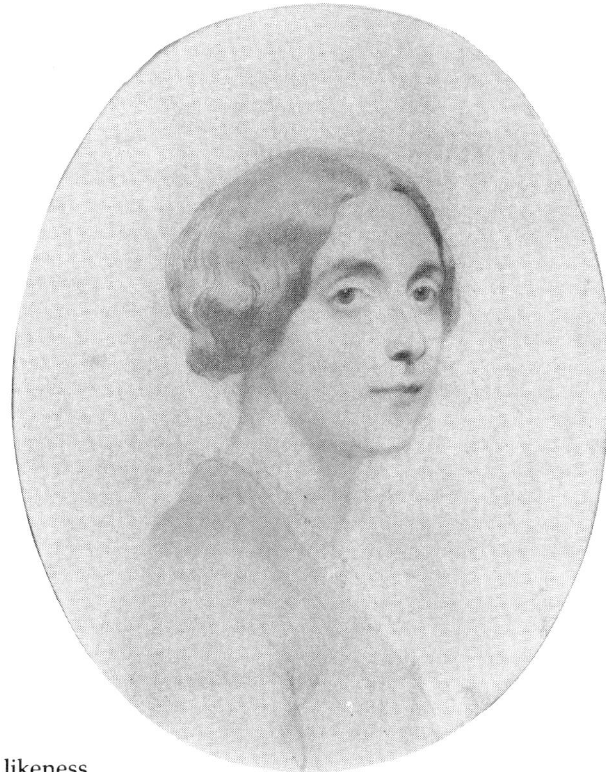

Sarah Walker: an early likeness

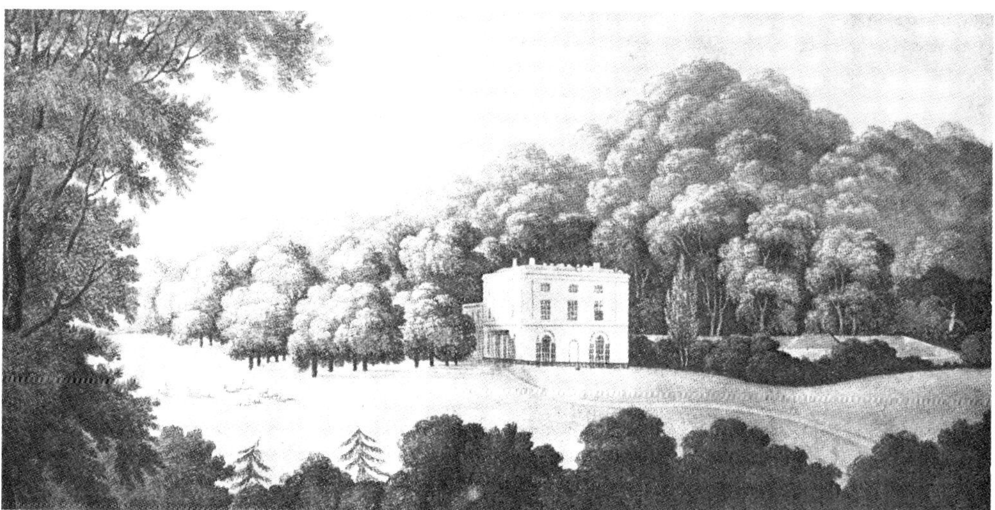

Ammerdown House, Radstock, Bath as it was in the 1830's when Robert, the artist's father, was reputed to have been a stable boy there.

for Bath as living at 7 Burlington Place: this street, up behind the Circus, is now called Julian Road. By this time the seven year old John was a scholar, and there was another son, James, who was eleven months old, and who had been born in Bath. Robert is listed as keeping a post office and stationery shop. Bath at that time still retained its eighteenth century elegance, although much of the fashionable world had deserted it for its new rival, Cheltenham.

Robert's business must have been brisk, for after three years he was able to give up the post office in favour of selling stationery and prints. Over the next seven years he ceased selling stationery and transformed the shop, so that in 1862 he advertised as purchasing for ready money 'Good old libraries, Missals, and early Manuscripts, engravings and Pictures, old China and Wedgewood Ware, Ancient Bronze, and carved Ivories, early works in

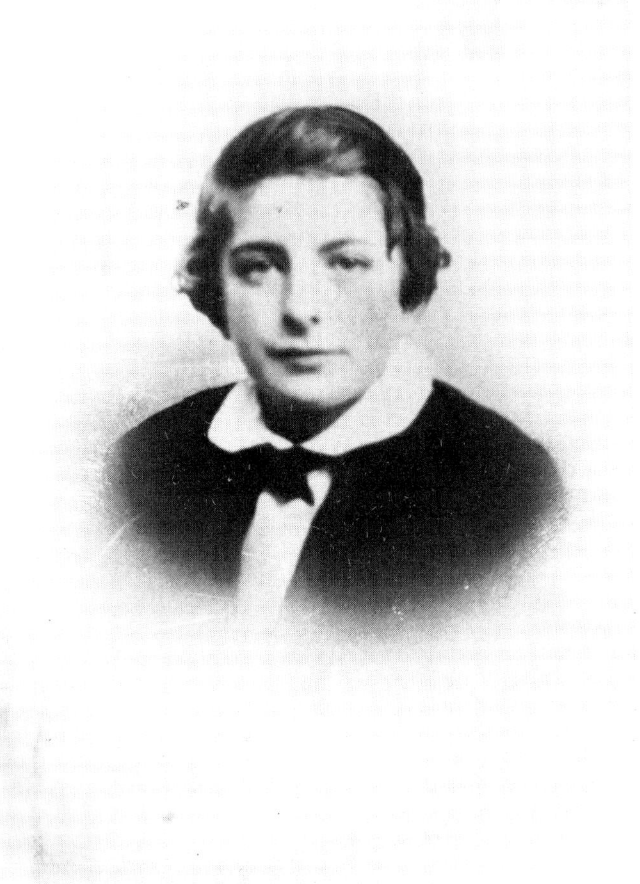

John Hanson Walker aged fifteen.

Enamel, Cabinets of Coins, and objects of Fine Art in general'. Besides this, Robert had had time to paint many charming small landscape paintings.

By the age of seventeen John Hanson Walker was acting as assistant to his father in the shop, while his brother James aged eleven was still a scholar. The family was completed by William, nine, and Mary Anne, aged six.

Although Bath was now deserted by the sort of society described by Jane Austen and Dickens, it was still a popular place for people of delicate health. Among those who moved to Bath for this reason were the Leighton family, who bought No. 9 The Circus in 1853, close to Walker's shop. Dr. Frederick Leighton had long ago given up his medical practice because of his deafness, and for the last thirteen years the family had lived in Frankfurt so that Mrs. Leighton could benefit from the climate there. In Frankfurt their son, Frederic,

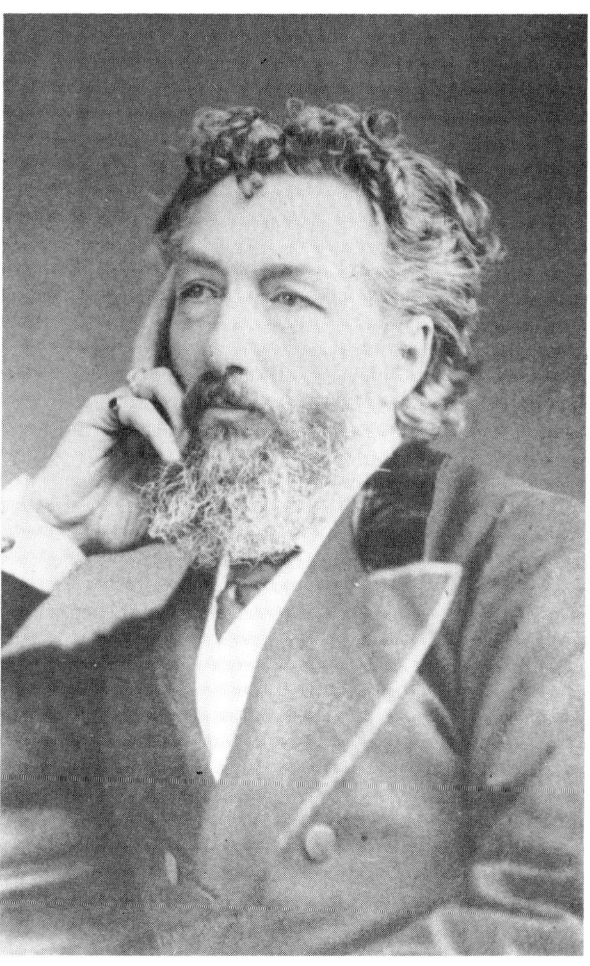

Leighton – *Carte de Visite* photograph 1869.

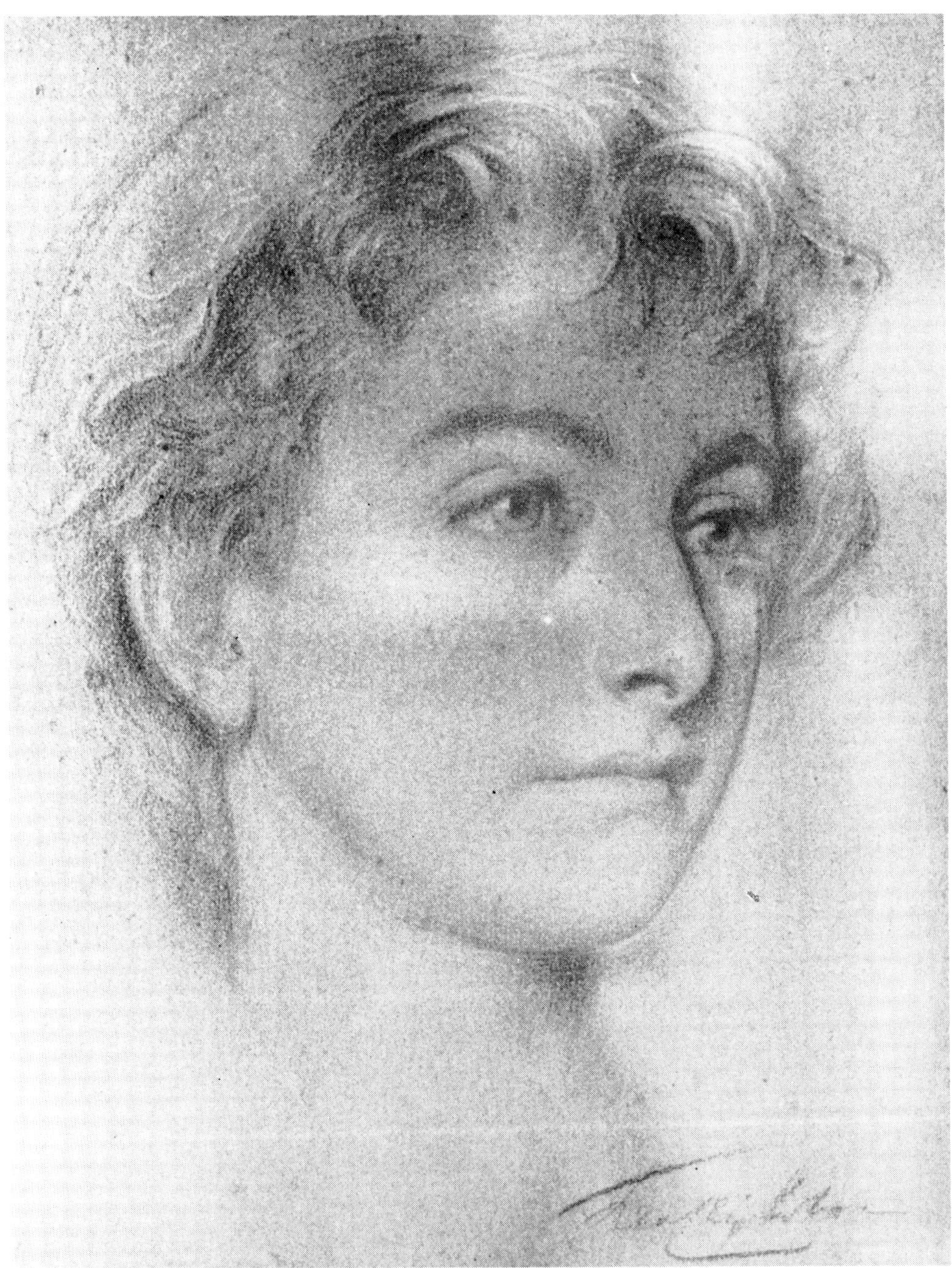

John Hanson Walker aged seventeen (Leighton drawing of 1861)

(who had already studied art in Berlin and Florence) had enrolled at the Städelsches Kunstinstitut, and had become the most admired and talented pupil of Edouard von Steinle, a leading member of the Nazarenes, a group of Germans who wished to replace the existing methods of art-teaching by something approaching the apprenticeship of medieval times. Many of them lived in Rome, housing themselves in a ruined monastery, calling themselves the 'Brotherhood of St. Luke'; 'Nazarene' was a nickname given to them because they were anxious to revive the medieval art of religious fresco painting. They anticipated the Pre-Raphaelites.

The year before his family left Frankfurt for Bath, Frederic Leighton moved to Italy to study in Rome, and had written in his diary, 'I really feel that I have taken the great step, that I have opened the introductory chapter of the second volume of my life, a volume on the title-page of which is written "ARTIST". He was right, for in 1855, three years after his arrival in Rome, he sent his first major painting, *Cimabue's 'Madonna' carried through the streets of Florence*, to the Royal Academy and it had the distinction of being bought by Queen Victoria herself on the first day for six hundred guineas!

It appears that Dr. Leighton was in the habit of walking up the steep hill from the Circus to view Robert Walker's 'antique prints and objects of vertu'. In the summer of his son Frederic's great success at the Royal Academy, he had somewhat autocratically summoned him back to England and Leighton had at once become a notable person in the London art world, making the personal acquaintance of Ruskin, Holman Hunt, Millais and Watts. It may have been during this summer that he accompanied his father for the first time to Walker's shop, and was deeply struck with the picturesque beauty of 'Johnny's' head.[1] Young 'Johnny' Walker (as Leighton always called him) was only eleven at the time, but already had an arresting mixture of good looks combined with intelligence.

During the following summers, when Leighton visited his family in Bath he continued his acquaintanceship with Johnny, and asked his father whether he might use him as a model. Fortunately Alice Corkran, Leighton's first biographer, gives first-hand accounts of this period, gleaned from Walker in 1904. Walker told her 'I was very eager to go. Leighton made the sittings enchanting; he whistled like a bird; he sang songs for me; he told me the most wonderful stories'.[2]

Johnny used to accompany Leighton to the country, and watched him painting the other children there. He was immensely popular with them. One small girl, Ann Boldwell, was allowed to sit on his knee as he painted and, unreproved, to dip her small fingers into his palette and wipe them on his coat and waistcoat. He was intensely fond of little children, and they responded keenly to his magnetic influence, and his drawings and paintings of children show the protecting, caressing tenderness he felt towards them.[3]

George Aitchison, (who was later to build Leighton House) describes Leighton, who was twenty-two in the year of his Academy triumph, as he was then: 'a light-haired, fresh coloured handsome dashing young fellow, with fine manners, who let the most brilliant as well as the wisest saying fall from his lips in his sprightly and animated conversation. In those days he was so gay and lighthearted that, when at friends' studios, he would often break off his conversation to sing a snatch of an Italian ballad or an air from an opera, and would sketch comic idylls on their canvasses.'[4] Although Leighton normally found his pleasure in mixing in sophisticated society, and in the friendship of well-educated people, he obviously found great relaxation playing for a week or two with the simple country children of the Bath area.

John Hanson Walker told Alice Corkran how sad it was for him when Leighton went back to Italy. Before leaving, Leighton had elicited from him the fact that it was his ambition to be a painter too. Leighton had spoken to him both of the difficulty of art and of the splendour of it. 'One day', said Walker, 'I remember it so well, a big crate came to the door, addressed to me. I could not think what it was and from whom it came. But when it was opened the mystery was cleared up. There were all the treasures I longed for; plaster casts of heads, hands and feet. There were drawing paper and drawing boards, pencils and chalk, everything a boy could want whose longing was to be an artist. It all came from Leighton, who had carried in his mind my wish to be a painter'.[5]

Leighton finally came back to London for good in 1860, and moved into a studio at Orme Square, just north of the Park. On his visits to Bath in 1860 and 1861 Leighton had made several studies of Walker's head. There has been considerable debate about how much he drew on these for his painting *Lieder ohne Worte*, which he probably began in the second half of 1860 and which was the most important of his Academy exhibits in 1861. *Lieder ohne Worte* was painted for Leighton's stockbroker friend, James Stuart Hodgson, and now hangs in the Tate Gallery. The title of the painting, taken from Mendelssohn's *Songs without Words* is suggested by the fact that the young girl portrayed in it sits dreaming by an ornamental fountain. She seems to be beguiled by the sound of the falling stream of water from it, which fills her pitcher, and the singing of a bird which is perched above her.

Mrs. Russell Barrington, Leighton's close friend and biographer, published the Leighton House drawing of the sixteen year old Walker's head in her autobiography, and says that Leighton used it as a study for his *Lieder*, although probably in the end in a fairly minimal way. As Leighton himself wrote to his father, 'I remember, it is true, telling you before I began to paint, "Lieder ohne Worte" that I intended to make it *realistic* but the moment I began I felt the mistake, and made it professionally and pointedly the reverse'.[6]

In changing the sex Leighton has made the girl's face narrower and more feminine in outline, although he has kept the heaviness of the eyebrows and even accentuated them. The shape of the eyes and nose are very similar to Walker's, as is also the mouth. In the British Museum Study for *Lieder* (Prints

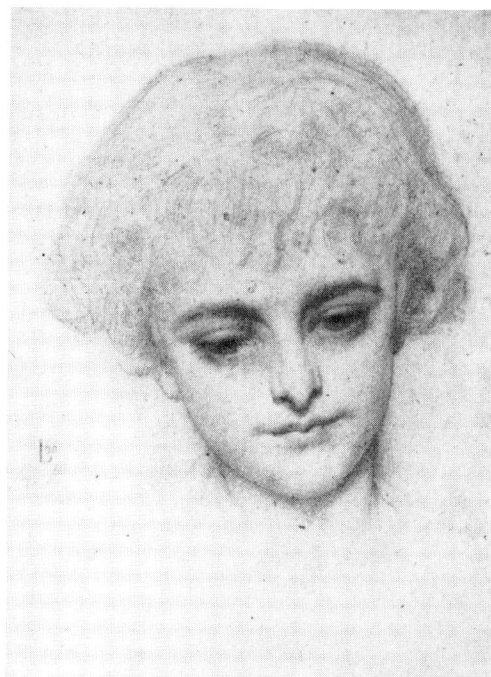

Studies for *Lieder Ohne Worte*:
Head of John Hanson Walker (Leighton House).
Hands: a Leighton Study (British Museum).

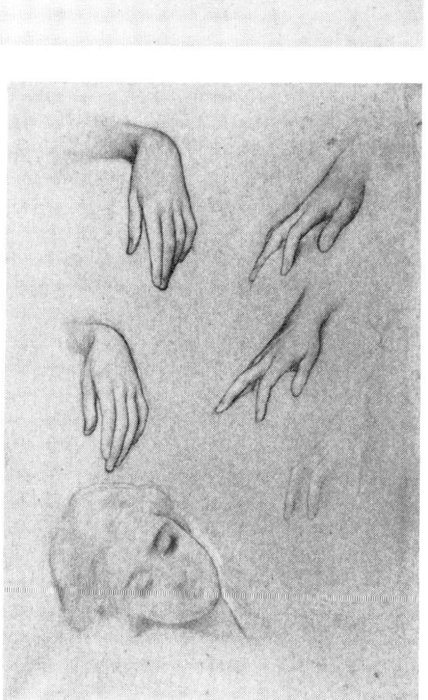

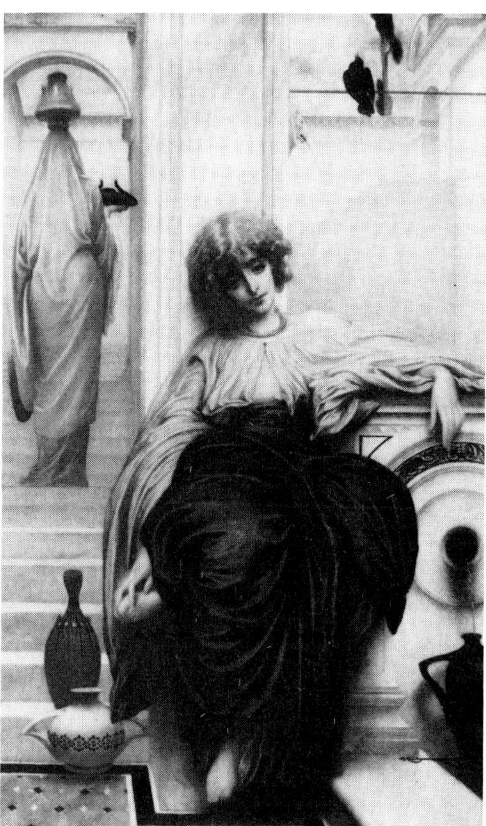

Lieder ohne Worte (Tate Gallery) exhibited by Leighton at the Royal Academy of 1861.

and Drawings, 1897:12:16) the face is very vaguely drawn, but the hands included in the study may well be Walker's hands. His were small and well-shaped, with filbert nails.

Another study of Walker's head (which now belongs to Commander Whitaker) was used as an illustration in Alice Corkran's biography of Leighton published in 1904. This study shows the same almond-shaped eyes and the ideal beauty which exactly fulfilled the type of features Leighton wanted in order to create his aesthetic effect.

In an article in the *National Review* of December 1896, Mrs. Russell Barrington says 'Lord Leighton first showed me some of his sketches more than thirty years ago when a friend took me to his studio in Orme Square. One sketch was of a boy's head with a heavy shock of curly hair from under which large almond-shaped eyes looked dreamily at you. As he held it up I

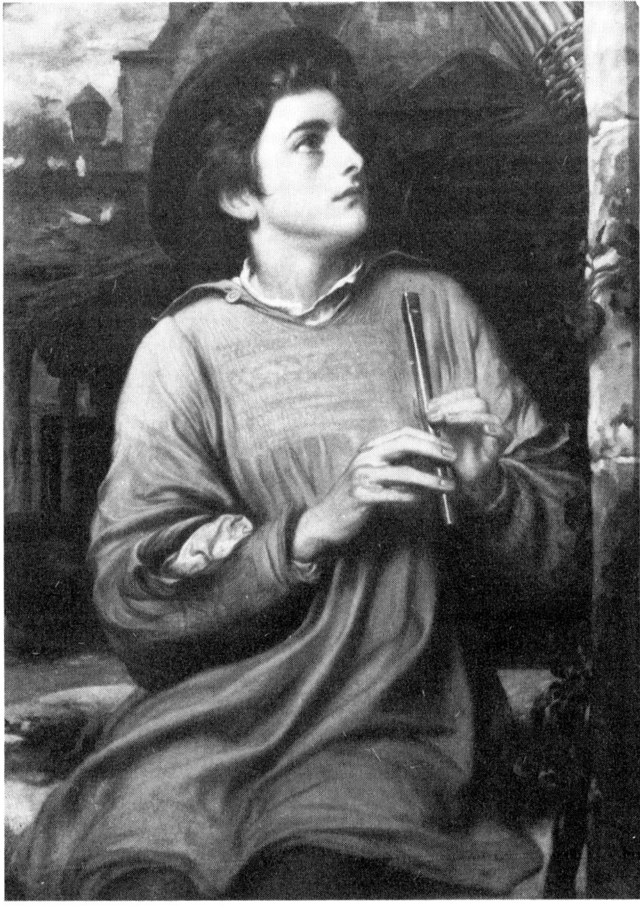

Duett: Leighton's 'Pot-boiler' of Walker (RA 1862) which was later bought by Queen Victoria for the Prince of Wales.

exclaimed "Lieder ohne Worte". This was the name of a picture by Leighton which I had seen and which had fascinated me when I was very young. I remember his quick look of surprise. . .'[7]

Leighton wrote to his mother 'I am very glad Gussy (his sister) liked the receding figure in "Lieder ohne Worte" as it was a favourite also with me, the tallness of the said figure was inseparable from the sentiment of it in my mind'. He went on to say that he would be coming to stay in Bath for three weeks at the beginning of September and, 'I have thoughts of painting a pot-boiler of little Walker if he is still handsome. I wish Papa would look after him, and let me know what he is doing and how he is looking.'[8] The answer was obviously encouraging, for in 1861 he painted two portraits of his young friend, *Duett* and *Rustic Music*. Both the portraits continue the theme of music: perhaps inspired by the fact that Johnny was a great whistler, both then and later in life as recorded by his grandchildren.

Duett shows John Hanson Walker as a shepherd boy, pipe in hand, about to play in concert with a blackbird. The background is a farm, while the shepherd boy is a surprisingly realistic study of Walker, as a contemporary

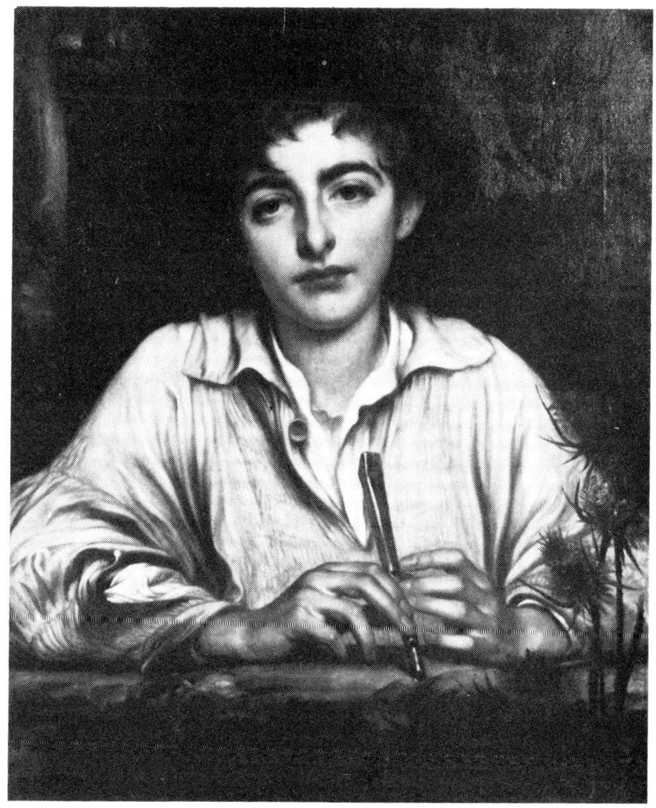

Rustic Music, 1861: the companion-piece to *Duett* Refused by the Royal Academy, it was re-discovered in an Indian Maharajah's collection.

photograph shows. *Duett* has much subtler colouring, and is a more sophisticated study than *Rustic Music*, but what it gains in charm it loses in the freer expression of the second painting.

Rustic Music is a larger painting than *Duett*. Again Walker is shown in a shepherd smock and hat, and holding the same whistle, which he rests this time on a wooden rail, against which he leans. To the right of the rail are painted beautiful thistles – very reminiscent of Leighton's study of thistles in the British Museum. It has been said that of the two pictures *Rustic Music* is the more revealing of Leighton's sources. 'It is clear that his early fascination with Florentine linearity, accentuated by his Nazarene training, has given way to a strongly Venetian response in colour and texture. From the same school Leighton has adopted the motif of the ledge on which the sitter leans. The picture, with its self conscious pastoral allusions, refers to the tradition of the fête champetre.'[9] Alice Corkran thought that both *Duett* and *Rustic Music* caught the personality of the sitter well, and were more freely handled than was usual with Leighton.

The frame that he found for the "large Johnny" as Leighton called *Rustic Music* pleased him. He wrote 'I found the frame for the "large Johnny" on my return. It improves the picture very much, and looks very handsome'.

Both paintings were sent, together with six others, for exhibition at the 1862 Royal Academy: *Duett* was accepted, but *Rustic Music* refused. To his mother Leighton wrote 'I have deferred answering your letter till now, that I might be able to inform you definitely of my fate as regards the Royal Academy. I have just been there; I must tell you at once the least pleasant of my news – they have rejected the large "Johnny" and "Lord Cowper". On the other hand, the other pictures are well hung . . . the small "Johnny" just below the line. I am sorry about the large "Johnny" because my chance of selling it is much diminished'.[10]

To his father he wrote 'You will be glad to hear that I have received congratulations on all sides; that two of my pictures should not have been accepted does not indeed surprise me, and least of all would it do so if they were rejected on the score of *number* but I have reason to suspect that they were not *liked*; in fact I know it'.[11] Leighton faced strong opposition from the Royal Academy during his first years back in England, because he had been trained abroad and painted in an alien style: he did not become an Academician until nine years after his initial triumph in 1855.

In 1863 Leighton sent *Duett* to the United States for exhibition, and in 1868 it was bought by Queen Victoria for the Prince of Wales and it is still in the Royal Collection. For many years *Rustic Music* remained untraced, but it was found by Leonée and Richard Ormond, Leighton's biographers, when it came up for sale from the collection of the Nawab of Nawanger. It was acquired in August 1984 for Leighton House, where it now hangs.

For John Hanson Walker, sitting for the two 'Johnnies' must have had its tedious moments, for Leighton wrote to his sister Gussy 'I am glad for the poor lad that the corvée of sitting is over; he was dying to get back to his work. If zeal and enthusiasm can make an artist, he ought to become one. . .'[12] It was probably at this time that Johnny, inspired and encouraged by Leighton to be an artist himself, had started to learn drawing at the Bath School of Art. During the time he sat for Leighton, he had brought him his own drawings, which Leighton had corrected. 'Leighton', he told Alice Corkran, 'made me come to his studio and work under him'.[13]

There has naturally been speculation about the nature of the relationship between Leighton and Johnny, and as to what drew Leighton, ten years his senior, to this good-looking but simple country boy. The many letters which Leighton was to write Johnny over the next few years show a fatherly attitude towards him, indicating that he filled the role of the son he would have wanted had he married. He does not seem to have supplied any more complicated an emotional need. Throughout his life Leighton suffered from creative depression, being unable to obtain the ideal that was always before him. In the young of both sexes he felt nearer to that ideal and he doubtless found John Hanson Walker's intelligent sympathy and youthful enthusiasm heart-warming. Johnny himself was affectionate, susceptible, and gifted with the art of friendship.

Leighton's mother was saddened that he did not marry. When he had reached thirty, he wrote to her 'About marrying, Mama you must remember that it takes two to play at that game. I would not insult a girl I did not love by asking her to tie her existence to mine, and I have not yet found one that I felt the slightest wish to marry; it is no doubt ludicrous to place this ideal so high, but it is not my fault – characteristically I should like to be married very well'.[14]

As Leighton returned to England for only a brief period in the summer when he was studying abroad, he can have had few friends of his own age with whom he had kept in touch, and he therefore treated Johnny in a more intimate and confidential manner than that which usually exists between an artist and his model: a friendship was thus established which was to last until the end of Leighton's life.

CHAPTER TWO

ART SCHOOL

Having learnt drawing at the School of Art in Bath, Walker progressed well enough to be enrolled at Leighton's suggestion and with his help at the Heatherley School of Art in London, at 79 Newman Street, just off Oxford Street. This was an area in which many artists lodged, including George du Maurier, who was living next door to the school when Walker began studying there.

The thirty-seven year old Thomas Heatherley was, by all accounts, an ideal art master, and lived only for his school. His pupils took to him at once. He had a high forehead, a straight nose, deep-set eyes, and hollow cheeks; his long lank hair and beard were almost colourless, like his complexion. His voice was quiet. Mild, benevolent and gifted with patience, he ruled his little kingdom well. He inspired respect and affection despite the faint sarcasm with which he taught. His gentle manners put his students in mind of Christ.

The Heatherley was one of the schools which prepared students for the Royal Academy, and had Elementary, Antique and Life Schools. Pupils could attend for as many days a week as they liked, and for any length of time. The school had been built over the garden of the house, and casts from the antique were ranged round the room, among them the death mask of Sir Thomas Lawrence, whose few remaining whiskers fascinated the students. The dressed models (the school had a valuable collection of costumes) sat at one end of the room, while at the other end the nude models posed behind the screen and curtains.

Mr. Heatherley used to pace up and down the school clad in a long black velvet gown and slippers, humming softly to himself as he went. He would often have difficulty in trying to convince a pupil that he was right and they were wrong over a detail of their drawing: but the sharpest thing he ever said to them was 'You see how strong is our confidence in our own infallibility'. When not instructing, he would work on his own canvas, *Laban and his daughters*, which never seemed to be completed![15] Samuel Butler, the writer and painter who was an adult student at Heatherley's in the 1860's depicts his master in his *Mr. Heatherley's Holiday* repairing the school skeleton: a job he

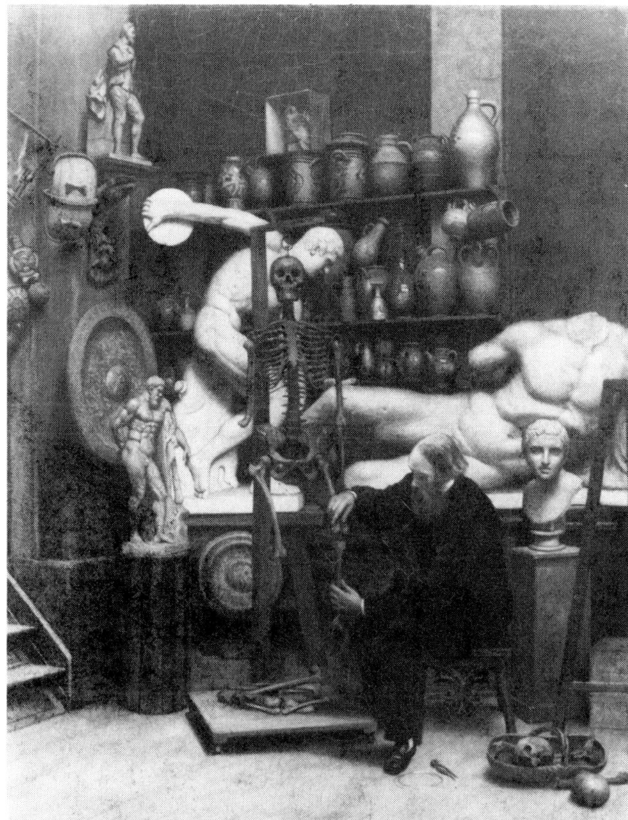

Mr. Heatherley's Holiday, 1874. Samuel Butler, the novelist and painter, who attended Mr. Heatherley's school, depicts Mr. Heatherley mending the school skeleton.

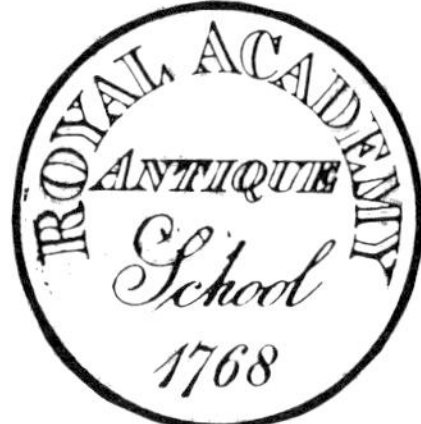

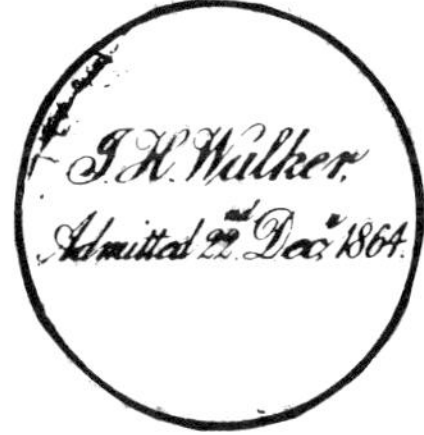

The Royal Academy School 'bone'.

often had to do, as it was the students' habit to dress it up and dance with it!

Frith (who had such a triumph with his *Derby Day* in 1858) had attended Sass's school, Heatherley's rival, and gives a graphic account of the grinding training there in his amusing *Autobiography*. 'Sass's course of study was very severe . . . the master had prepared with his own hand a great number of outlines from the antique, beginning with Juno's eye and ending with an Apollo. The young student was compelled to copy outlines that seemed numberless; some ordered to be repeated again and again, until Mr. Sass could be induced to give the long-desired 'Bene' at the bottom of them. When a pupil was considered advanced enough he was allowed to study the mysteries of light and shade from a huge white plaster ball, standing on a pedestal. Then came a gigantic bunch of plaster grapes, intended to teach differences of tone . . . after which permission was given for an attempt at a fragment from the antique in the form of a hand'.[16]

While at Heatherley's Walker lodged with Mary Ann Green, a young

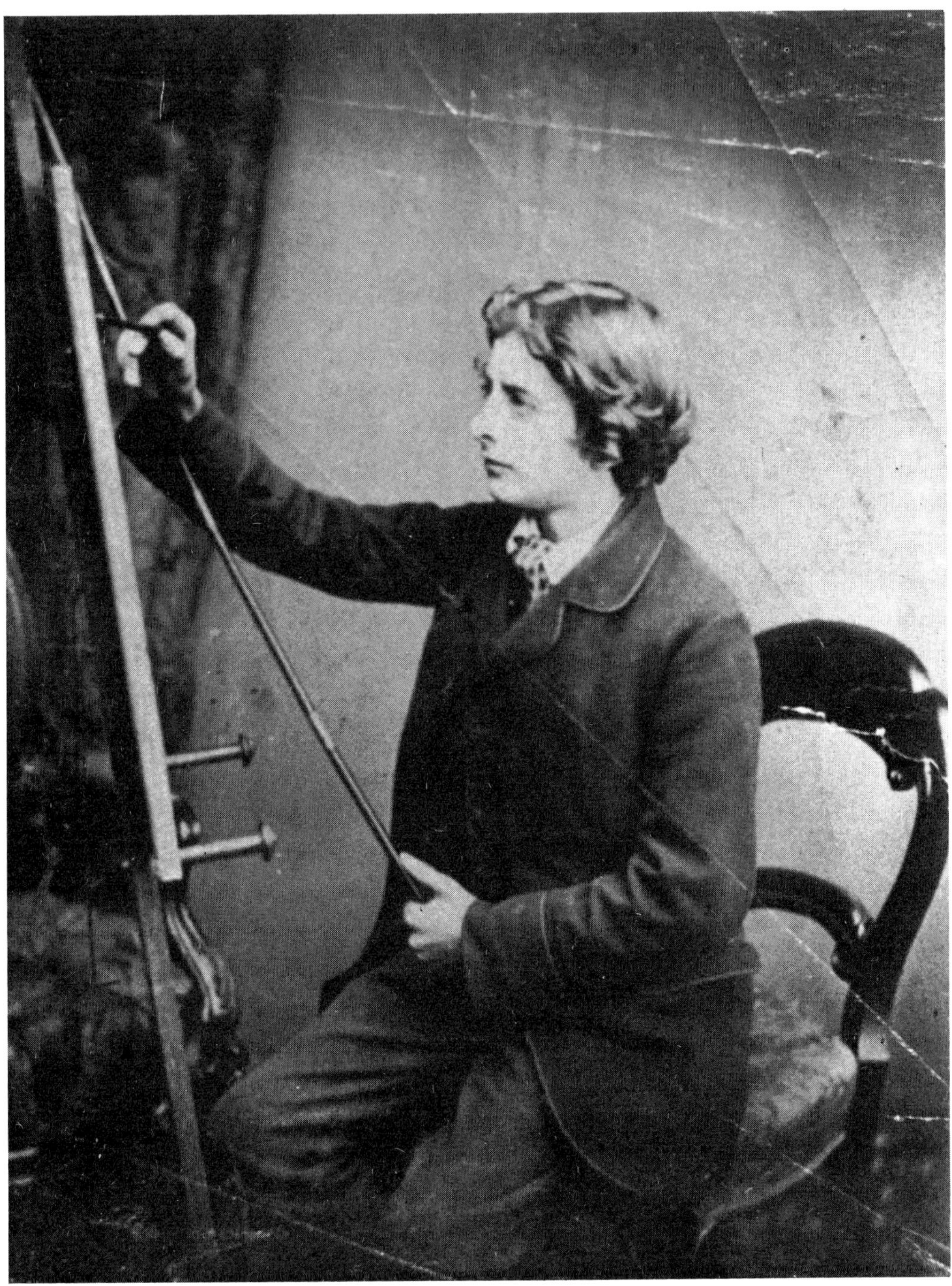

John Hanson Walker at his easel, *circa* 1864.

widowed cheesemonger, at 43 Beaumont Street. This was near the school, and not far from Leighton, at Orme Square. Leighton was living in comparative poverty, for his father had limited his allowance to £250 a year. He continued, however, to support Johnny by finding him commissions, and arranging for him to copy paintings. His help was most delicately given. He wrote 'Dear Johnny, supposing a *proper* price were given would you care to copy (for a man of position) a portrait by William Beechey and one or two by Sir Thomas Lawrence? I am not asking you to do it for a moment – I only want to know whether you would *care* to do the work – if so please let me know what you would ask. Yours sincerely, Fred Leighton'.[17]

In the spring of 1864 it was decided that Johnny should apply for admission to the Academy school, and Leighton allowed him to work in his studio on the drawing he had to submit. This had to be a finished drawing in chalk, about two feet high, of an undraped Antique statue, showing that he was able to draw and was acquainted with anatomy. Entry to the school was very competitive as tuition was free, and in the previous year only 43 of the 70 candidates who had applied for probationership had been successful. Luckily Johnny proved to be one of the successful ones!

Once a probationer, Walker had three months to prepare, in the Academy building itself, three further drawings, of a cast, a skeleton and an anatomical figure with all the bones, muscles and tendons indicated. Finally, on December 22, 1864 he was formally admitted to the Antique School and given his ivory admittance ticket, or 'bone' with the date of his entrance on it. His name is registered in the students' register immediately after that of the fifteen year old Theodore Wirgman, who was to become a successful portraitist, and one of his close friends. Each student enrolled faced a seven year course of study.

Leighton wrote a letter of congratulation: 'My dear Johnny, One line in a great hurry to say that I am delighted to hear that you have got in to the life school at the Royal Academy, and to thank you for the photo, which is capital. (This was probably the photograph of him sitting at his easel). I have not touched my Venus since you went away (his *Venus Disrobing*). I have been a good deal out of town myself and have spent most of my time in painting two large decorative figures which have now gone home. I am sorry you did not see them. Come as soon as you can to begin Mr. Greville's picture. Yours in haste and sincerely, Fred Leighton'.[18]

Henry Greville was one of Leighton's closest friends, although he was thirty years older than Leighton. He had retired at a young age from the Diplomatic service and had become Private Secretary to his brother-in-law, Lord Francis Egerton, (later the Marquess of Ellesmere). He also added to his modest income by acting as a gentleman usher at Court. Before Leighton came to live permanently in London he would stay with Henry Greville. They shared the same love of music and art. Greville, who never married (he was thought to have other leanings) moved in the highest society, and his diaries show how he went from one great house to another, joining in house parties with all the noblest aristocratic families.[19]

Johnny completed several commissions for Henry Greville and many of the letters Leighton wrote to him, (unfortunately rarely dated) concern them. For instance he wrote: 'Mr. Greville wants to know if you can think of any good picture – (Sir Joshua or Gainsborough would be best) that would make a good companion to the one he has already bought of you. If you could suggest something suitable, he would give you the commission'. Leighton then adds a warning note – 'I am very glad you should have encouragement but I trust you will not flag in your zeal about more important studies'.[20]

Walker's first term at the Academy would have started at the beginning of January 1865. At this time the Royal Academy and its schools shared the National Gallery's premises in Trafalgar Square. Students entered from a door at the east end of the front and made their way up to the Antique School, a handsome room in the Greek style, but where space was so much at a premium that the casts from which they drew overflowed into the hall outside. These casts (which are still used today) included the limbs and torso of Thurtell the murderer (nicknamed 'Gigman' by Carlyle, because he kept a gig) and 'Smugglerius', an eighteenth century cast by Carlini of a smuggler who had been flayed, and his bones then set by the famous Dr. William Hunter. In the summer their classrooms had to be vacated for the annual exhibition, and they were taught instead in the 'pepperpot' or dome.

W.S. Spanton, who was Walker's senior by one year and had also been at Heatherley's, wrote an interesting book, *An Art Student and his Teachers in the Sixties*, in which he described his time at the Academy. The school seemed to him very similar to Heatherley's but on a much larger scale: he found it just as cheerful and stimulating. Students were taught by Visitors, who were Academicians, and each attended the school for a month, teaching the method he himself used. It was thought that in this way pupils were saved from becoming mere imitators and mannerists. Spanton found the Visitors a fine set of men, easily accessible, kindly and communicative, but there were others who were deeply critical of the system. The Visitors sat with the students for two hours at a time, and some of them were very neglectful of their duties. The students themselves were not obliged to attend classes and only about half of them attended regularly. When Leighton was elected President of the Royal Academy in 1878 he made the reform of the Academy Schools one of his main objectives.

Charles Landseer (brother of Sir Edwin) was the Keeper, and used to walk round the Antique School and inspect their drawings every day. Landseer was of middle height and his features aquiline and well-formed, although his dyed hair was a source of student mirth. He was usually good-natured, courteous and dignified, but his voice could be heard all over the building owing to his habit of laying stress on the last word he spoke. Landseer caused Walker the deepest embarrassment at the start of his Academy career. He called the students together to address them and said 'I hear there is a Genius here, recently arrived, a Genius of the first order, and his name is Walker, comes from Bath'. He repeated this three times amongst giggles from the students and confusion on Walker's part. Poor Johnny was overcome with shyness at this gibe, which must have referred to his being Leighton's protégé.[21] It is known that Leighton was not lacking in reticence when it came to declaiming the merits of those he championed.

Students were expected to draw in silence, a silence only broken from time to time by the sound of the Guards, who had their barracks in the yard behind the Academy and often marched out into Trafalgar Square to the sound of their band. Order was kept (more or less) by an old retired sculptor called Lofft, who prevented the dome being used too often for boxing and wrestling matches, but who otherwise spent his time in a small office peeling and consuming innumerable apples.

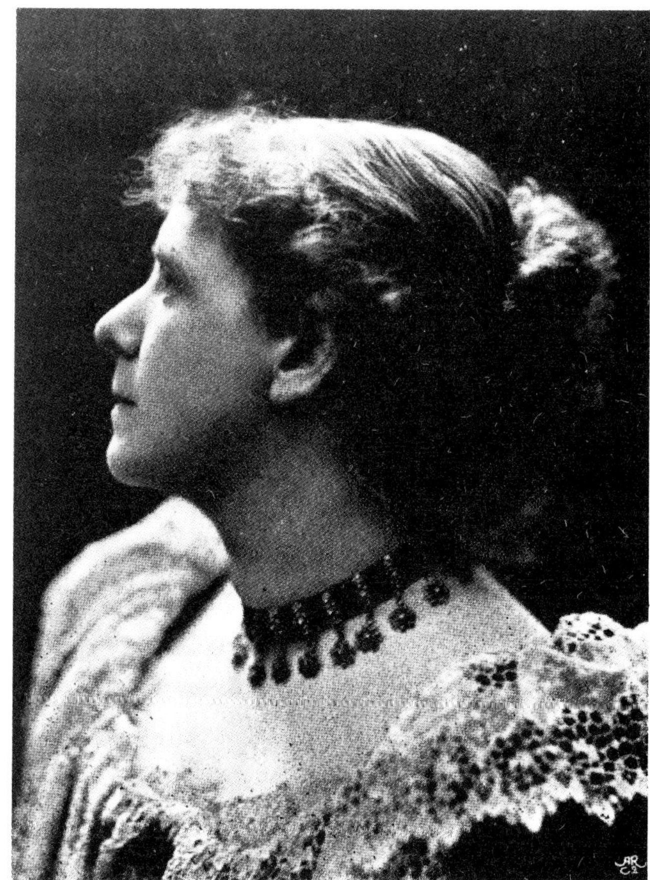

Madame Louisa Starr Canziani: as a young girl the Academy elected her by mistake as their first female student.

Among the students were six girls. Their presence at the school was due to Louisa Starr, who two years before had signed her entrance drawings 'L. Starr'. Her sex was not suspected, and there was general amazement and consternation when she appeared and was found to be a girl! The President, Sir Charles Eastlake, said that the admission of ladies was not permitted by the constitution. However Louisa (a small fair-haired girl of Titania-like proportions but with an iron will, who had also been at Heatherley's) asked to see the clause in question, and it proved to be non-existent! The Academicians had no authority to dismiss ladies and so six other students were admitted to chaperone each other. As their number increased, it led to further controversy, and at the end of two years the Council passed a rule preventing the reception of any more women until they could be given separate accommodation.[22]

Students progressed from the Antique School to the Life School, where they studied from 6–8 p.m. each evening. Visitors there included Cope (who had painted many of the frescoes for the newly built Palace of Westminster), Horsley (nicknamed 'Clothes-Horsley' by *Punch* because of his puritanical advocacy of draping the nude figure), and Solomon Hart, who lectured in a deep bass voice. Other Visitors were John Phillip, Thomas Faed the Scottish painter, who was humorous and racy, and Frith, who would stand no nonsense. When Frith found fault with a student who said he was 'only doing it for fun' Frith replied 'Don't you think you might do it *well* for amusement?'[23]

There was great excitement at the Academy school when it became known in 1865 that Millais was to be a Visitor. The Pre-Raphaelite Brotherhood rebellion of 1848, of which he had been a leader, was still very much in the students' minds, as was Ruskin's championship of him. His subsequent marriage to Effie, Ruskin's wife, made him a romantic figure in the students' eyes. Louisa Starr records how she 'went to the R.A. – model already sitting, and Mr. Millais there. The place crowded to suffocation, – in that little room in the dome I counted 23 painters, and the master says it only holds three or four properly. The discomfort is so great I can hardly work at all, they all come now Mr. Millais is a Visitor'.[24]

John Hanson Walker was also taught by Millais, who had almost as much influence over his painting as Leighton. Millais was now thirty-seven, and was handsome, curly-headed and genial. He was an egoist, and could also be brusque. He had been elected an Academician in 1863, and that year had gained popularity with his highly successful painting of his little daughter Effie in *My first Sermon*. During the 1860s his own style was changing, and he was seeking new channels for his technical mastery, trying to accomplish with a single stroke of the brush what in former years he had only attained through hours of hard work.

W. S. Spanton describes the way he taught: 'Under Millais we drew in charcoal, fixed the outline in ink, and when dry, brushed away the charcoal, rubbed white thinned with oil over the surface, and painted in the colours at once, a method he had learned from Etty'.[25]

Louisa Starr also describes what it was like to be taught by Millais: 'Mr Millais is very kind. So handsome, and such a bright smile! He speaks with a 'go' in his voice, as if he were feeling the most intense enjoyment for the moment, in the occupation of teaching and pointing out mistakes. He is what Italians call 'Simpatico' in the fullest sense of the word, for he carries one with him quite, but then he is simpatico for himself – not for you – he makes one feel with *him*, he does not feel with *you*. And he frightens one also, he is so abrupt and impatient, if he asks for a brush or a paint, he will not wait a second, but does without. He said to Miss Phillot "A rag, a rag", so sharply, that it made me jump and long to run away. But then while he has been so sharp a moment after he will turn upon you the brightest sparkling smile in his eyes, and all over his face; so spontaneous, and as if he enjoyed his own conceit of your work so truly – that it makes one's very heart smile in sympathy'.[26]

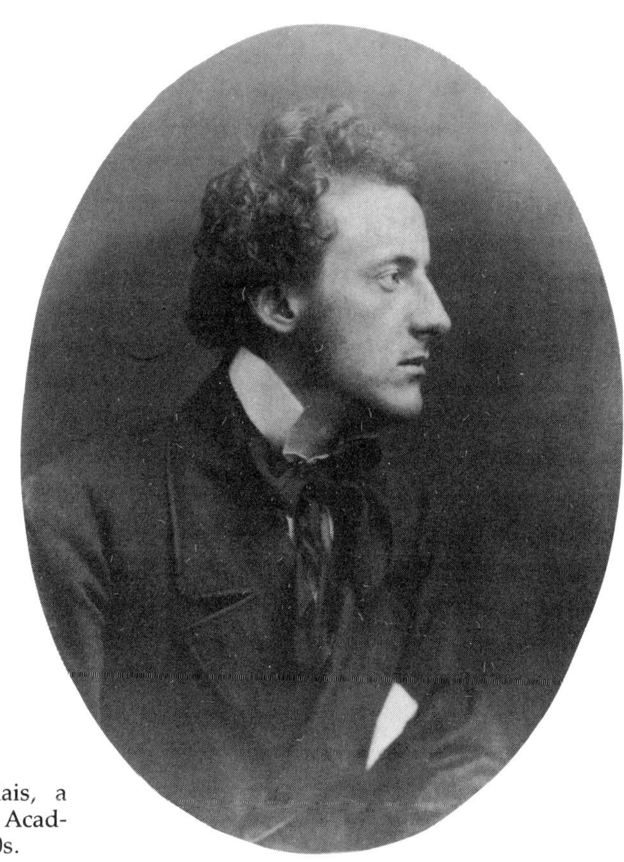

Sir John Everett Millais, a 'Visitor' at the Royal Academy School in the 1860s.

Students studied anatomy in detail and also attended dissecting classes at King's College. As they walked up the Strand to these classes they would have passed Charing Cross station in the process of being built on what had been the site of old Hungerford Market, where Charles Dickens had worked as a small boy in a blacking factory: an old tumbledown building, full of rats and mice.

Of the thirteen fellow painting students admitted to the Academy school with Hanson Walker in December 1863, ten get a mention in Christopher Wood's *Dictionary of Victorian Painters,* but none became outstandingly famous. Among them were Alfred Grace, a hunchback who later did well painting landscapes and cattle, and portraits in miniature. Alfred Grace was one of the students to gain the Turner Gold Medal. Gold and Silver Medals were awarded annually for various categories of painting and students took great trouble over the pictures they submitted. In 1865 Louisa Starr gained the first medal awarded to a woman by the Royal Academy for her copy of Murillo's *Beggars* and in 1867 went on to win the Gold Medal for the most successful historical painting with her *David with the head of Goliath before Saul.* In the same year John Hanson Walker won the Silver Medal for his copy of Rembrandt's *Servant Maid.*

Louisa Starr describes the ceremony of Prize Giving vividly. On the night itself, she went to the Academy and, not daring to hope, sat as far back as she could, in the crowded lecture room. The students sat at some distance from the Academicians, behind several tiers of benches. 'After they had tramped in the students gave three cheers for the ladies . . . following this with three for the perpetual student, and three for the gentleman with his hat on – who directly took it off!' She continues 'There were various awards. Then suddenly I heard Mr. Boxall say in a clear, low voice the words "To Miss Louisa Starr . . . a gold medal is awarded . . ." In a second or two I had risen, and was making my way round and down, with clapping in my ears. We stayed some time, – everyone came up to look at my copy particularly, and Mr. Leighton came with Mr. Walker and looked at it, but we could not hear what he said'.[27]

Leighton's biographer, Edgcumbe Staley, says 'Perhaps no class of persons did Leighton's whole loving kindness go out to more sharply than to young students, both boys and girls. His kindly words, his helpful advice, his patient judgements were no less warmly received than his magnificent gifts and constant kindly tips'.[28]

Johnny one day told Leighton about one of his fellow pupils at the Royal Academy, a youth of talent, who was in poor straits financially. Leighton walked to a drawer and took out a £5 note, saying, 'Give that to him, and ask him to make me a little sketch in exchange'.[29] Perhaps this was the way Johnny, too, thanked Leighton for kindnesses, for Leighton wrote 'My dear Johnny, On returning home last night I found your generous present – I am really quite ashamed to rob you of your sketch which I think is charming. Accept the sincere thanks of yours always truly, Fred Leighton.'

During the time that he was at the Academy School Walker changed his lodging from Beaumont Street to Oxford Street, and then to Great Castle Street, all three addresses being within the same small area. As he walked down Regent Street to the National Gallery he would have passed the many photographers' shops there, for Regent Street claimed a greater number than anywhere else in London. The fact that of his year at art school only he, Theodore Blake-Wirgman, Charles Gogin and Alfred Grace took up portraiture probably reflects the rapid spread of photography. In 1857 'Carte de Visite' photographs had been introduced, taking the place of miniatures, and for a time portrait painting was threatened, despite the fact that in the Great 1862 exhibition photography had been excluded on the grounds that it was not a fine art. However, colour photography had not advanced sufficiently to be used for photographing paintings, and there was still a demand for good copyists. A copy of a good painting was preferred by the public to an indifferent original, and copywork was lucrative work for a painter.

Students at the Academy School were allowed to copy the paintings in the Wallace collection, which was then housed in the Bethnal Green Museum, and Leighton kept Johnny well provided with copy work, as correspondence shows. Leighton forwarded him a request from Henry Greville to copy a portrait of his mother, Lady Charlotte Greville, for him. This was presumably to be a copy of Leighton's portrait of her, made in 1856. The portrait belonged to his sister, the Countess of Ellesmere, and the copy was to be given to the Countess Grey. Leighton wrote to Johnny forwarding him the £10 due to him for the work, and said 'I send you the money from Mr. Greville for the portrait of his mother – I am very glad you should have this new commission but you must thank *him, not me* for it was entirely his idea and desire. He is indeed one of the kindest and best men possible – I look on him myself as a second father. To save time I shall make arrangements for you to work in my studio on the four first days of January if you can manage it – I shall be out of town and you will have the place to yourself. I wish you a happy Xmas and New Year'.[30] This letter was probably written to the twenty-two year old Johnny in December 1865.

Leighton appears to have been in the habit of lending his studio to Johnny to work in, and continued to give encouragement: 'Tomorrow (Thursday) or Friday you will have the place to yourself – I am delighted to hear that you have sold your boy and so good a price. It will give you courage. Yours truly, Fred Leighton'.[31]

The Academy school year was divided into three terms, which ran from the beginning of January to the end of March, from the end of May until the end of August, and from the end of September until the end of December. It was during one of these breaks that Walker went to the Isle of Wight to do some landscape painting. His grandparents, James and Jane Walker, who were seventy-eight and sixty-four respectively were still alive and living in Brighstone, although they had moved out of 'Willes', their little farmhouse.

The earliest painting of John Hanson Walker's which still remains in the family is a small landscape, 5 × 9 inches only, which he painted on wood when he was twenty.

Leighton approved of his efforts to paint landscape, for he wrote 'I am much obliged to you for your letter telling me of your doings in the country. I think you will do wisely in going to the Isle of Wight to paint landscape. The danger of copying the old Masters too exclusively, as you have been forced to do lately, is that one is apt to fall into mannerism by trying to see Nature with the eyes of them – painting landscape direct from Nature is the best possible corrective against this tendency. I shall be glad to see you and what you have done on your return – if you are here before the 20 or 22 August – if not we shall meet in October when I return from the East. I am working away on my picture which will be under-painted before I leave England. I wish you joy of your summer trip'.[32]

Leighton himself made exquisite studies from Nature. In 1859 he had amazed Ruskin with the delicacy of his *Study of a Lemon Tree,* which he had made in Capri, and his understanding of its structure and growth. Ruskin had written to Leighton 'Dear Leighton, Unless I write again I shall hope to breakfast with you on Friday, and see and know for evermore how a lemon differs from an orange leaf. In cases of doubtful temper, might the former more gracefully and appropriately be used for bridal chaplet? Most truly yours, J. Ruskin.'[33]

CHAPTER THREE

MARRIAGE

One day, when Johnny was sitting for Leighton he told him that he was engaged to a Bath girl, Fanny Whitaker, whom he had met at drawing classes in Bath, but that he was too poor to think of marrying her. He records that 'Leighton became greatly interested. He questioned me about my prospects. He would not hear of my marriage being put off. "You must work", he said, and I shall help you to get commissions'.[34] From that time on, Leighton kept a fatherly eye on both Johnny *and* Fanny, and did all in his power to see that they got married.

'Miss Nan', as Leighton always called her, was the eldest of the eleven children of John Hector Whitaker and his wife Mary Ann (Gee). Christened Frances Elizabeth, she was nine months younger than Johnny, having been born on September 7, 1844. She had long auburn-brown hair, blue eyes, and the fresh complexion of a country girl, despite the fact that her family lived in Bath. The Whitakers had, since coming to Bath at the end of the eighteenth century from Cononley, near Skipton-in-Craven in Yorkshire, been involved in the upholstery and cabinet making business, doing a brisk trade furnishing the elegant rooms of Bath. At the time Johnny and Fanny met, her father was running the Kingston Steam (Cabinet) Works at 7 Dorchester Street, Bath, making reproduction antique furniture. John Hector Whitaker was too much of a perfectionist to be a good businessman – he was by nature a poet, but through industry and integrity he kept the firm going and was later able to move the works to the de Montalt Mill, high above Bath on Combe Down. The Whitakers added to their income by running a number of lodging houses. They bought houses, or leases of houses, furnished them and then put in managers or landladies.

The Whitakers, longer established in Bath than the Walkers, opposed their daughter's engagement to Johnny and while the latter was still continuing his drawing classes in Bath, had sent Fanny up to London to live with her father's sister, Fanny Unwin, a rich widow. They little knew that shortly afterwards Leighton would arrange for Walker to come to London to pursue his career at Heatherley's!

Encouraged to persevere with his suit, Hanson Walker set to work successfully, for Leighton wrote 'My dear Johnny, You will forgive me I am sure for not writing to you to thank you for your letter received some weeks back – but the fact is I have been so very busy as to make writing a matter of very great difficulty. – I heard from your father not long ago that you have been very fortunate in getting capital commissions for portraits where you have been staying. – I am very glad indeed to hear it and trust sincerely that you feel you are progressing as steadily in proficiency as in prosperity. – To the commissions you have had in the country I have one to add here – Mr. Henry Greville wishes you to paint for him a copy of a head of a relation of his – I believe of poor Lady Ellesmere his sister – whose recent death has been such a terrible grief to him. You will I am sure be glad to undertake this painting even tho' it may not in itself be very interesting – the size a sort of oval kitcat – not large, – he proposes to offer you ten pounds for it. How is Miss Nan? I hope you have good accounts of her and that all goes smoothly between you. I send this letter to Bath to be forwarded as I do not know your present whereabouts. Yours very sincerely, Fred Leighton'.[35] This letter must have been written just after April 1886 when Lady Ellesmere died.

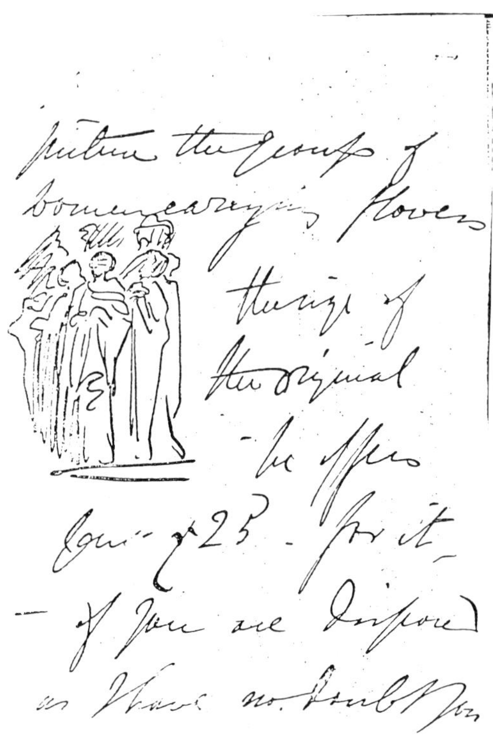
picture the group of
women carrying flowers
the size of
the original
– he offers
you £25 – for it –
– if you are disposed
as I have no doubt you

A page from one of Leighton's letters to his protégé.

Johnny must have written reassuringly of his progress to his master, for Leighton replied 'I am just off to Paris and write one line in hot haste to thank you for yours and to say that I am delighted to hear that you are conscious of progress – come back as soon as you can *conveniently* please because Mr. Greville has *borrowed* Lady Ellesmere's portrait for you to copy and wants to return it as soon as possible to the Duke of Devonshire. Come to see me when you return, and believe me, with kind regards to Miss Nan, – Yours always, F. Leighton'.[36]

Henry Greville was generous over the commissions he gave Walker, for another followed the request for Lady Ellesmere's portrait. Leighton wrote 'My dear Johnny, Mr. Greville has very kindly desired me to give you another commission – this time a larger one. He wants you to copy from my large picture the group of women carrying flowers the size of the original – he offers you £25 for it. – If you are disposed as I have no doubt you will be I would if I were you, write him a line of thanks for the kind interest he shows in you. In great haste – Yours very sincerely, Fred Leighton.'[37]

The 'large picture' Leighton wrote of was his *Syracusan Bride leading Wild Beasts in Procession to the Temple of Diana* (a subject suggested by the passage in the Second Idyll of Theocritus), which was painted by Leighton 1865–6.

In his letter Leighton sketched the little group of women to give Johnny an idea of what he wanted, and added his advice as to how to proceed: 'My dear Johnny, I leave town Saturday next and shall not see you till Saturday the 6th January, so I write a line to say you will set to work for yourself – the maid will light you a fire and give you the key of the studio. I have written direct to Eatwell to order the canvas or it would not have been ready in time. You are to paint the group life size – *trace it* to get it quite accurate – put the head of the centre figure, the woman in *yellow* about four inches or 4½ inches from the top of the canvas – and it will give you all the rest – *leave out* the little child *sitting* go slap at the colour, *vigorously but not quick* – the slower you work, if you work with energy, the sooner you get through and the better the result. I hope you are enjoying yourself.'[38]

Leighton's method of painting, which he probably expected Johnny to follow, was extremely painstaking, and followed this pattern:

a) His idea for a composition was jotted into a notebook; every line in the pattern having its relation to other lines carefully worked out.
b) A sketch of the composition was made in black and white chalk on brown paper.
c) The model was posed, and drawn from the nude.
d) A first sketch of the entire composition was made, and 'squared off'.
e) A small oil sketch followed to determine the colour scheme.
f) The squared drawing was traced on to the canvas, then the whole figure was sketched on from life in monochrome, and every muscle and joint (later to be painted over with draperies) was painted in.

g) Separate studies of the draperies were made, over a slightly enlarged scale drawing of the figure, in great detail on brown paper.
h) The draperies as worked out in the above studies were painted on to the nude monochrome figures, each fold being exactly fitted into its place on the figure.
i) The background and accessories were next added to the canvas, which had already been underpainted in a grey tone.
j) Certain areas of the picture were prepared with a flat tinted wash, i.e. a blue sky might be underpainted with a soft ruddy tone, and lastly the colour, which was applied fairly quickly, was added.

The Whitaker family's opposition to Fanny's engagement to Johnny may have affected his health, for Leighton wrote solicitously: 'I write one line in haste to say how sorry I am to hear that your health has been unsatisfactory of late. I earnestly trust you won't disregard your doctor's advice and that you will *at any sacrifice* do something to recover strength, even tho' a long sea voyage were necessary – health is the *first* thing. Talk it over with Miss Nan – if her love is as sincere as you believe – and I don't for a moment doubt it – she will give you the same advice. For myself I begin to think my studio will never be ready. I have not done a stroke of work. *I hope* by the end of next week I shall be at it again. In October I am off to Rome'.[39] As a young man Leighton had suffered with eye trouble and was somewhat obsessed by his state of health, always beginning his letters home with a report on it.

The reference to Leighton's studio being unready indicates that the above letter must have been written in the summer of 1866. Two years previously Leighton had bought a plot of land from his friend, Lady Holland, on the edge of Holland Park and, despite remonstrances about extravagance from his father, had commissioned his old friend, the architect George Aitchison, to build him a studio house. Building had started in 1865, and Leighton put many of his own ideas into it. Every stone and brick was inspected, and all the wood and metal work was minutely checked. He climbed on to the scaffolding and peered through window frames, carefully checking each ornament and detail. Whenever he went abroad he left minute details specifying the size, shape and decoration of the furniture, much of which was especially designed for the house.

Leighton's new home was at No.2 Holland Park Road; it was only later that it was re-numbered No.12 and called Leighton House. It was, when first built, much smaller than it is now. The front had only three windows, but it was planned so that it could be extended later to five. The house was dominated by the studio, which was on the first floor at the back and faced north, towards Holland Park. It originally measured forty-five by twenty-five feet, and had a gallery at the east end. A stair led from this end of the studio to the side entrance, which was intended for the use of the models. In this Leighton showed a conventional sense of social propriety – his neighbour, Val Prinsep, allowed the models to use the main staircase. Apart from the studio there was a lofty hall, lit by a large skylight. Only one main bedroom, Leighton's own, was included in the plan, perhaps to deter visitors who might distract him from work. The servants' bedrooms were over his first floor apartments and were reached by a back stair.

The interior decorations were boldly colourful. Much of the woodwork was lacquered black and the delicately incised leaf and flower mouldings of the door and window architraves were often picked out in gold. The stone columns of the entrance hall had their capitals silvered and supported the beams of the ceiling, which were painted blue. The studio walls were painted red. The famous Arab Hall, which is now the best known part of Leighton House, was not added for ten years, until 1877.[40]

Leighton was an indefatigable collector and it may have been on his behalf that his father, Dr. Septimus Leighton, visited Robert Walker's antique shop in Bath, for Leighton gave to Johnny the portrait of Dr. Leighton which he had painted in Frankfurt at the age of nineteen. The painting now hangs in Leighton House.

On August 27, 1866 Leighton wrote to Johnny, 'My dear Johnny, On returning from the Continent I find your letter for which best thanks. I am very glad indeed to hear a favourable account of your health and work. Of myself I have absolutely nothing of any interest to tell you except that I go into my new house on *Friday* next. I went to Switzerland, as you know, for my health and therefore did no work; – now that I have returned I am entirely engrossed with moving and buying and ordering furniture so that I have not touched a brush for ages and you will find my work just where you left it I regret to say. I shall, however, finish Venus next month and I go to Italy in the beginning of October – I don't feel very flourishing in health I regret to say. When do you come back? Remember me to Miss Nan and believe me very kindly yours, F.L.'[41]

All this time Nan had been living with her father's sister, her godmother, Mrs. Unwin, to whom she had been sent from Bath. Fanny Unwin (née Whitaker) was a very remarkable person. A good artist in her own right, she was also a pioneer in the field of education in design for women. At the time her niece came to live with her, she was fifty-two years old, twice widowed and had lead a very eventful life. As a young girl she had eloped with, and married, a Scottish actor, Robert Ronald McIan, whom she had met while he was playing at the Bath Theatre. On the London stage McIan was famous for his spirited character studies, especially of 'the Dougal Cratur' in Rob Roy. He appears to have been a wild, warm-hearted, impulsive but lovable man.

Fanny had exhibited at the Royal Academy from the age of twenty-two, and after one or two years of marriage McIan gave up the stage and, tutored by his wife, became a painter too. He had a passionate love of everything connected with the Highlands, and he and Fanny illustrated and exhibited scenes from

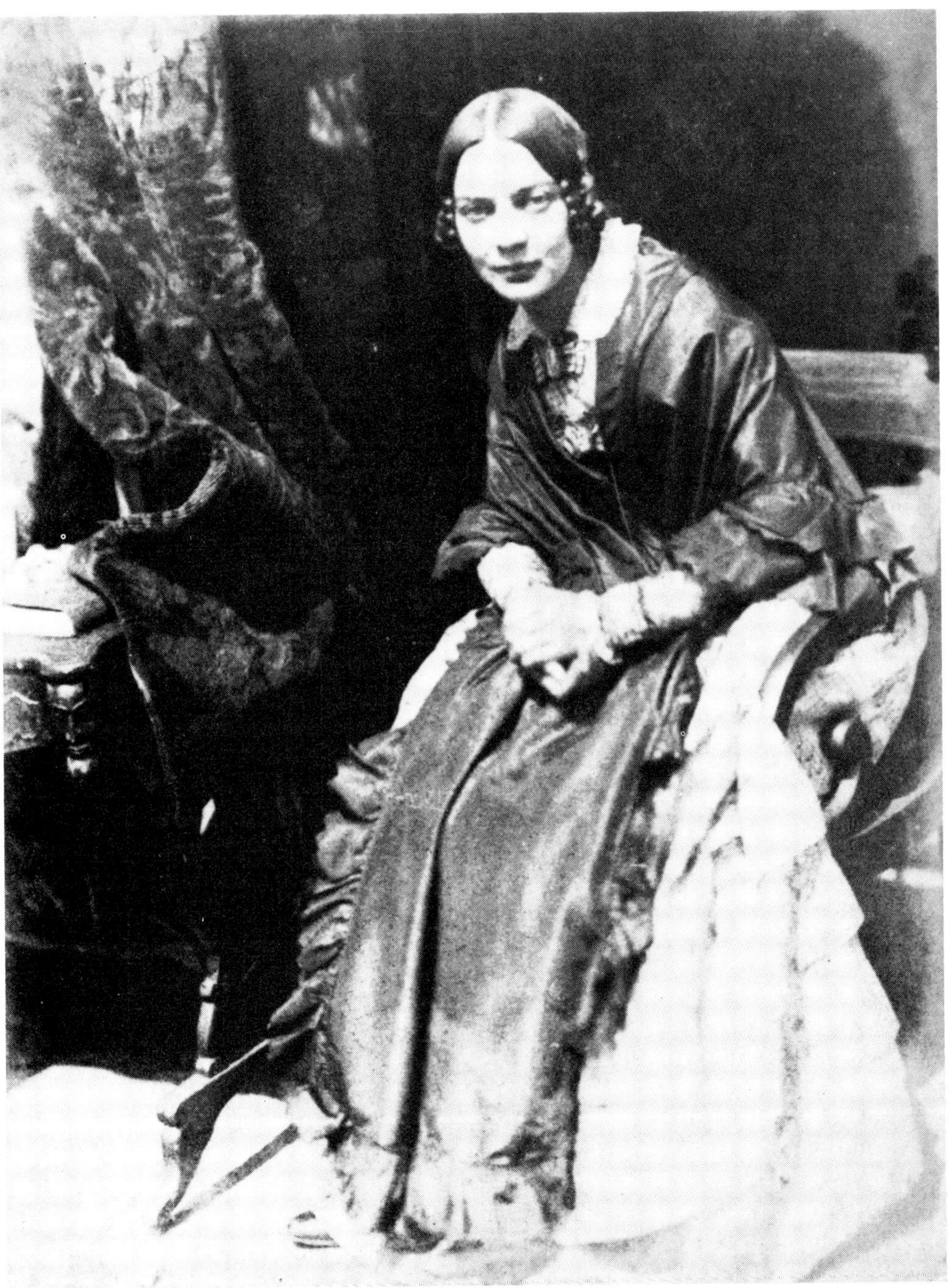

Fanny McIan, first Superintendent of the Female School of Design, Somerset House.

Scottish history and battles. Fanny's *Highlander Defending his family at the Massacre of Glencoe* was considered her masterpiece, and in 1854 she was given the great honour of being the first woman to be elected an Honorary Member of the Royal Scottish Academy 'in consideration of her eminent talents as an artist'.[42] She remained the only woman to be elected to the Academy for the next sixty years!

In the early 1840s the McIans were on intimate terms with Charles Dickens and his family, and visits were exchanged between the McIans at Great Coram Street and the Dickens' at Devonshire Terrace. On New Year's Day 1842 Dickens wrote to thank Fanny for illustrating the scene of 'Little Nell reading the inscription on the tombstone', and for presenting it to him. He sent her an inscribed copy of *The Old Curiosity Shop* and wrote 'My Dear Mrs. McIan, The enclosed book belongs of right to you for you have beautifully perpetuated it. You who have done so much for the love of the fiction will accept this volume I hope, for the sake of its author. Ever believe me Faithfully and Truly Yours, Charles Dickens'.[43] The painting was exhibited at the Royal Academy in 1842 under the title *Nell and the Widow* and later Dickens hung it in his dining-room at Gad's Hill.

In his *Memoirs* Frith recalls how he met John Leech, (who later illustrated the novels of 'Surtees' and who was a regular contributor to *Punch*) for the first time in Fanny's studio, where she was giving him some of his early lessons in oil painting. She was predicting that while Leech would go far, *Punch* was not a periodical destined for a great future![44]

When the female branch of the Government School of Design was founded at Somerset House in 1842 Fanny, who was then twenty-eight, was appointed its first Superintendent. The object of the school was to train designers and so to improve ornamental design in manufacture. It was the only school in London where the principles of design were to be taught both in theory and in practice, and the first students were only asked to pay the low fee of 2d. per month. Design in manufacture in England at that date was very poor indeed, (a state of affairs obvious at the Great Exhibition of 1851), and moves were soon being made to establish further schools of design all over England.

Fanny was a very spirited Director, taking great trouble to learn each craft before teaching it to her students. For instance, she visited Paris in the summer vacation of 1843 in order to study porcelain painting at Sèvres. She said 'I saw the artists at work, observed their method of using colours, and obtained a knowledge of their technical modes of proceeding, and of the media they employ in the process. The result of my observations at that time was a conviction that I could readily learn this art, and could easily teach it'.[45]

Fanny received many tributes for the work she did; in 1845 her pupils presented her with an address expressing their deep sense of the benefits they received from her able and efficient instruction. She worked under great difficulties: after a year or two the school, having petitioned for more space, was moved from Somerset House to two dark and ill-ventilated rooms over a soap manufacturer's in the Strand; Charles Dickens was so appalled by the overcrowding that he took up their case in an article published in his *Household Words*. Having described the unsavoury area, the overcrowding and lack of light, the article went on to compliment Mrs. McIan on the drawings which had been produced under circumstances so disadvantageous. This was written in 1851, the year of the Great Exhibition, to which her pupils had contributed several exhibits and won many prizes. Fanny McIan directed the school, (which in 1852 amalgamated with the Central School of Arts and Crafts) until 1857, when it was said that it could 'challenge comparison with any school of art in the United Kingdom'.[46]

During the two years prior to this Fanny had been nursing her husband, who was suffering from a brain disorder and was violent. At her own insistence, she looked after him single-handed until his death at their home in Hampstead on December 13, 1856. The *Art Journal* paid a touching tribute to both of them: 'McIan was keenly alive to the watchful tenderness of his loved and loving wife; who, before and after her daily duties at the Female School of Design, was blessed with strength to watch him day and night; her presence became more and more his light, his joy, his life, and nothing could exceed his gratitude to her. His deep and earnest affections remained in full activity to the last – they were the strongest elements of his nature . . . their friends feared that Mrs. McIan's devotion to her husband would have brought her to a premature grave before *his* time for departure arrived'.[47]

Fanny later married again, a rich Scottish stockbroker, Richard James Unwin of Ardbeg, Kilmun, Argyll and Albert Gate, London. By the time her niece Fanny Whitaker came to live with her he too had died, but she was still living at Albert Terrace, a large house which stood on the site of what is now the Hyde Park Hotel. In it she kept the superb collection of furniture, porcelain and paintings that she had built up.

Fanny Unwin knew many people in London, particularly in the art world, and she entertained a great deal. She was childless, and so was pleased to have young Fanny to stay with her, and seems to have encouraged the romance with Johnny just as much as did Leighton, promising the young couple that if they married she would always see that they lacked for nothing.

It is thought that while she was living with her aunt (who was a friend of Leighton's) Fanny, like Johnny, also modelled for him, although always fully draped! During this time he would have been working on the five classical works which he exhibited in 1867, and also his *Syracusan Bride*. It is quite possible that Fanny did some modelling for studies for this painting, which illustrated the Syracusan practice of sending young girls who were to be married in procession to the Temple of Artemis, to propitiate the Virgin Goddess. Fourteen women are portrayed walking in the procession. This was a key painting in the development of Leighton's classical style.

John Hanson Walker was learning from Leighton and studying at the Academy School at a particularly interesting time in Victorian art, for in the

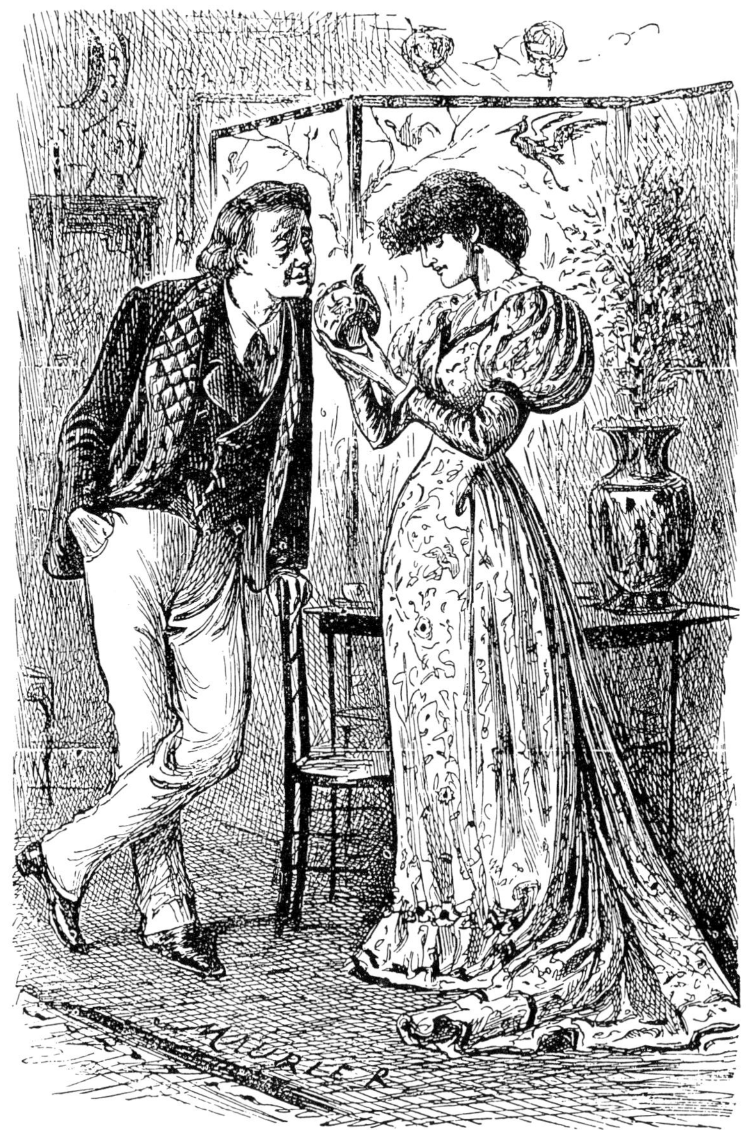

THE SIX-MARK TEA-POT.

Æsthetic Bridegroom. "IT IS QUITE CONSUMMATE, IS IT NOT?"
Intense Bride. "IT IS, INDEED! OH, ALGERNON, LET US LIVE UP TO IT!"

George du Maurier's humorous view of the 'aesthetic' movement.

1860's there was beginning to be a reaction against the predominance of Ruskin and the Pre-Raphaelites, resulting in a classical revival centred round Leighton and to which Watts, Alma-Tadema, Edward Poynter and Alfred Waterhouse were the main contributors. It was a romantic classicism, looking wistfully back to a golden age as if to escape from Victorian materialism. This movement soon became inextricably interwoven with an 'aesthetic' movement, led by Burne-Jones, whose participants believed beauty in itself to be a moral force, – 'Art for Art's sake' was their cry. The two movements ran parallel to each other, but of the two the aesthetic movement was more of a literary force for it included writers like Pater, (who wrote *Marius the Epicurean*), Swinburne, Rossetti and later, Wilde. The movements began in the 1860s and flourished in the 1870s.

From the start Leighton had held firmly to the classical ideals of order, harmony, unity and perfection. He was by nature an aesthete. He was not

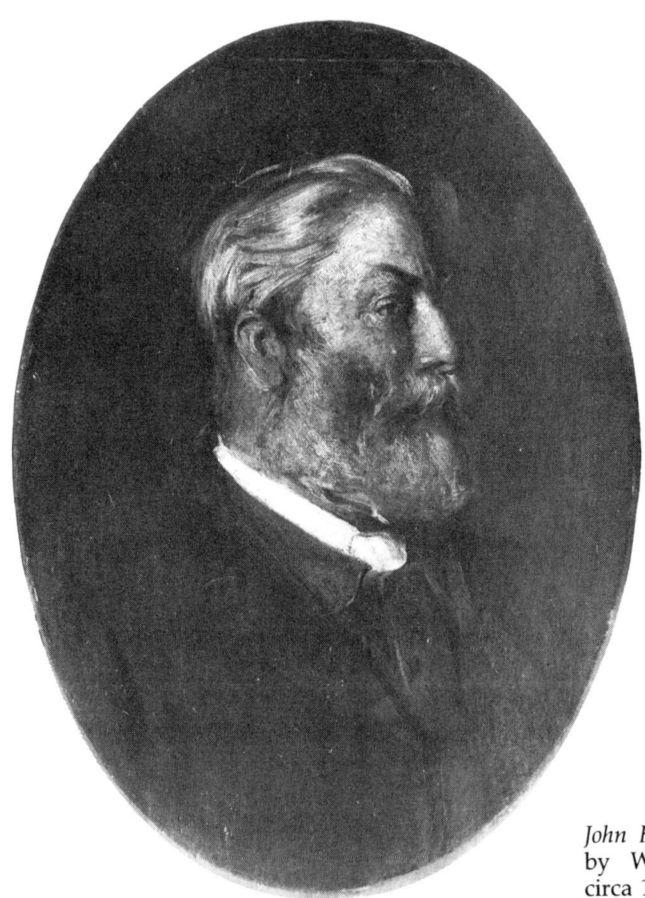

John Hector Whitaker painted by Walker, his son-in-law circa 1872.

religious, as his father had brought his children up to be free thinkers, and when Johnny first met Leighton he had been shocked by Leighton's suggestion that Johnny should model for him on a Sunday. Both the classical and the aesthetic movement were later mocked. W. S. Gilbert referred to one of the rooms in his house as the 'Flirtarium', and the fashion for living 'intensely' by 'Passionate Brompton' was ridiculed by George du Maurier. In one of his most brilliant cartoons for *Punch* he shows a young couple gazing rapturously at a blue and white Chinese vase, the wife saying to her husband, 'Oh Algernon, let us live up to it!'

It is not known how much modelling Johnny did for Leighton after he had sat for *Duett* and *Rustic Music* but Leighton probably used him at various times between 1861 and 1867. For instance, he may have modelled for the head in *The Knuckle Bone Player* which Leighton painted around 1867. This shows a

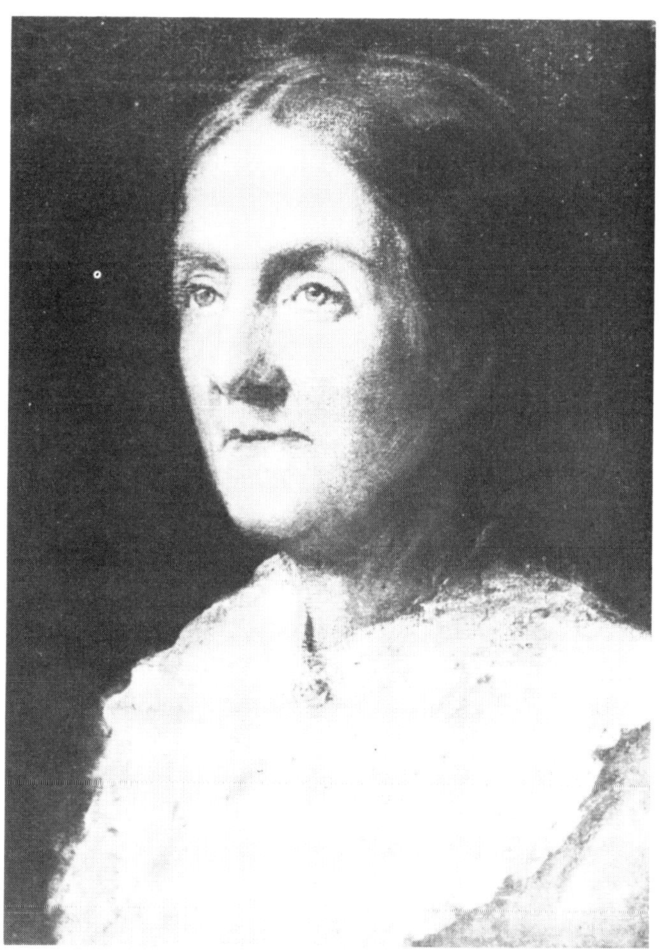

Sarah Walker painted by her son circa 1874.

Grecian girl sitting on a wall tossing up four bones from the back of her hand. Although it is the painting of a feminine subject, the eyes, eyebrows, nose and mouth are very similar to Walker's in the Leighton House Study (No.959) which Leighton made for *Lieder ohne Worte* and again Leighton may have drawn on his features, despite the change of sex eventually depicted.

Leighton wrote two amusing letters to Johnny enlisting his help in getting 'props' for his paintings: 'I want very much, before they have quite disappeared, to get for myself and for a friend a couple of old-fashioned country bumpkins' smocks; you know the sort of thing. Do you chance to know any one in any of the villages about Bath who could pick up a couple? I should like a brown one (NOT a white Sunday one) and a green one, and they should *not* be washed – well worn, untidy things. If you saw your way to getting me such garments, I should be very grateful, but don't *trouble* about it.'[48] Again he wrote 'My dear Johnny, If you have leisure to think of anything but Miss Nan just at present will you do me a favour? Will you get for me a peasant's *wide-awake* in shape like the one I painted in your portrait only really old and *soiled* and *stained* – bought in fact if possible off a bumpkin's head? Can you do this for me and either send it or bring it if you are about to return shortly? I will pay you when we meet. – When is the wedding to be? Or is it already over? I wish you all happiness and prosperity and remain with kind remembrances to Miss (or Mrs.) Nan, Yours truly Fred Leighton. I hope you can read this, my hands are so cold I can scarcely hold the pen'.[49]

The search for the above garments must have been successful, for Leighton wrote on Boxing Day, 'Dear Johnny, I have got your note and enclose little cheque. This is as it should be; – it is absurd that because I am old friend you should be a loser by me in time and pocket. With a Merry Xmas & New Year to you and Nan, Written in haste, Yours sincerely, Fred Leighton.'[50]

The New Year of 1867 was ushered in by severe snowstorms on January 2nd and 3rd but for Johnny and Nan it was a happy month, for at last her family appear to have been reconciled to their union, and they were married in St. Mark's Church, Lyncomb, Bath on January 8. The Register was signed by the two respective fathers. John Hector described himself as cabinet maker of Dorchester Street, and the church was very near to his works. Robert Walker gave his profession simply as 'artist' and it is possible he had given up his business. Five years after the marriage he and his wife Sarah disappeared from the Bath street directories, and it is thought that he may have lost money and so left Bath to work for one of the Somersetshire families of Malets, Mallets or Malletts (of Antique fame) as a butler cum art adviser, but it has unfortunately been impossible to trace him further.

For John Hanson Walker, aged twenty-four, and his young bride of twenty-three it was the start of a long and industrious life together, during the course of which he would carve out for himself with Fanny's help a career as a portrait painter based in London.

CHAPTER FOUR

THE START OF A CAREER

Walker told Alice Corkran, Leighton's early biographer, that Leighton asked him what he would like for a wedding present, '"Should it be a piano or some silver?" "I said", said Johnny, "What I should treasure most would be a slight pencil sketch of my wife". "All right", he answered; "as soon as I have got my Academy pictures sent off you shall have it". After that I got a letter from him saying he wished to speak to me about my wife's portrait. I went to his studio, and there were three canvasses displayed – a large full-length, a medium-size, and a kit-cat. "Choose which size you will have", he said. I was overcome; I could not speak. I had only hoped for a sketch. "Nonsense", said Leighton, when I told him. "It shall be a picture; we must do Nan justice". I chose the least of the three canvasses'.[51]

Leighton kept to his word and wrote to arrange sittings: 'My dear Johnny, Many thanks for your letter. I have had absolutely no time to answer sooner and now can only do so most briefly. I am extremely glad to hear of the success of your labours at Dorchester and think you were very right to take for yourself and "Mrs. Nan" a refreshing little holiday on the hills. I will begin the portrait next week when you return – at which time also I hope to show you some underpainting work which I think may interest you. I shall certainly call and see your screen – it will no doubt be a very useful bit of "property" to you. Remember me very kindly to your wife and believe me, Yours very sincerely, Fred Leighton'.[52] So Nan went to Leighton House, which was then, as Leighton put it, in 'little more than a mews' with old stables and lined with trees, to have her portrait painted – a portrait that was to be considered later as one of Leighton's best, and which is now on loan to Leighton House, from the Tate Gallery.

Leighton greatly admired Nan, and in his portrait he captured her likeness exactly. He painted her as the unsophisticated country girl she was, and the picture has a wonderfully airy quality to it. Leighton has shown 'Nan' with a half-dreaming look, perhaps almost subconsciously harking back to the mood he captured in *Lieder ohne Worte*. The feeling of freshness (noted by Hugh Marles, who catalogued this painting for the Tate Gallery) is achieved by the base colouring, which is relatively warm for Leighton, and strengthens the blues in 'Nan's' dress and the sky. Interestingly Marles feels that the painting reflects a gain in professional assurance on Leighton's part since painting the two 'Johnnies' following his election as A.R.A. and the general change in his fortunes from 1864. The flesh painting of the portrait, and its 'sweetness, breadth and pure naturalness' found favour when it was exhibited at the Grafton Galleries at the end of the century, in 1897.[53] Towards the end of his life John Hanson Walker was to write to Mrs. Russell Barrington, Leighton's second biographer, 'the picture I treasure most of the ten that I have by my old master is the portrait he gave me of my dear wife as a wedding present – a truly noble gift! G. F. Watts said it was the best thing he had ever seen painted by his old friend'.[54]

In 1867 Watts was living next door to Leighton, with Mr. and Mrs. Thoby Prinsep at Little Holland House. W. S. Spanton in his book describes Walker as 'the friend and pupil of Leighton and Watts'.[55] This remark is borne out by Walker's son, Jolliffe, in his unpublished memoirs, who claims that 'Watts was a great friend of my father's and helped him considerably in his work, and got him a number of commissions'. He continues that 'thanks to the kindness of these two great friends, Leighton and Watts, Dad was well

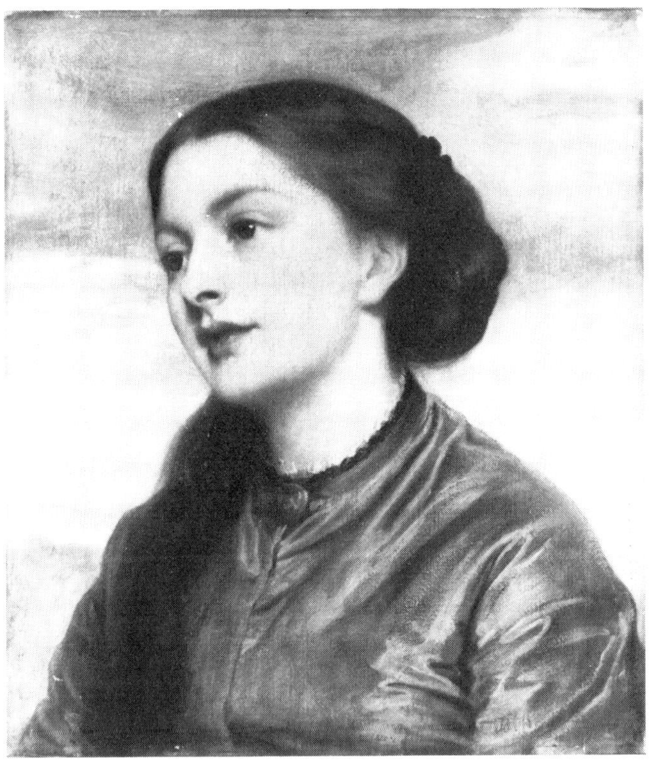

Mrs. John Hanson Walker (Nan) painted by Leighton 1867 as a wedding present for his protégé.

grounded in Art both in drawing and painting, and began to form a style of his own'.

Unfortunately, nothing in the Leighton/Watts correspondence refers to John Hanson Walker. In the year that Johnny married, the high-minded Watts was fifty and success had not yet fully come to him. Three years earlier he had made a brief and unhappy marriage to the sixteen-year old Ellen Terry, and was now parted from her. The only memento of their marriage was the beautiful portrait of her, *Choosing*, which now hangs in the National Portrait Gallery.

Watts lived cocooned from the world by the Prinseps, revered by younger artists as a sort of father-figure of Victorian classicism, and both Spanton and Louisa Starr record calling on him for advice. Spanton asked for his help when he was preparing his painting *Ulysses being recognised by his nurse* to enter for the Academy Gold Medal competition, and tells of being graciously received and given advice. Louisa Starr was sent several commissions by Watts, who, when he saw her portrait of J. E. Pfeiffer badly hung at the Academy in 1870 replaced it with one of his own, so that hers was hung 'on the line'. She consulted Watts as to what she should charge for her paintings and he replied 'With respect to the matter of prices I really am unable to give you advice; it is long (unfortunately) since I was a beginner, and you must be guided in some degree by that consideration, though there is no necessity you should paint *cheap* pictures. I am the less able to give you an opinion, having painted portraits in a very irregular manner with regard to terms, never having looked upon portraiture as my branch of the profession'.[56]

Watts had evolved an extremely personal colour scheme and technique to convey the mood of his pictures. He used very stiff dry paint, and worked with rough stumpy brushes, or even his fingers, developing a range of peculiarly iridescent, glittering colours, although many of these are now sadly faded.[57]

It appears that Walker continued with his classes at the Royal Academy after his marriage, for he won his Silver Medal for copying Rembrandt's *Servant Maid* in that year. He also exhibited his first painting at the Suffolk Street Galleries. It was called *Study of a Head* and he asked twenty pounds for it, which was a high price for a beginner. It may have been about the sale of this that Leighton wrote 'Dear Johnny, tomorrow (Thursday) or Friday you will have the place to yourself – I am delighted to hear that you have sold your boy and so good a price. It will give you courage. Yours truly, Fred Leighton'.[58]

On marrying, John Hanson Walker and Fanny had taken 26 Thurloe Place at a very low rent, and soon found that it was haunted. One night Johnny was summoned by the maid who had heard strange noises downstairs. Armed with a poker and followed by Fanny he proceeded to investigate. The sounds came from the drawing room, and it was as though heavy furniture was being moved across the room. The door was flung open, but all was silence. By the light of the candle they found every piece of furniture in its usual place. When they closed the door, however, the noises were resumed. The servants left the next day and some time afterwards, workmen who came to see about a leak in the roof told Johnny that they were the first tenants to remain in the house for any length of time, because of its reputation. They were its last tenants, for after two years the house was demolished![59]

Four days before their first wedding anniversary a son was born to Fanny and Johnny: Leighton stood as godfather to him, and he was named Frederick after him. With added family responsibilities, Johnny wrote to Leighton for advice on how much he should now try to exhibit, and got the following reply: 'Although I certainly think it is a pity to exhibit too soon; nevertheless I think that your particular situation just now does justify you in doing so as long as you confine yourself to the Suffolk Street gallery. I sincerely hope you may sell your pictures. With kind regards to Mrs. Nan and love to my godchild. I am in haste, Yours always F. Leighton'.[60]

Walker was to exhibit a great deal at the Suffolk Street galleries of the Society of British Artists. They had been founded in 1824 to provide more space for the ever growing number of artists wishing to exhibit, and for

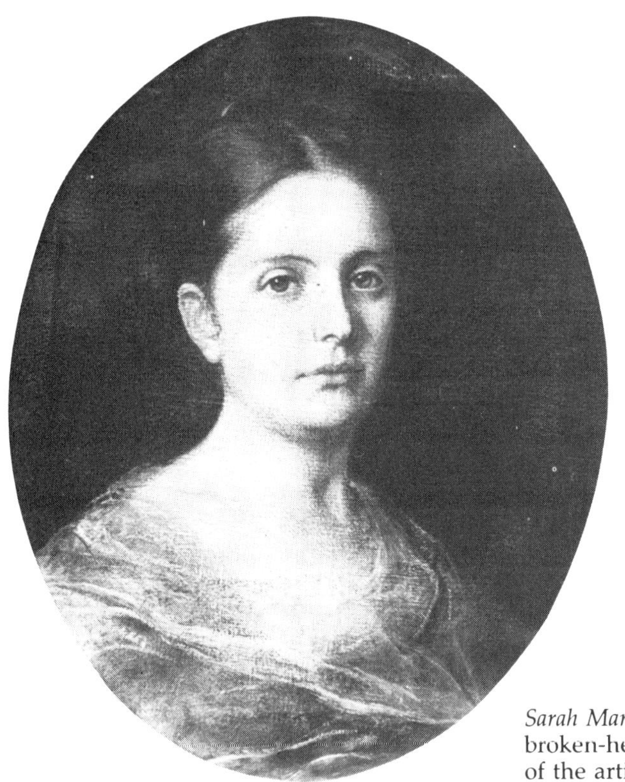

Sarah Marion Whitaker 1872: a broken-hearted sister-in-law of the artist.

whom, until that date, only the Royal Academy and the British Institution catered. It was founded to complement the Academy rather than compete against it. John Nash had been commissioned to build the galleries, which were in a cul-de-sac off Pall Mall East, and his handsome doric facade led into a suite of six well-proportioned rooms. Exhibitions at the gallery were held from April to July.

In 1868 Leighton was elected a full Academician, and on receipt of Johnny's congratulations, wrote the following: 'Many thanks for your amiable note on the subject of my election. I am very glad to hear that you have been enjoying a holiday – I wish I could say as much for myself for the work one does in this tryingly sultry weather is really not worth much, and the pictures are progressing only very slowly. I shall not get clear away till the middle of September but I shall be obliged to take *some* holiday before that; I shall probably leave town for a few days on the 24th, and go backwards and forwards during August. I am charmed to hear that you have sold your Rembrandt so well, and very much obliged by your kind thought about the Barkers. Remember me very kindly to Mrs. Nan and give my love to Master Freddy and believe me Yours very truly, Fred Leighton.'[61]

In his early days Walker exhibited mainly heads, landscapes and subject pictures, although he was already painting family portraits. His earliest existing portrait is a pastel he made of Fanny during their engagement, which shows her wearing a black bonnet tied with blue ribbons. It is one of his best works, and it is interesting to compare it with Leighton's portrait of her. In 1870 he painted his wife's youngest sister, 'Nell', who was only two years older than their own baby! He also painted another sister-in-law, Sarah Marion Whitaker, who died a year or so later of a broken heart, or so it was said, because she was refused permission to marry her first cousin. These early portraits show Walker's style to be direct, with an excellent facility for catching a likeness. The face is always carefully drawn and painted, the flesh tones are particularly good, as is the texture of the hair. The painting of the clothes is more freely handled, garments are outlined and special emphasis is achieved with impasto. There is a Leightonian influence in the way in which frills and folds are painted, and there is considerable underpainting. On the whole his colours are muted and subtle, but he often uses a spot of strong colour in the middle of a relatively sober picture to emphasise a point, something which he may have learned from Millais.

It must have been difficult for a painter who had had a modest education to grapple with the new vogue for classical subjects. Walker tended to keep to short titles, such as *Greek Girl* or *Ariadne* for his paintings. Besides oil, he also worked in watercolour and pastel, and in 1872 he exhibited a watercolour entitled *Dolly Varden*. The popularity of Dickens' *Barnaby Rudge* had brought in a 'Dolly Varden' craze: it was the fashion to wear dresses made of chintz or cretonne which the wearers fondly imagined to be a kind of eighteenth century costume. A hat tilted over the forehead completed the outfit.

Victorians were self-conscious about the clothes of their own age, which they felt were ugly.

In 1870 Fanny's third child in three years was born, for Frederick had been followed by a second boy, Robert, and now a daughter, christened Frances Sarah Marion (but nicknamed Sissie) appeared. This had necessitated a move to 14 Montpelier Square, Kensington. The census of 1871 opens the door of the house to show their very full household, headed by John Hanson Walker, now aged twenty seven and Fanny, one year his junior. Also there were the two youngest children, Robert aged one and 'Sissie' – 4 months, but there was no mention of the two-year old Frederick. They had a boarder, William Drury, the young Curate of the nearby All Saints Church, Knightsbridge, and two visitors. The latter were George Brightwell, a landscape artist from Brantham

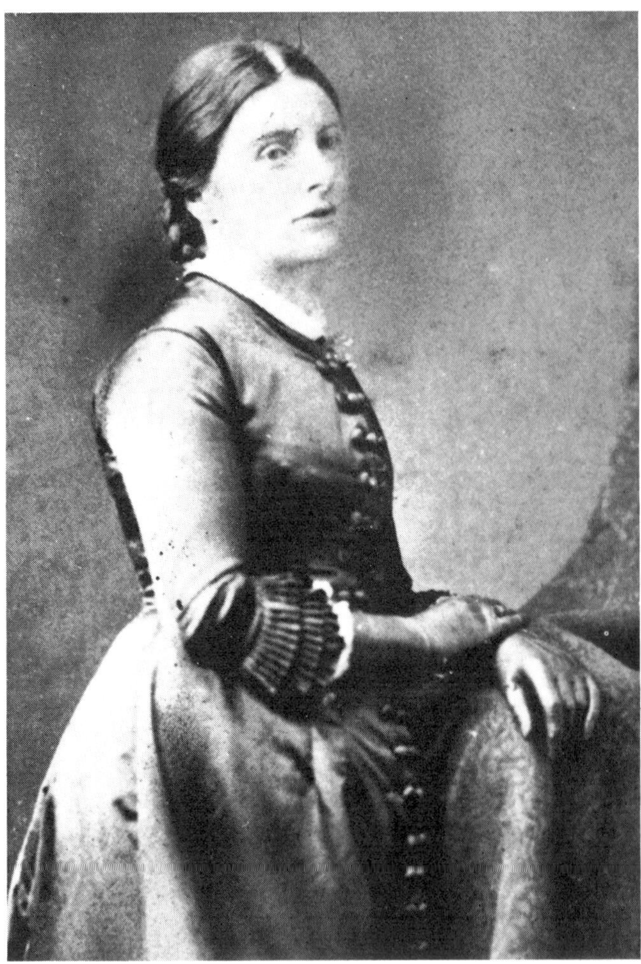

Fanny Walker: photographed *circa* 1872.

in Suffolk, who flourished as an artist for the remarkably short space of only four years, and George Goodson, an eighteen year old hatter from Colchester. Fanny's living-in maid, Grace Martin, a twenty-one year old London girl, completed the household.

From the beginning of their marriage, Fanny had taken over full responsibility for the house, leaving her husband free to paint – she had the better head for business of the two, and a photograph taken at about this date shows the toll that hard work and child-bearing had already taken of the beautiful girl Leighton painted. The care of a growing family, and the struggle to get a footing for Johnny must have caused her many headaches. She suffered, too, from a jealous temperament, and so like many Victorian artists' wives (Mrs. Briton Riviere, for example) she refused to allow Johnny models.

Painting alone could not easily support their growing family, and John Hanson Walker thought about getting other employment. In 1870 the Academy Schools were being re-organised to introduce an improved system of instruction, wherein a preliminary painting class was introduced, to give special tuition in the knowledge and use of pigments prior to students entering the upper school of painting. The Curatorship of the school was advertised with a salary of £200 per annum, and it appears that Walker decided to apply. He wrote to Leighton for a testimonial and got a firm reply: 'I have just received your note, and hear with sincere regret that you have not been prospering lately in your affairs. I am in great difficulty as to what I can do for you in the matter of the Curatorship. If it were only a question of testifying to your character, zeal, industry, etc., etc., I should have real pleasure in giving you that testimony in the highest and fullest degree. But, my dear Johnny, if I am not very much mistaken, the Curator is expected when required *to advise and direct the pupils*, and I cannot in candour conceal from you that your age and experience do not appear to me yet to qualify you for that part of the duties. If it were not so, why does the candidate send in some of his works for inspection? You must not be angry with me, Johnny; you know I have always spoken the plain truth to you, and am always ready and desirous to help you when it is in my power. I should be only too glad to think of you obtaining some post that should relieve you from all immediate pecuniary care. Give my love to your wife and children, and believe me always, yours most sincerely, Fred Leighton. P.S. I shall be back on Wednesday or Thursday'.[62]

In the kindness of his heart, Leighton wrote again the next day, 'My dear Johnny, In case any alteration should have been made in the arrangements of the schools during my absence, and that *teaching* is not expected as part of the duties of a curator, I send you a letter to the Council, as I should be sorry you lost any fair chance by my absence. You heard from me no doubt yesterday'.[63]

In the years 1867–1872 Walker exhibited only eleven paintings, and probably supplemented his income during that period by doing copy work at both the National Portrait Gallery and the National Gallery, where W. S. Spanton mentions having often worked with him. To work in the gallery, painters needed a special ticket and recommendation. Unfortunately these records are now missing, but copywork was lucrative, and many well-known artists did at least some.

Walker also probably wrote to Leighton to ask if he might copy Nan's portrait, for copies still exist by him. Leighton replied on September 6th: 'I have just got your letter, and scribble a line in haste (for I am very busy) to say that you are wholly at liberty to do whatever you choose with Nan's picture, and that I am glad for your sake that people like it. I am also much pleased to hear that you have an interesting portrait on the easel, in which you see progress and improvement in the matter of breadth and light and subordination of half tints; nothing is more important in painting; I think that after accuracy and refinement of form, it is the quality you should most strive for. I am myself tolerably well, but not by any means brilliantly. I have got to work at a few small heads, which you will see before long. In haste, with love to Nan and the children'.[64] This letter shows that Leighton still took an active interest in Johnny's progress, and that they were still in fairly close touch, seeing each other from time to time.

Johnny is remembered by his family as having a happy, out-going temperament, while Leighton was lonely and withdrawn, despite his public life. The two were about the same height – 5 feet 7 inches, although Leighton with his leonine head, must have seemed taller. Disraeli, who took Leighton as his model for Mr. Phoebus in *Lothair*, described him as 'crowned by a countenance aquiline and delicate, and by . . . a remarkable radiancy'. Johnny was lightly built, with blue eyes, dark and rather bushy eyebrows and a fresh complexion. He talked in a very precise way and was neat in all his movements, which must have pleased Leighton, who had a passion for precision and punctuality. Johnny is remembered as being very gentle and almost childish in his sense of humour, although endowed with the energy and zeal which seem to have impressed Leighton from the start.

The two men shared a love of collecting. Leighton collected furniture, Tanagra figurines, Italian renaissance statuettes, Chinese bronze bowls and vases, needlework, silver and weapons, and when he was abroad, particularly in the Middle East, pottery and porcelain. Walker had inherited his father's love and flair for collecting antiques, and from childhood days had grown up with considerable knowledge of them.

Leighton was very solicitous for Johnny when he was ill, as he appears to have been in these difficult years, with a bad knee. Leighton wrote 'Dear Johnny, Thanks for your note, I am glad Prescott Hewitt was kind to you I thought he would be – take great care of yourself – as for me it will be weeks not days before I walk again as I did. In haste, Yours always truly, Fred Leighton'.[65]

Johnny was still thinking up new ways of making work, and in doing so approached Leighton about the possibility of copying a work owned by

Leighton's patron, the stockbroker Hodgson. Again the artist had to be firm with him: he writes to Johnny from Malinmore, in co. Donegal 'I have got your note, in regard to which I feel some little embarrassment. I am, as you know, always pleased when it is in my power to be of any use to you, and I should therefore wish to help you in this matter concerning which you write. I own, however, to having some hesitation in asking this favour of Mr. Hodgson, because I fear that the granting of it would be a source of a good deal of inconvenience to him, and he might, out of his old friendship, be put in an awkward position; he would be equally loth to say "yes" or "no". The picture hangs in his dining-room, *and cannot possibly be moved*. The copy would be a lengthy affair, for there is an enormous amount of work in the group you speak of, and you would have, therefore, to be established for a long time in a room which is in daily use by the family. I do not at all say that he might not grant the favour you ask, but I own I feel that *I* cannot, discreetly, ask it of him. I am sure you will not misinterpret my declining, and I shall be very sincerely glad if you yourself succeed in your direct appeal. I trust you and yours are thriving, and that you have not suffered lately from your leg. This is a wild, wind-swept corner of Ireland in which I am staying, and abounding in matter for studying, especially rock forms, but the inconstancy of the weather puts sketching almost out of the question. This is a matter of comparative indifference to me, as I came here purposely for rest, and not for work. Give my love to Nan and the chicks. Sincerely yours, F.L.'[66] The painting referred to must be the *Daphnephoria* which Leighton painted for Hodgson in the early 1870s.

In May 1872, after four lean years, John Hanson Walker at last had two paintings accepted by the Royal Academy. These were *Idol Worship* and *La Tarantella*. The latter painting shows a small boy of three of four, (probably his eldest son, Frederick) clapping his hands as if in time to music, in a Spanish setting. *Idol Worship* appears to have been the more important of the two paintings: it was re-exhibited at the autumn exhibition at the Liverpool Museum, and he asked £126 for it. It has, unfortunately, vanished.

John and Fanny Walker must have been thrilled to be part at last of the opening of the Academy exhibition, which was one of the most important events of the London 'season'. The merits of the 'pictures of the year' were hotly discussed in the press (*The Times* reviewed the Academy Exhibition on at least four different dates) and at dinner parties. On the Sunday before the opening it was the custom of well known artists to open their studios to their friends, for a preview of their work. The *Art Journal* describes the difficulties that artists, lacking the benefit of modern lighting, often had in getting their canvases ready, as a result of winter darkness and fog, and the furious activity that reigned as March drew to an end to get work completed. The article describes how canvases were collected by a frame-maker's van, which was always in a tearing hurry, so there was hardly time to wrap a cloth round them. Two days were allowed for the sending in, and works were received by the Academy far into the night on those days. Vans were unloaded at the west door of the building, and by the second day there was an unbroken line of traffic in Piccadilly. The new hands often accompanied their paintings as far as the lift, gazing as it bore the fruit of their labours away with mingled feelings of love and fear.[67] 'Varnishing Day' was on Tuesday, a private view day for the press on Wednesday, and on Thursday royalty was received, before the public were admitted on Friday.

The Times reviewer, Tom Taylor, reported that the 1872 Academy Exhibition was the largest to date. Sir Francis Grant had just acquired Burlington House, in Piccadilly, for the Royal Academy on a 999 year lease at the rent of one pound a year, and the Academy and the school had newly moved there, gaining valuable exhibition space for the summer show. There were 1,072 works on view, whereas only 1,000 had been shown six years previously. Altogether 3,674 works were submitted, and apart from the 1,072 accepted, 909 had been made doubtful, and 1,693 rejected. Of the paintings, 933 had been oils, 217 watercolours, and 57 miniatures. If a painting were 'made doubtful' it meant that works necessary to complete the hanging for the exhibition would be taken from the 'doubtful' pile.

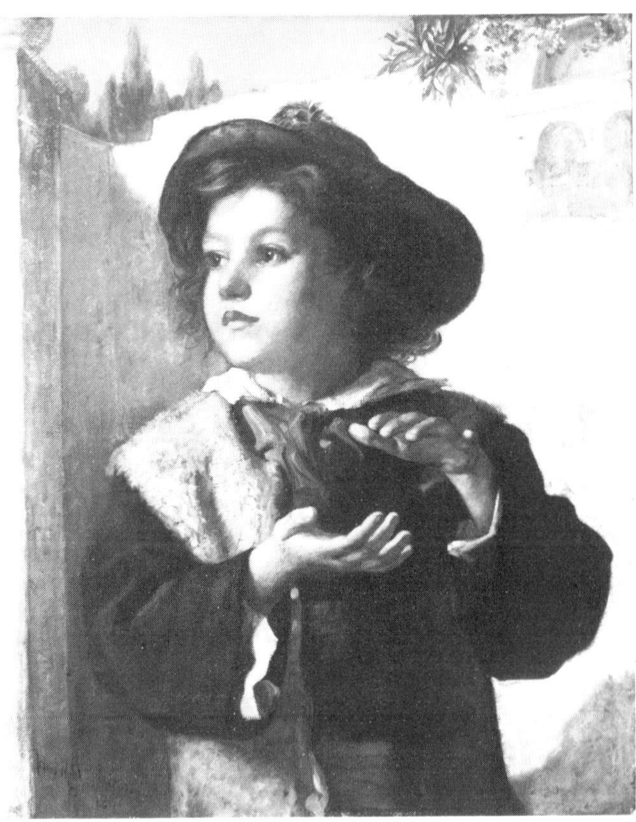

La Tarantella Walker's first exhibit at the Royal Academy, 1872.

The Times review opens 'A brilliant sun brightened the pictures for the critics. Of the general character of the Exhibition it is not easy to express any decided opinion . . . the exhibition contains a vast deal of indifferent work made to sell . . . with a predominance of the namby-pamby nursery element. As a whole it is considerably below the average in artistic merit, the prevailing type of thought is of a lower order than that which was attained in several recent years and a duller, if not a coarser art pervades the show'.[68]

Leighton exhibited *Summer Moon* (which portrayed two girls sleeping on a marble garden bench), while his other protégé, George Mason had a favourable review for his *Harvest Moon*. All the while he had been helping Walker, Leighton had looked after George Mason, whom he first met in Italy. Despite the fact that Mason was nine years his senior, Leighton protected, nagged and encouraged him, pushed him to work, found him patrons, and when these failed, dipped into his own pocket for him.[69]

Also exhibiting in 1872 were Frith, Orchardson, E. M. Ward, Tissot and, of course, Watts and Millais. The latter exhibited his painting of the three daughters of Walter Armstrong playing cards. His *Hearts are Trumps* was much praised for his magical power of dealing with flesh tints, the forms and contours of the flesh, and his mastery over colour. It seems that Walker adopted Millais' style of painting flesh rather than Leighton's, which tended to make each limb look as if it were carved from marble. The works of Briton Riviere, Alma-Tadema, Poynter, C. R. Leslie, Philip Calderon and Landseer were also exhibited, and Walker must have felt justly proud of being, at last, of the company.

1872 ended sadly for on December 12th Leighton's great friend, and Johnny's good patron, Henry Greville, died after a lingering illness. By giving Walker so much copy work for his relatives, he had done him an untold service, for his introductions were to act as a springboard for Walker as an up-and-coming young portraitist. His first big commission, gained in 1874 was to paint the Egertons of Tatton Park, who were related to Greville through his sister, who had been the wife of the 1st Earl of Ellesmere. This commission was to come two years after Greville's death, and will be described later, but it was to lead to a network of good portrait commissions for Johnny in the future.

The paintings which Walker exhibited at the Academy 1872–6 included subject pictures as well as portraits, and the titles of these, I fear, would qualify for *The Times* 'namby-pamby' school of painting. Titles like, *The Catechist*, *Luck* and *5 o'clock p.m.* probably pandered to the sort of painting the public wanted to buy, – paintings that exemplified the cult of 'home' as a haven of rest and protection, with the joy of domestic happiness. When he exhibited *A Beggar Boy* at the Suffolk Street galleries in 1873, it is doubtful whether this was an attempt at social realism (his *Beggar Girl* of 1882 certainly was not). Social realism had been explored earlier by Ford Madox Brown with his *Work* exhibited in 1865, and by Frank Holl, who wanted to bring the crime of poverty to the attention of the minds of Mayfair. However the public had been uninterested: *Work* was badly hung when re-exhibited at Leeds in 1868 and then vanished for a decade, while Holl's *Newgate Prison* was ignored, though the public raved over his portraits. The art criticism of Thackeray indicated the role that art must play – elevating, doing good, making decent people more decent and warm and happy; an art from the heart to the heart.[70] Thackeray felt that paintings should be kindly, beautiful, inspire delicate sympathies and awaken tender good humour.

Leighton still gave Johnny introductions for commissions, as can be seen from the following short letter, written from Warsash: 'Dear Johnny, Your kind note has been forwarded to me in the country; I am happy to say that I am getting on considerably better in the country air and that I hope before very long to get to work again. I am however in doubt whether I shall get through my picture for the Exhib. You tell me of a Mr. Brentnall who has called on you – I don't think I ever heard that name; he does not come from me, but I earnestly hope he may give you a commission – whoever sent him. I am sorry you say nothing of your own knee – I hope that it is a sign you are right again or at least much better. In haste – with kind regards to your wife. Yours very sincerely, Fred Leighton.'[71]

Walker still painted the occasional picture which was very Leightonesque in style, but with mixed results. For instance his *Neapolitan Fruit Seller* exhibited at the Suffolk Street galleries in 1873 and now hanging in the Victoria Art Gallery, Bath as *Italian Fruit Seller*, shows a slightly clumsy attempt to follow his master. It depicts an Italian girl with a basket of grapes on her lap, and holding a bunch of them in her hand. He used a great deal of white, in the girl's peasant smock and in the sky. This copied the effective use of white made by Leighton, particularly in his *Countess Brownlow* where the white of the dress is reflected and accentuated by the cloudy whiteness of the sky behind the figure.

In *Italian Fruit Seller* the features of the girl are very similar to Walker's own, and so the sitter may have been a relative, or the painting may even have had an element of self-portraiture to it. He exhibited a far more attractive painting at the Royal Academy in the same year, entitled *Mary*. It is a portrait of a girl with long auburn-brown hair sitting in a woodland clearing, dressed in a grey cloak with a straw hat on her arm. The sitter is thought to be his sister, Mary Ann, then aged eighteen, as she bears a strong likeness to the painter. Mary Ann was a dressmaker, and her pink sprigged muslin dress, probably made by herself, just shows beneath the cloak. A small spray of fresh poppies and wheat ears on the hat give a tiny patch of bright colour to the muted tones of the painting. The picture conveys a feeling of 'mood' more clearly than do others painted at this time, and this may be an indication that Walker's most successful portraits like those of Leighton and many other portraitists, were of friends or people he knew well.

Walker continued to paint landscapes, and these he exhibited at the Dudley

Art Gallery, which specialised mainly in watercolours. The gallery had been founded in 1865 with the landscape painter and watercolourist Walter Severn as one of the founder members. Severn, who was a contemporary of Leighton's, was a friend of Walker's; he was married to Ruskin's niece, and was much influenced by the great critic. Ruskin had prophesied in 1848 that the Pre-Raphaelites would found 'a school of Art nobler than the world has seen for three hundred years'; but the movement, revolutionary though it was in England, was destined never to spread further than the country of its origin. 1874 saw the birth of what was to become a world-wide revolution in art, for it was in this year that the first 'Impressionist' exhibition was held in Paris; the derisory nickname was given to the group by a mocking critic, Louis Leroy, on seeing Monet's painting of the sun seen through the mist of the harbour at Le Havre entitled *Impression: Sunrise*. Leighton much admired the landscapes of a supporter of Renoir, Cezanne and Monet, called Charles-Francois Daubigny. Daubigny, (who was nine years older than Leighton) was of the Barbizon School, and painted with a feeling of light and space similar to the effect Impressionists tried to achieve. Leighton had invited

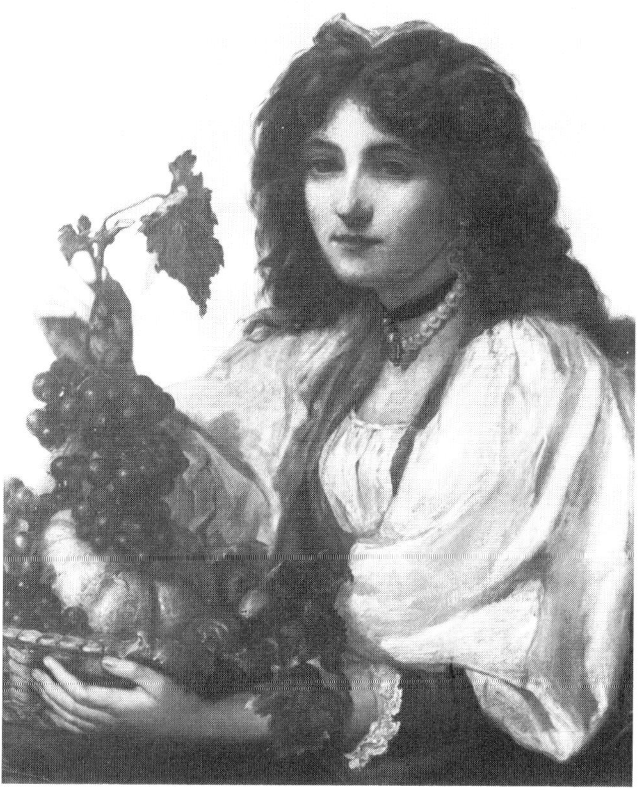

Italian Fruit Seller 1873 (Victoria Art Gallery, Bath).

Daubigny to England in 1866 and owned one of his paintings. He was therefore among the first to acknowledge the value of this new sort of painting, and one wonders how much he would have discussed it with his young protégé, Johnny.[72]

John and Fanny had a fourth child in 1872, a second daughter, whom they christened May, and two years later another son, named John Hanson after his father, was born to them. The increase in their family necessitated a double move, first to 68 Earl's Court Road, and then to 4 Penywern Road, (just off the Earl's Court Road) which they were to occupy for the next seven years. Penywern Road was developed in 1873, and so the Walkers moved into a brand-new house with a 99-year lease, which had three storeys above ground and a basement. It had a doric portico and bay windows on the ground floor, and a stucco facade. Charles Booth wrote 'the tide of fashion and favour which flowed towards Brompton exhausted itself in the Wild West of Earl's Court!'[73] In reality the Walkers' neighbours were mainly lawyers, clerks and military men, but they also included a ship owner and a railway contractor, all good solid middle-class citizens!

CHAPTER FIVE

THE DOOR OPENS

The year 1874 opened with a great opportunity for John Hanson Walker, for he was commissioned to paint four members of the Egerton family, whose seat, Tatton Park in Cheshire (now belonging to the National Trust), was a Regency house built by the Wyatt family standing in beautiful grounds laid out by Humphrey Repton. He was asked to paint a large portrait of William Tatton Egerton, the 1st Baron (1806–1883), and a trio of three portraits of the 1st Baron's son, Wilbraham and his wife, Mary, and their only child Gertrude Lucia, which were to be the same size.

The Egertons were distant cousins, through marriage, of Henry Greville's sister Harriet Catherine, who was married to Francis Leveson-Gower, 1st Earl of Ellesmere, who had taken the name and arms of Egerton in 1833. The two families were both descended from John Egerton, 2nd Earl of Bridgewater.

Walker must have felt extremely honoured by this commission for the Egertons were great patrons of the arts, the bulk of their collection being built up by the two Wilbrahams: the father and the son of the first Baron. The elder Wilbraham had purchased a valuable Van Dyck altarpiece, *The Martyrdom of St. Sebastian,* and his grandson shared with him his interest in classical Italian paintings and an appreciation of the Dutch school.

Hanging at Tatton today are Walker's portraits of William Tatton Egerton, the 1st Baron and his daughter-in-law, Lady Mary Egerton. A portfolio of miscellaneous photographs there includes all four paintings: the portrait of Gertrude Lucia is still in the family, but the portrait of Wilbraham has disappeared.

The painting of William, the 1st Baron hangs in the Family Entrance Passage at Tatton. It shows a youthful and keen looking seventy year old, dressed in a black jacket and white wing collar, sitting holding a letter in his hand. Until he was created Baron Egerton by the Whig Prime Minister Lord Palmerston in 1859 he had sat as Member of Parliament for North Cheshire for twenty-six years. He was married to Lady Charlotte Loftus, the eldest daughter of the 2nd Marquess of Ely (noted for her sharp tongue and nicknamed 'Tatty'), but at the time the portrait was painted he had been a

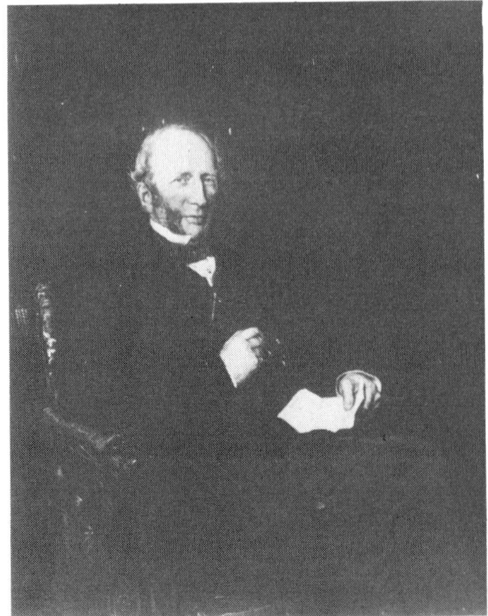

William Tatton, 1st Lord Egerton, 1874.

Lady Mary Egerton, 1874

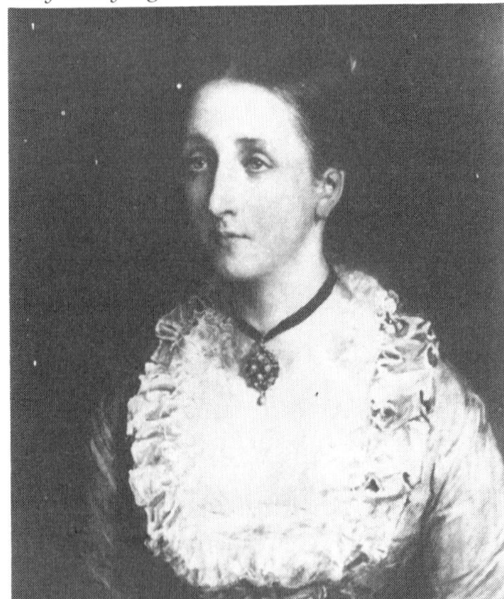

widower for four years. Walker has painted this portrait in a very direct way, and the flesh tones are excellent. The face is very accurately painted, and conveys an immediate impression of the 1st Baron. The clothes are outlined in, with heavy impasto to emphasise parts of the dress in places.

The portrait of Lady Mary Egerton now hangs in the Chintz bedroom at Tatton, although originally the trio of portraits hung in the Little Dining-Room. Lady Mary is shown wearing her brown hair plaited and coiled on the back of her head. Her dark cream dress has a low neckline, and she wears a black velvet neck ribbon from which hangs a pendant of emeralds, diamonds, pearls and rubies. Lady Mary was the eldest daughter of the 2nd Earl Amherst. She married Wilbraham Egerton in 1857, and their only daughter Gertrude Lucia was born in 1861. Lady Mary interested herself in the Primrose League and the Red Cross, but like many Victorian women she may have felt herself a captive in her own home. The portrait is made memorable by the sad and haunting eyes which Walker has given his sitter, investing her with an almost despairing, vacant, look. She died in 1892, and after her death her husband was re-married to Alice, Duchess of Buckingham and Chandos. Lady Mary's portrait is more subtly handled than that of the 1st Baron, and seems to be painted with a more authoritative touch. Again the flesh tones are excellent, but this time the portrait is very softly painted, and there is less

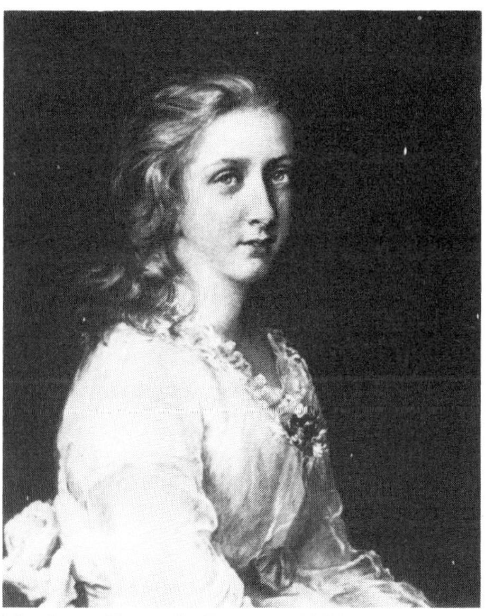

The hon. Gertrude Egerton, 1874.

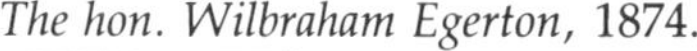

The hon. Wilbraham Egerton, 1874.

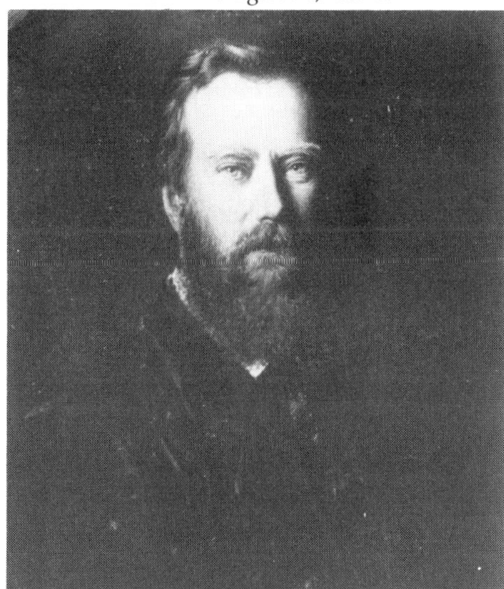

outlining. The colouring of the dress is very subtle and gentle, and there is a good comparison between the cream beige of the material and the pink flesh tints. The ruffles on the dress are beautifully executed.

Gertrude Lucia was fourteen when Walker painted her, and like her mother, has a pensive look. However, a touch of gaiety is aded to the picture by the pink carnation pinned to her white dress. In 1881 Gertrude Lucia married the 8th Earl of Albemarle.

It is sad that Wilbraham Egerton's portrait is untraced at present, for according to his grand-daughter, the Lady Elizabeth Matheson, it was a brilliant likeness of her grandfather. Wilbraham Egerton (1832–1909) succeeded his father in 1883, and was created Earl Egerton of Tatton and Viscount Salford in 1887. He followed his father into politics, and sat as Liberal-Conservative candidate for North Cheshire 1858 68, and then for mid-Cheshire until his elevation to the House of Lords. Wilbraham Egerton played a prominent part in furthering the Manchester Ship Canal project, travelled widely in his role of art collector, and was also an authority on weapons. He was for a time Lord Lieutenant of Chester, although later in life he became somewhat of a recluse.

From the Tatton Park commission Walker obtained several others, and was launched as a portraitist into the highest circles. The fact that he later painted so many Members of Parliament must stem partly from the introductions he was given through the Egertons. It also seems likely that Wilbraham Egerton suggested him for his next commission, which was to paint a presentation portrait of James Crossley for the governors of the Chetham Hospital and Library in Manchester (where it still hangs), for Wilbraham Egerton was among the subscribers to the portrait. The resolution to have James Crossley commemorated in this way was passed in March 1875, and the painting was to be presented to the library 'in recognition of Crossley's services rendered to the library over many years, and for his valuable contribution to literature'.

The presentation ceremony was held on October 4, 1875 with Hugh Birley, M.P. officiating as Chairman, and Wilbraham Egerton was among those gathered to witness it in the black and white timbered Elizabethan style room of the library. In his presentation speech the chairman said 'It would be difficult to suggest a more appropriate gift to the library, or as he thought, a more appropriate tribute of respect and esteem to Mr. Crossley himself, than the portrait now offered to the governors. For a period of fifty years, at least, Mr. Crossley had been devoted in his attention to the Library; for more than twenty years he had been a Governor of the College; but he claimed their regard not only as a student and a governor, but also, and more especially, as one who, since the library was instituted by Humphrey Chetham, had drawn from it larger stores of learning, and had better known how to assimilate and apply that which he had learnt, than any other man. As President of the Chetham Society, and always the presiding genius, Mr. Crossley had illustrated with notes many of its valuable publications, and nothing that he touched had he failed to adorn. Of the portrait itself he would only say that it did great credit to the artist, and that it satisfied, and even more than satisfied, all the reasonable expections of Mr. Crossley's friends.'[74]

It was considered that Walker had achieved an excellent likeness of James Crossley, whom he represented three-quarters life size, sitting with a half-open book in his hand, and he obtained favourable notices of it in the Manchester press.

James Crossley had been born in Halifax in 1800 and on leaving school at the age of sixteen he had decided to spend six months reading all the Latin poets. For this he had used the Chetham Library, using the large gothic reading room which his portrait was now to adorn. After this period Crossley was articled to Mr. Thomas Ainsworth, a Manchester solicitor (father of Harrison Ainsworth, the novelist), and remained a partner in the firm until his retirement in 1860. He was a frequent contributor to *Blackwood* and a number of other journals and became a figure of some importance in the literary circles of Manchester. He founded the Chetham Society, established for the 'publication of Historical and Literary Remains connected with the Palatine Counties of Lancaster and Chester' at his house in Booth Street in 1843 and was closely involved with the society for the remainder of his life. With the surplus money raised from the subscription, Walker had also been asked to paint Thomas Jones, the Librarian, who had held the office for thirty years.

Crossley must have written to Walker to congratulate him on his portrait, for Walker replied on October 12, 1875 'Dear Sir, Many thanks for your kind letter, which really makes me feel quite conceited after the great amount of praise you were so good as to bestow on my work. I quite feel that a very great share of the success of the work is due to the great patience and amiability of my sitter. I much regret I cannot find the same qualities in *everybody* who sits to me. It strikes me the people of Manchester are particularly gifted in these virtues, hence my great success with most of the portraits I have painted about there'.[75]

Walker wrote to Crossley again two months later to commiserate with him on the fact that Jones the Librarian had died. 'December 8th, 1875. Dear Sir, I deeply regret to hear the sad news of the death of Mr. Jones. What a shock it must have been to you and all those who knew him so well. I believe you told me that you had known him intimately for thirty years. He did not appear to

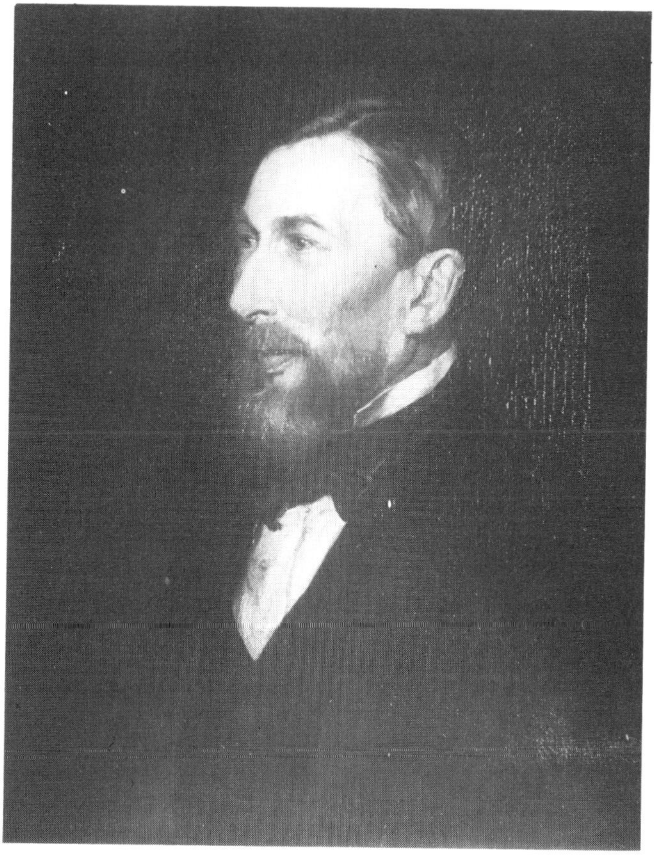

Thomas Jones, Librarian of the Chetham Society, 1875.

me to be so near his end the last time I had the pleasure of meeting him, indeed he was quite jolly and bright the night before I left Manchester. I am so glad that through your kindess I was enabled to make a portrait of Mr. Jones, which I hope is still liked'.[76]

In March the following year the Governors approved a written request from Walker that he be allowed to exhibit the portrait of James Crossley at the Royal Academy, but for some reason the portrait was exhibited at the Manchester City Art Gallery in 1876 instead, where the portrait of the 1st Lord Egerton of Tatton had been exhibited the previous year. Walker exhibited frequently in Manchester. Those who had made fortunes out of the industrial revolution in the north donated money towards building imposing art galleries. Leighton took a great interest in the foundation of these galleries, and spent a great deal of his time organising huge exhibitions for them. To exhibit in the north was lucrative, and current works of art were avidly snapped up by an enthusiastic but sometimes undiscriminating public.

Johnny now felt confident enough to ask Leighton if he might paint his portrait, and Leighton agreed, despite the fact that he had to juggle sittings to find time for them. He wrote 'Would you *very* much mind postponing our sitting till *Tuesday* at 3.30. I will also give you *Wednesday* at the same hour if you like. I have remembered that there is a ballot at the Athenaeum on Monday'.[77] The portrait was exhibited at the Royal Academy in 1877 (342) and several times elsewhere after, including the Queen's Silver Jubilee 'Victorian Era' exhibition at Earl's Court in 1897, but has sadly disappeared. It appears to have been ignored by all the reviewers except the *Art Journal* which said 'The portrait which we most affect in Gallery IV is that of F. Leighton, Esq., R.A. in a brown velvet jacket. We are glad to see that the artist, J. Hanson Walker, has really risen to the height of the subject'.[78]

The portrait was well timed, for the following year, Sir Francis Grant, who had become President of the Royal Academy during Walker's time at the Academy School, died, and in November Leighton was elected as his successor by an overwhelming majority, obtaining thirty-five votes to his rival Horsley's five. The Prince of Wales, worried by the apparent deterioration in the standard of the Academy exhibitions had actively campaigned for him. During his time as President Leighton worked tirelessly to promote the Arts, and under his leadership the Academy attained a level of prestige, power and prosperity that has hardly been equalled since.

One of Leighton's duties as President of the Royal Academy was to advise on artists for patrons who wished commissions fulfilled. In 1879 he wrote to Walker 'Dear Johnny, Do you know of any one who would do a life size *copy* of a portrait of the Queen in robes for the sum of £100? I have been asked to enquire. It is I believe for the Chelsea Hospital – in former days it might have been worth *your* while – now it no longer is – it would not pay you, but you perhaps know some less prosperous artist who would undertake it who could do it *well* for of course that is expected. Yours sincerely, Fred Leighton'.[79]

Johnny felt it *was* worth his while to do the copy, and in March 1879 the Governor of the Royal Hospital and the Chairman of the Board of Commissioners went to Buckingham Palace and selected a portrait of Queen Victoria by Winterhalter for him to copy. It fell to poor Fanny (her son later recorded) to sit for hours posing in the royal robes! Walker's copy hangs today in the Great Hall of the Royal Hospital.

John Hanson Walker could well do with a fee of £100, for the Walker home in Penywern Road was overflowing with children. Elsie Walker, their sixth child was born on New Year's Day 1876 and the following year another son, Jolliffe, was added to the family. The Walker children were pressed into service as models, and he used to paint them time and time again, just as Millais also used his own family. Like Millais, (who said that children should be 'blown' not painted on to canvas)[80] some of his most successful paintings were of his child sitters: he managed to convey the quality of soft silkiness of their skin and hair very well.

One of his most successful paintings of children was *The Bubble Company* exhibited at both Glasgow and Liverpool in 1877. The subjects were his two eldest daughters, Sissie and May, who are seen watching their brother (either Frederick or Bob) blowing bubbles from a clay pipe. This is a clever composition, and particularly interesting because it precedes Millais' famous painting *Bubbles* by nine years! The colouring of *The Bubble Company* is very clear and bright, almost reminiscent of Leighton's *Rustic Music*, and there is a lot of underpainting. The delineation of the children's faces and limbs is sharp, but the skin and hair convey their especial soft childish quality. The faces are very carefully painted while the brushwork on the dresses is free. There is a very good characterisation of the children, and a feeling of humour to the painting. A spot of very bright red at the end of the boy's clay pipe forces the eye up in the bubble's direction. The painting of the soap bubbles is particularly effective, especially when it is realised what difficulty Millais encountered ten years later when painting the bubble being blown by his four year old grandson. It is recorded that in the end he got over the difficulty by having a crystal sphere made, from which he could capture exactly the lights and colours of its aerial counterpart.[84] Millais was horrified when Pears Soap bought his *Bubbles* from the *Illustrated London News* and used it as a nationwide advertisement.

The Walker children must have found modelling as tedious as the Millais children. Mary Millais, who posed for her father's paintings *Sleeping* and *Waking* in 1867 wrote 'It was so horrid, just after breakfast, to be taken upstairs and undressed again, to be put to bed in the studio'.[82] After hours of gazing seraphically at the ceiling she would get her revenge by kicking the bedclothes off just as her father was painting a particular fold – a trick he never seemed to appreciate!

It is impressive to see how beautifully Fanny Walker dressed her children, for in every painting they appear in clothes which are full of imagination and taste. It must have been a great relief to her that her husband was now becoming more secure in his profession.

In 1878 John Hanson Walker had six paintings accepted by the Royal Academy. It is interesting to note that of the 6,138 works sent in that year, only 309 were accepted, and 1,445 made doubtful. He scored a great success with his portrait of Colonel Davies, of Elmley Park, Worcestershire which was picked out for an especial mention by *The Times* reviewer, as were also his paintings of the Hon. Home Browne and Miss Laura Fletcher. The reviewer wrote 'The (1878) exhibition brings to the front other young portrait painters of style not unlike, and in merit not far below Ouless, in particular Cyrus Johnson whose portraits all display the excellent quality of honest truth, and grapple in strong straightforward fashion with the facts before the painter, without conventionality or carelessness. Another young portrait painter of similar merit, whose work has been crowned, in one case, at least, with one of the most signal successes in the portraiture of the year, is J. Hanson Walker, whose Colonel Davies[95] in Room 2 is one of the keenest and most life-like renderings of a head on canvas in these rooms, some of the interest of which is no doubt due to the soldierly physiognomy the painter has had to deal with, but much to the force with which he has felt, and the truth with which he has expressed, the best and most characteristic points of his sitter. We see the same quality in all that bears the same painter's name, and in particular in a simple standing half-length of the hon. Home Browne (1373) in which no attempt is made to get anything out of *pose* or accessories. We should infer, besides, from a head of Miss Laura Fletcher (145) that Mr. Hanson Walker has the still rarer power of recording beauty without any undue recourse to millinery for showing it off'.[83] This review was echoed by the *Magazine of Art* which said 'Mr. Hanson Walker, whose name has not hitherto attracted much attention, has a remarkably well-painted "Portrait of Colonel Davies".[84] The *Athenaeum* commented on 'Sound honest work by our youngest artists'.[85] The committee of arrangement who had selected the paintings for the 1878 Academy Exhibition were Davis, Sant, Wells, C. R. Leslie and Sir John Gilbert.

The *Magazine of Art* reviewer in 1878 was so bold as to say 'Mr. Leighton paints trivial subjects for his admirers, and great ones for the love of art'.[86] It is pointed out that Leighton's particular skill in his portraiture was to isolate, by psychological as well as physical means, the subject of his paintings. In his portraits this allows a strong sense of the character of the sitter without the distraction of subordinate detail, and this is something that he managed to pass on in some degree to his protégé, Walker.[87]

The Times reviewer who gave Walker such a good notice in 1878 was Tom Taylor, who was the influential Art Correspondent of *The Times* from 1857 to 1880. He was also Editor of *Punch* and a playwright, writing more than seventy plays for the London theatre, mainly domestic comedies. He did much to discover and encourage talent in the young, and as his obituary in

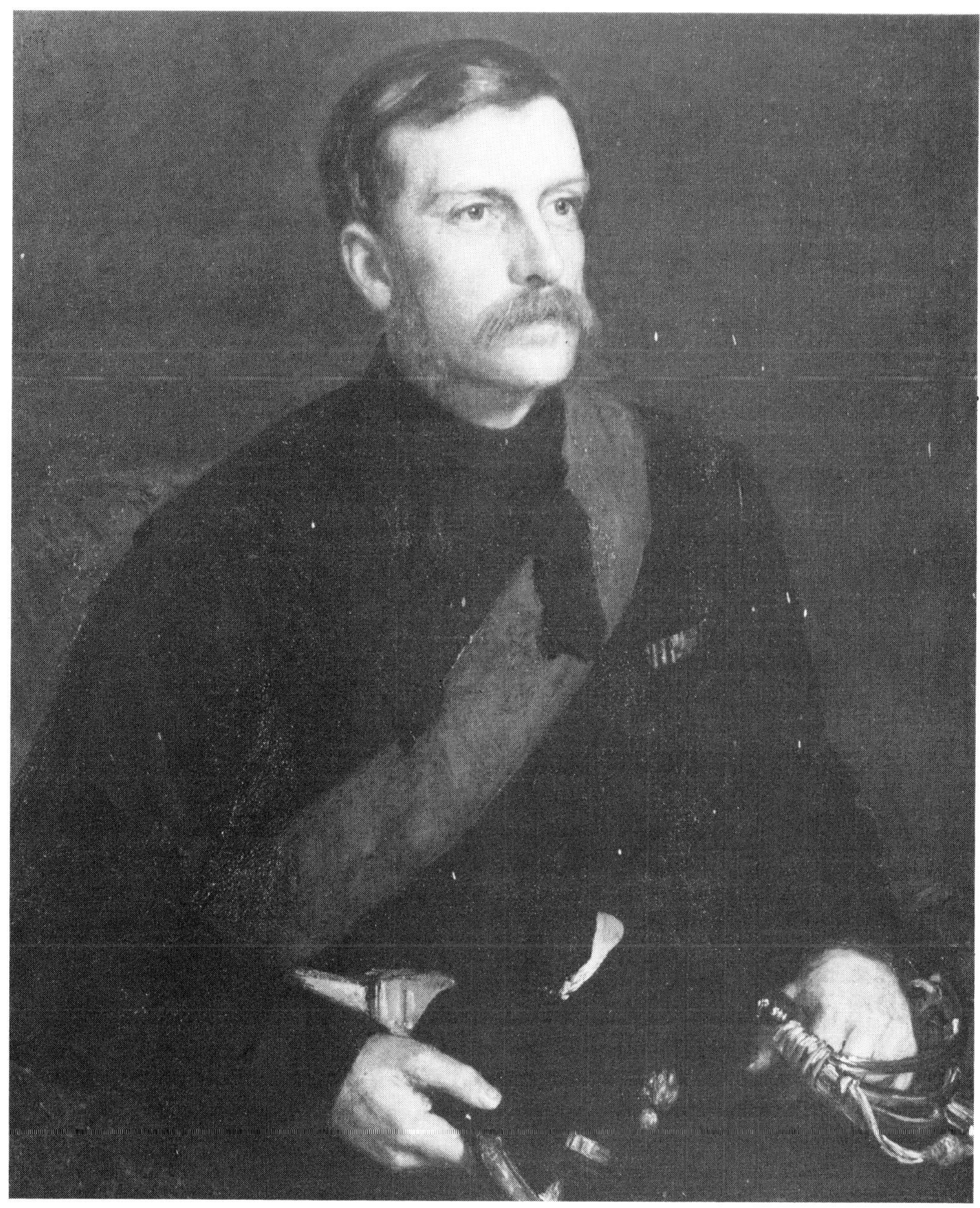

Colonel Davies of Elmley Park, 1878.

The Times said when he died in July 1880, he had 'an intimate knowledge of art, in theory and in practice, and a strong sense of justice'.[88]

Until 1877 the Royal Academy had had immense power in influencing the picture-buying public, who tended to buy there rather than through dealers. However, the system by which each Academician had the right to exhibit eight paintings, leaving the choice of outsiders' work to the mercy of the council, came under attack, as did also the type of paintings they selected. Walter Crane accused them of having 'irresponsible power' and 'corrupting influence'.

In 1877, in order to break the monopoly of the Academy, Sir Coutts and Lady Lindsay founded the Grosvenor Gallery (Lady Lindsay had been born Blanche Rothschild). The gallery was in Bond Street, and was built in a grandiose Italianate style, – richly decorated and furnished. In deliberate contrast to the Royal Academy the pictures were hung widely spaced apart, with groups of one artist's work placed together. This enabled the spectator to form an overall impression of the artist's style. Burne-Jones sent eight paintings to the opening: they were an immediate success, and he rose to sudden fame. The Grosvenor Gallery also showed Whistler's work, and became the headquarters of the aesthetic movement, giving rise to W. S. Gilbert's song in *Patience* about the 'Greenery-yallery, Grosvenor Gallery, Foot-in-the-grave young man'. Artists were asked to submit paintings to the gallery, and Walker exhibited his first painting there three years after its inauguration.

In 1879 Walker sent two portraits of women to the Royal Academy, – these were of Viscountess Sidmouth, (142) and Mrs. John Hill. (299) This year the *Athenaeum* reported that an unusual proportion of the portraits were of high quality, and *The Times* agreed. *The Times* said 'In portraiture the exhibition is particularly strong, and among the young men who most conspicuously distinguish themselves in this field are F. Holl, G. F. Gregory, J. Collier, Blake-Wirgman, Cyrus Johnson and Hanson Walker, to say nothing of the more known portraitists as Sant, Wells, Ouless, J. Archer, etc.'[89] The *Art Journal* also heartily commended his portraits of Richard Matthews, Esq. (130) and Mrs. John Hill.[90]

With both his portrait of Lady Sidmouth and that of Mrs. John Hill Walker has captured a certain quality of emotion which is not always apparent in his portraits of men. With his gentle nature, and susceptibility to feminine charm, Walker could probably relate well to his female sitters.

The portrait of Mrs. Hill is particularly appealing. She was John Hill's second wife, and had married him when he was a widower with five children. This was her wedding portrait, painted when she was barely older than her eldest stepchildren. Her fair hair is parted in the middle, and she wears no jewellery: the painter has concentrated on her youthful face, and the large lace collar of her low cut dress, accentuated by a red velvet bow to one side of it.

Both Lady Sidmouth's and Mrs. Hill's portraits are still in their beautiful original frames. At this period artists very often designed their own (this hadn't been common practice before), with the idea of the frame adding to the decorative effect, and even re-inforcing the message of the painting, so that symbolic elements might be included. Rossetti very often used this device, so that in his painting of Jane Morris as Proserpina, for instance, the sensual painting of the face, extended to the colour and rhythm of the drapery, is continued to the frame, which has a pomegranate motif.

Leighton, too, took great trouble over his frames, for many of his works had frames he had designed in his own classical style to suit them, with fluted pilasters at each end, a base and cornice or pediment above, decorated with classical mouldings and borders. These often echoed the architecture in the picture, thus producing the overall aesthetic effect he wanted.[91]

Walker exhibited five portraits at the Royal Academy Exhibition of 1880 – these included Viscount Sidmouth, who had followed his beautiful wife by having *his* portrait painted, and Maud and Gwendoline, the step-daughters of Mrs. John Hill. He also painted Mrs. Moncrieff, wife of Colonel Alexander Moncrieff, who followed his wife by being painted himself the following year. Like many of Walker's sitters, the Hills and the Moncrieffs were to become close family friends, and to found friendships which exist still in the present generation.

The Academy Review in *The Times* of May 3, 1880 relates that the winter had been such a gloomy one that it had interfered with painting to the extent that many important pictures never reached completion. (The enormous amount of coal burnt led to the notorious London 'pea-souper' fogs). Gloom had also been cast by the fact that the Grosvenor Gallery was proving a rival to reckon with, and had never been so formidable as in this year, so that the Academy Exhibition fell conspicuously below the average.

The reviewer now openly classed Walker as of the Millais school: 'Millais . . . has made an excellent school, headed by W. Ouless and numbering many as yet outside the Academic pale: Lowes Dickinson, John Collier, Cyrus Johnson, Hanson Walker, Blake-Wirgman. . .'[92] Walter Ouless, who figured so conspicuously in all these reviews became known as 'the pocket Millais'. He was four years younger than Walker, and had been admitted to the Academy school one year after him. He quickly built up an enormously successful practice as a portrait painter, and was made an A.R.A. in 1877 and a full Academician in 1881. During their time at the Academy school Walker and Ouless formed a friendship that was to last to the end of their lives, and continued with their children. Walker painted portraits of all three of Ouless' daughters, one of whom, Kitty, became a portrait painter like her father.

Although he was singled out for mention with a group of other young artists for three years running, Walker sadly faded from reviews after this, rather as a racehorse fails to keep up the pace to the end of the race. It is hard to put a finger on exactly what caused a slackening in his progress – it was probably a combination of reasons. Like Millais, he was primarily a painter who had a manual and material dexterity rather than an intellectual or emotional excellence, and being denied models by Fanny meant that he had little fresh inspiration to work on for his subject pictures. He had a large family to support, and was therefore forced to play safe, and not to experiment with a new style or method of painting. Much of his painting seems to look backward for inspiration rather than forward. A good example of this is his portrait of Lord Aveland, painted in 1881. In this painting Lord Aveland is shown seated, dressed in stalking clothes. Over his shoulder is a stalking telescope, and he has a mackintosh cap in his hand. The treatment of the tree under which he sits, (which is part of Glenarty forest) and the view of Ben Vorlich in the background, seem to be influenced by the eighteenth century portraits Walker would have seen so often in Bath and studied and copied in the National Gallery.

When the 1881 census was taken, the Walkers were still living at 4, Penywern Road. The entry for their household included John and Fanny themselves, now aged 37 and 36, and their children, Frederick aged 13, (no

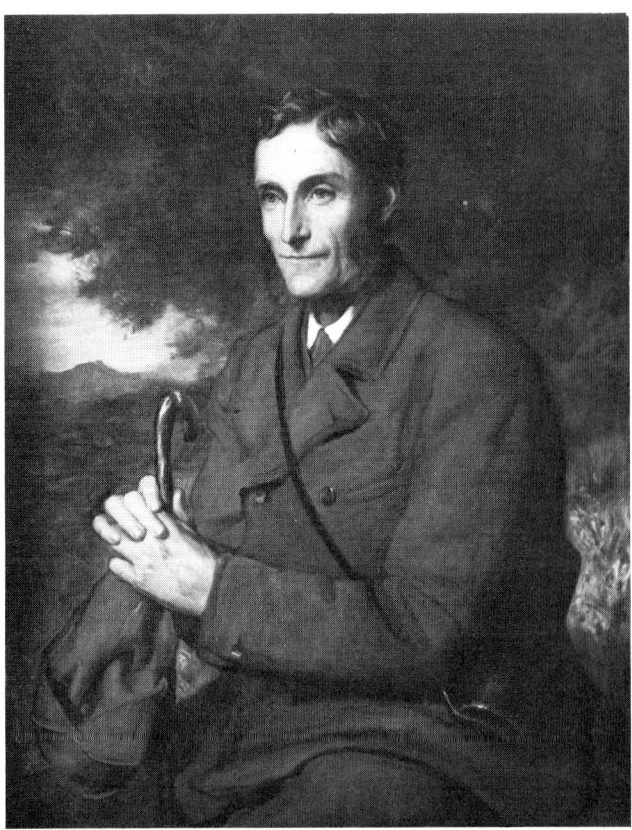

Gilbert, 2nd Lord Aveland, 1881.

mention of the next son Bob, who would have been 12), Fanny 10, May 8, John 7, Elsie 5, Jolliffe 3, and a new son, Churton, aged 2. To look after the children there was a twenty-one year old governess, Isabel Pettery, and three domestics, Fanny Brown aged 27, Anne Britten 21, and Anne Tomkins, 17.

Living next door to the Walkers at No.6 Penywern Road was the student who had been enrolled immediately before Walker at the Academy School: Theodore Blake-Wirgman. He had been born in Belgium, was living with his widowed mother and unmarried sister, and was a bachelor. He had achieved success as a portrait painter, but his most notable subject was called 'Peace with Honour' and showed Disraeli being interviewed by Queen Victoria after the signing of the Berlin Treaty in 1878. Although this painting was never shown at the Royal Academy, an engraving was made of it which became very popular. Blake-Wirgman exhibited a portrait of John Hanson Walker at the Royal Academy in 1885 (no.357) and also painted his friend, Walter Ouless.

This was the last year at Penywern Road for the Walkers, for in the following year they moved to a large brand-new house at Vicarage Gate, which was a fasionable area not too far from Leighton House in which many artists lived.

CHAPTER SIX

16, VICARAGE GATE

John Hanson Walker took a seven year lease of 16, Vicarage Gate, which was built in a newly formed cul-de-sac on land that until then had been a builder's yard. The house was imposing, with a huge porch supported by imitation granite pillars and several steps leading up to the stained glass front door. On the left of the hall was a large dining-room with stained-glass windows facing the street. The morning room, whose windows faced a blind alley at the back, took up the whole width of the house. Up the wide staircase there was a first-floor landing, where Walker had placed on a pedestal a figure of the *Dying Gladiator* which he flanked with two very large blue and gold Crown Derby vases.[93] The studio, which was such an important part of the artist's life, was built over an annexe to the north of the house. The studios of Leighton, Watts and Alma-Tadema were works of art in themselves, and Walker would have tried to emulate them.

John Hanson Walker's sixth child, Elsie (grandmother of the author) always remembered Vicarage Gate with great affection. She was six at the time of the move, and as an old lady still talked of the afternoons she spent with her parents at Leighton House, and the glory of living so near the Millais', who were at 2 Palace Gate.

Leighton kept open house on Sunday afternoons, and Walter Crane wrote of the 'princely and courteous way Leighton received his guests at Leighton House, and the crushes he had at his studio – Holland Park Road blocked with carriages, and all the great ones of London flocking to see the artist's work'.[94] Leighton gave an annual music party in the spring, and Mary Gladstone wrote after attending it in March 1882, 'Enjoyed it immensely, and the surroundings were most impressive. The King and Queen of Fiddlers (Joachim and Neruda) playing together there, and standing beneath the arch, – a background of palms, through which tiny dazzling rays of sun pierced and danced. Pictures and pretty people all in picturesque confusion, tapestry and lovely screens with hangings and a gallery with beautiful children gazing down'.[95]

The Walker children (all of whom were very good looking) may well have been among those in the gallery. Louisa Starr's daughter, Estella Canziani, who later wrote the delightful memoir *Round About Three Palace Green*, said of Leighton 'My remembrance of him was always of something big and friendly, with a soft black or brown velvet coat, and a nice long curl for me to hold on to when he danced me up to the ceiling or took me for rides. He showed me the stuffed peacock at the foot of the stairs, with its gorgeous coloured tail and throat, and also the beautiful tiles on the staircase and in the Arab Hall'.[96]

The Arab Hall, Leighton's spectacular addition to his house can still be seen there today. It was completed three years before the Walkers' move to Vicarage Gate. It was built 1877–9 to house the collection of tiles Leighton had acquired during his visits to the East, and others which had been collected for him by the explorer, Sir Richard Burton. According to Aitchison and Walter Crane the design of the hall was based on the palace of La Zisa in Palermo. The numerous seventeenth century tiles were complemented by the carved wooden Damascus lattice-work of the same period in the windows and

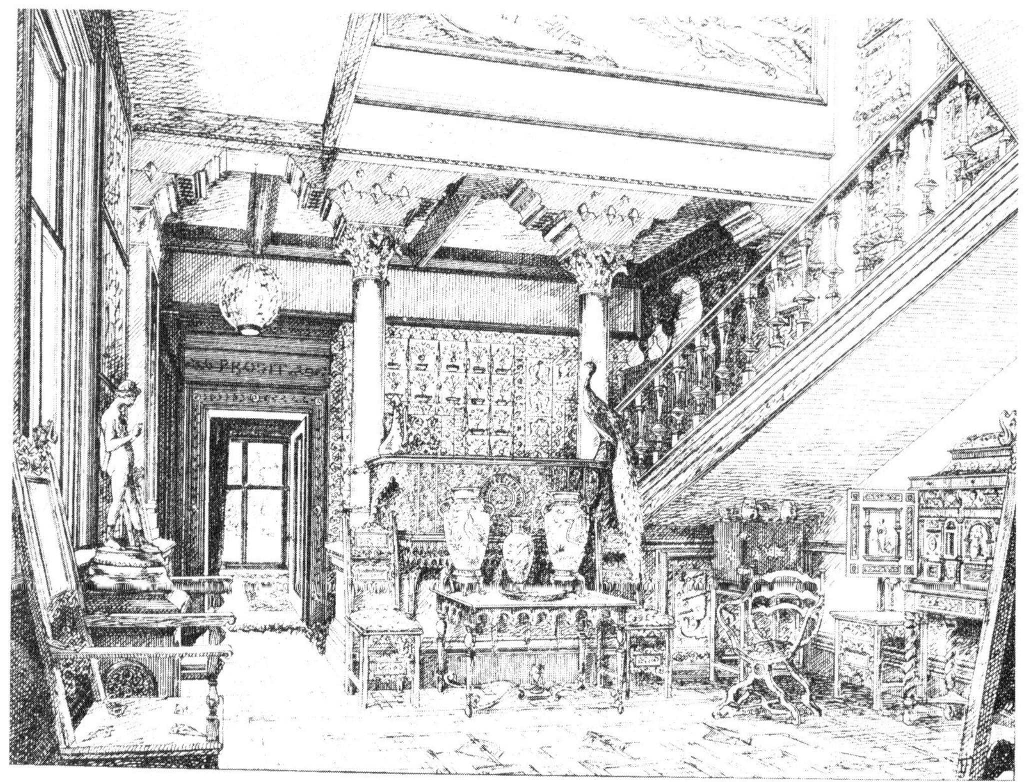

Leighton House: an early print (prior to the addition of the Arab Hall)

gallery above and a pool and fountain below. Apart from the tiles, the Arab Hall contains the work of several outstanding Victorian artists, for the capitals of the smaller columns were modelled by Boehm, and the birds in the gilded caps of the large columns by Randolph Caldecott. The mosaic frieze was designed by Walter Crane. At the time the Arab Hall was built the ground storey at the front of the house was extended to the west, and the entrance was moved from the westernmost of the original three bays to the easternmost.[97]

By this time a whole artist's colony had grown up round Leighton House. Hamo Thorneycroft, the sculptor, had come to live next door to Leighton at number 2a, a house built for him by Norman Shaw. Valentine Prinsep (son of Thoby) and his wife lived at number 1, a magnificent house designed for them by Philip Webb with a gold-panelled entrance hall and elegant rooms which they filled with objets d'art. (Mrs. Prinsep was the daughter of Leyland, Rossetti's patron from Liverpool). At number 6 lived Mr. and Mrs. Russell Barrington. Emilie Russell Barrington, who later wrote Leighton's biography, was the sister-in-law of Walter Bagehot, the period's most eminent writer on financial and constitutional matters, and not only wrote herself, but also painted. The house bought by the Barringtons had been brought to Emilie's attention by Watts, and when she had persuaded her husband to take it she wrote 'I felt this was indeed a delightful opportunity of entering into the highest precincts of art under the most helpful auspices'.[98]

In 1875 Little Holland House, where Watts had lived with Mr. and Mrs. Thoby Prinsep was pulled down to make way for the building of Melbury Road, and Watts asked Cockerell to build him New Little Holland House, at number 6, Melbury Road. He was living there when in 1886 he married the thirty-six year old Mary Fraser-Tytler.

Norman Shaw built new houses in Melbury Road for Luke Fildes (exhibitor of the enormously successful painting *The Doctor* in 1891) and Marcus Stone, who like Luke Fildes illustrated Dickens' works. William Burges, another friend of Leighton's, built an eccentric 'Tower House' in Melbury Road just for his own amusement.

These houses were followed by a number of other buildings representative of the advanced aesthetic ideals of the late 1860's and 70's. Inside them might have been found, creeping into the decor, a Japanese influence. There was a growing interest in Japanese art, much fostered by Whistler. This had started in the early 60's after there had been a Japanese stand at the 1862 exhibition, and in 1875 Liberty had opened up his oriental warehouse.

Both Leighton House and 16, Vicarage Gate, and indeed all the houses in the area stood in beautiful surroundings, on the edge of Holland Park and Kensington Gardens. Leighton said that 'not a sound reached him in his garden save the singing of the birds'.[99] In *Round About Three Palace Green* Estella Canziani, (Louisa Starr's daughter), remembers that every morning cows came down from Kensington Palace Gardens accompanied by milkmaids carrying milk in pails which were suspended from wooden yokes over their shoulders. They wore black bonnets, plaid shawls and coloured aprons, and called 'Milk oh' as they went. Every evening a lamplighter would go round lighting up the gas lamps.[100]

It was probably after one of Leighton's spring musical parties that he wrote to thank Johnny for a little sketch – the letter, written from Leighton House, and postmarked 1882 on the envelope reads: 'Dear Johnny, I am absolutely ashamed to rob you but you offer me the drawing so kindly that I can't possibly refuse it; I am delighted with it only you must let me give you a little drawing one day in return. With my best thanks, Yours affectionately, Fred Leighton'.[101] At some time during their friendship Leighton gave Johnny an early comic drawing that he had made when young in Frankfurt, and this is illustrated in Mrs. Russell Barrington's biography.[102]

Vicarage Gate where the Walkers now lived, had been turned into a cul-de-sac when the building of a new vicarage there necessitated the formation of a new street. The church, St. Paul's, Vicarage Gate was a unique oddity, for it was built of corrugated galvanised iron! Whether it was aversion to this building, or for some deeper motive, the Walkers began to attend the Church of New Jerusalem, in nearby Palace Gardens Terrace. They must have known about this branch of religion founded by Swedenborg (who was born in Stockholm in 1688) through Fanny's uncle, James Keene, who besides editing *Keene's Bath Journal* was Minister of the Church of New Jerusalem in Bath. The Swedenborgians (who were strongest in the industrial towns of the north of England) believed with their founder that he had witnessed the Last Judgement in 1757, and that he had been sent to preach the doctrine of the New Jerusalem (prophesied in *Revelations*) which would follow it.

Swedenborg (who published his beliefs in his *Heavenly Arcana* in London 1749–56) was a Unitarian, regarding God (in whom he saw Christ) as the sole object of worship. It was a religion that might appeal to an artist: Swedenborg believed the natural world to be an outbirth of the spiritual world, and the spiritual world of the invisible mental world, therefore unseen evil was manifested in things hurtful and ugly, and unseen good in things useful and beautiful.[103]

It was therefore at the Church of New Jerusalem that Dorothy Walker, the artist's ninth child, born on October 26th 1882 was baptized. She may have been given the name because earlier in the year Walker had painted another Dorothy, the five year-old daughter of Viscount Hood. This Dorothy, painted by Walker in profile, wearing a huge mob cap, was evidently a great character, even at that tender age. Her distinctly retroussé nose gives her face a look of defiant willpower, to the extent that it seems possible that artist and sitter had had one or two battles! The painting has much humour in it. Like Leighton before him, Walker was good with his young sitters, being well supplied with jokes and quips to keep them amused. Dorothy was the Hoods' youngest daughter, and her portrait was exhibited at the Grosvenor Gallery, (no.1). She never married, but became the family historian, writing *The Admirals Hood* and *Looking back on London,* a book full of her extensive knowledge of the city, which was published between the two world wars.

Walker exhibited five portraits at the Royal Academy in 1882, among them a portrait group of Dulciana, Ethel and Jeanette, the three daughters of C. L. Wood. Unfortunately this remains untraced, as it would have been interesting to compare it with a painting he did of his own three daughters several years later. *The Times,* reviewing the 1882 exhibition, felt that it was 'above the average'. On the Hanging Committee that year were Herbert, Millais, Ouless, Riviere and Barlow. Among the paintings shown was Whistler's *Nocturne in Black and Gold.* For ten years now he had been giving his paintings only musical titles, believing, as he himself put it, that 'Art should be independent of all clap-trap – should stand alone and appeal to the artistic sense of eye or ear without confounding this with emotions entirely foreign to it. . . .' Simon Wilson, in his *British Art* quotes this, and goes on to say 'not only did Whistler

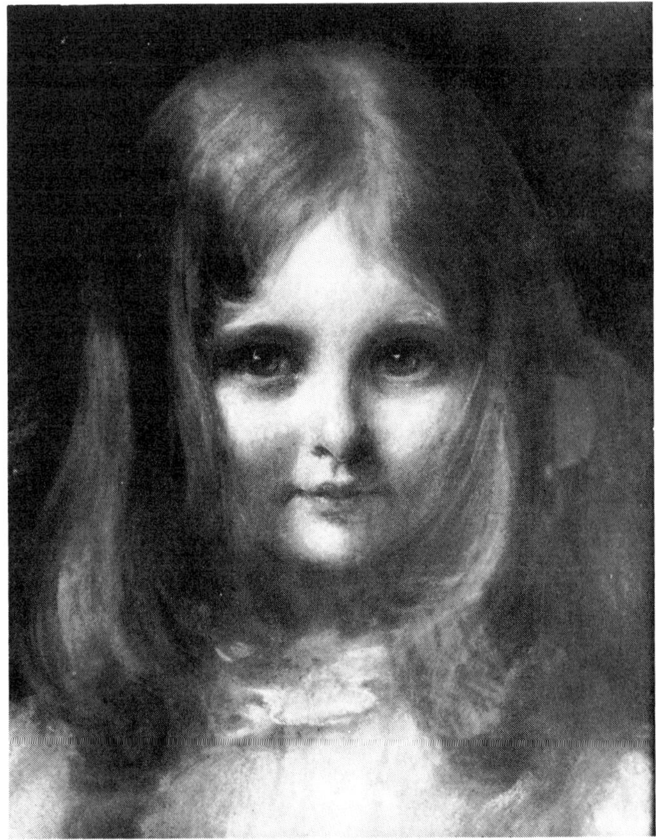

Dorothy Walker, 1885

create an art which can be seen as the only real counterpart in England in the 1870's of French Impressionism, he was, too, a tireless and vociferous propagandist of this art and the theories and ideas that lay behind it'.[104] Five years previously, there had been the famous libel case Whistler v. Ruskin, when Ruskin, reviewing the very first Grosvenor Gallery exhibition had slated Whistler's work, saying he 'never expected to hear a coxcomb ask two hundred guineas for flinging a pot of paint in the public's face'.[105] The award to Whistler was one of the most famous in English legal history – one farthing!

Leighton and Whistler had known each other well as young men, and Whistler had altered a head in one of his early masterpieces *At the piano* at Leighton's suggestion. Later, Whistler was to make many quips at Leighton's expense, but never lost his esteem for him. As the Ormonds put it, the two painters sought to achieve the same ideals from their work, – formal balance, harmony of tone and colour, and decorative effect.[106]

Leighton, despite his incessantly busy life as President of the Royal

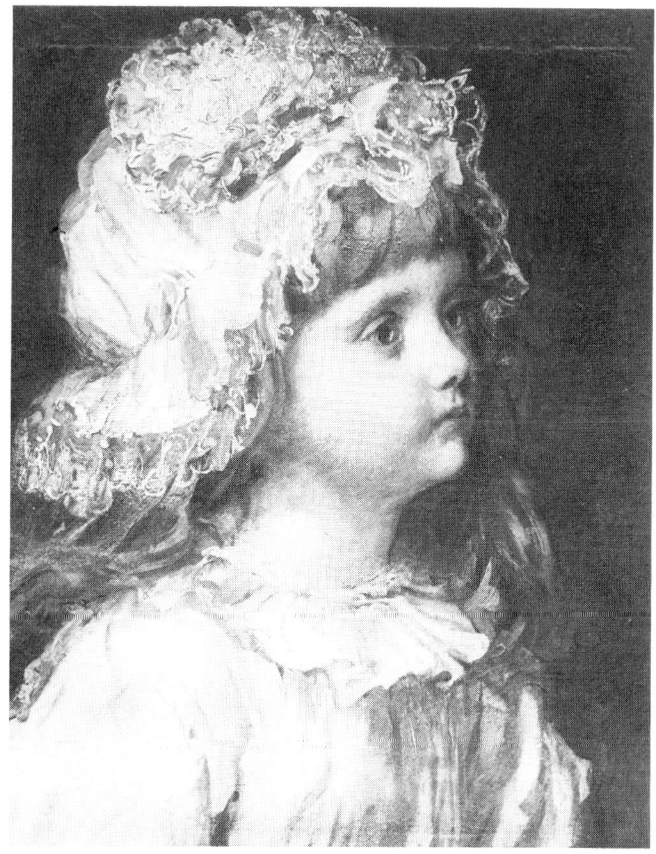

The hon. Dorothy Hood, 1882.

Academy never ceased to help Johnny by giving him recommendations. In 1882 Queen Victoria asked him to recommend a young artist to paint a picture of her son Leopold's wedding, stipulating that she wanted a good artist, but at a reasonable fee. From the list Leighton sent her, she selected the name of J. D. Linton, and Leighton recommended she pay him a fee of five hundred pounds. Victoria (who was a hard bargainer where art was concerned) thought this price much too high, and tried to negotiate a better one through her secretary, Sir Henry Ponsonby. Leighton refused to give in, and Victoria capitulated on condition that Linton painted a complete representation of the scene – at which point Linton decided to resign the commission! Victoria then asked for further recommendations, and Leighton suggested Gregory, F. G. Cotman, Claude Calthorp and T. Blake-Wirgman and added: 'another excellent colourist is young Hanson Walker a sort of pupil of mine'.[107] However, nothing came of this, as the Queen decided to use Linton after all!

Leighton's own painting, meanwhile, was moving into a new and exciting last phase, for fresh inspiration had been found for him by a new model,

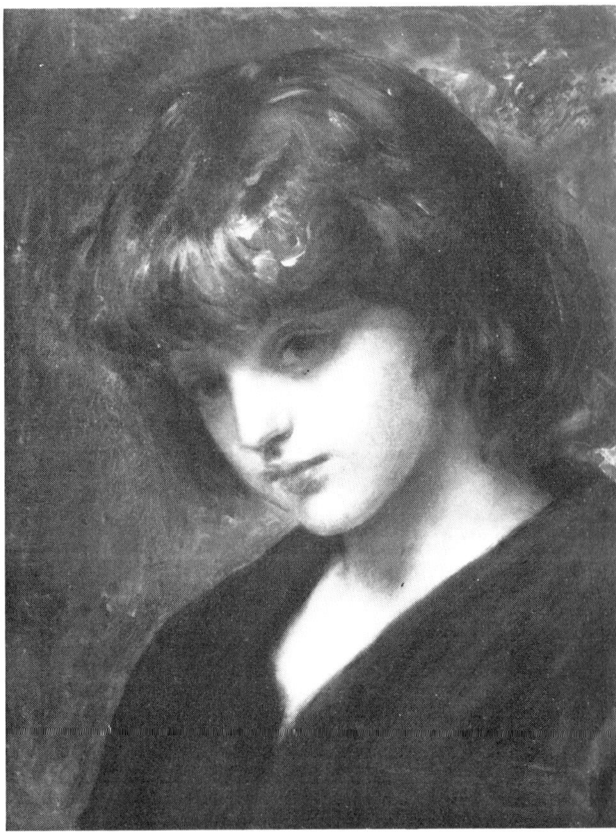

Beggar Girl, 1882.

Dorothy Dene. With the discovery of Dorothy, his ties with the Walker family may have gradually loosened.

Mrs. Russell Barrington had first discovered Dorothy (whose real name was Ada Alice Pullan) in 1879, when she had noticed 'a young girl with a lovely white face, dressed in deepest black, evidently a model' standing on the doorstep of the Holland Park studios[108], and told Leighton about her. Leighton discovered that she was sitting for Louisa Starr (now Louisa Canziani) and he and Mrs. Russell Barrington both began to use her as their model. They found that Dorothy (who was twenty, but looked much younger) was modelling in order to support her deserted mother who had a fatal spinal disease, and her eight soon-to-be-orphaned brothers and sisters. Soon Leighton began to paint three of her younger sisters as well as Dorothy, whom he had also introduced to Watts. At first Lena, the youngest sister seemed to be Leighton's favourite model, and it was only when he began to pose Dorothy naked, or thinly draped, in the mid 1880's that she woke some latent physical emotion in him, and became the presiding genius of his art, inspiring his work with an altogether more emotional and profound note. This led to Leighton's wonderful late works such as the *Garden of the Hesperides* and *Flaming June*.

Mrs. Russell Barrington had learned from Dorothy that her real ambition was to be an actress. She had however, Mrs. Barrington says 'a voice with a singularly unpleasant Cockney twang to it'.[109] Despite this, both Leighton and Emilie Barrington decided she should have her wish, and go on the stage. Leighton with characteristic generosity arranged that she should stop modelling for a period and go to Mrs. Glyn's acting school. Dorothy made her London debut in 1885, (with 'Dorothy Dene' as her stage name) and from that time on Leighton supported her every appearance on the stage, and was quite uninhibited in seeking work and introductions for her, to the extent that it was thought he might marry her. Although this never happened, Dorothy was able to release much suppressed affection in Leighton and, in visiting the girls in their own home, he was able to relax and enjoy a warm private life.

The first exhibition, at the Institute of Painters in Oil Colours at the Galleries, Piccadilly was held in 1883, and Leighton exhibited there, also Walker, who showed two paintings, *Interrogated* (294) and *Beggar Girl* (781). At this time, too, Whistler revived the galleries of the Society of British Artists at Suffolk Street, and they were granted the right to call themselves 'Royal'. Here Walker exhibited *Industry* (which he had exhibited at Manchester the previous year, with an asking price of £105), and which was a companion painting to his *Indolence* exhibited at the Walker Art Gallery, Liverpool.

Louisa Starr wrote to her future husband in the 1870's saying 'as regards income, I thought that if, as you said you have about £500-£600 a year, I could in one way or another add £300 or even £400, and we could be *very comfortable indeed'*![110] As prices remained relatively stable in the second half of the nineteenth century, falling, in fact, in the consumer's favour during and after the 1870's, it is interesting to compare this with the fact that Hanson Walker probably made between £1,000 and £2,000 annually in the late 1870s to '80s from his painting, while Leighton, at this time made about £4,000 to £6,000 every year. (£1,000 in 1880 can be equated to nearly £40,000 in 1986). For popular artists there were enormous rewards, – Millais made £30,000 to £40,000 per annum, and Landseer died a near-millionaire in today's terms.[111]

Walker exhibited three paintings at the Royal Academy in 1883, and his portrait of General Sir George Willis at Kassassin was hung 'on the line' (275). He also showed his portrait of the Hon. Ashley Eden (390), who was Lieutenant Governor of Bengal 1877–1882. This portrait, which was painted for the Bengal Chamber of Commerce and Industry, Calcutta and still hangs there, shows the Governor three-quarter length, holding a rolled document inscribed with his name at the top, which was presumably his presentation

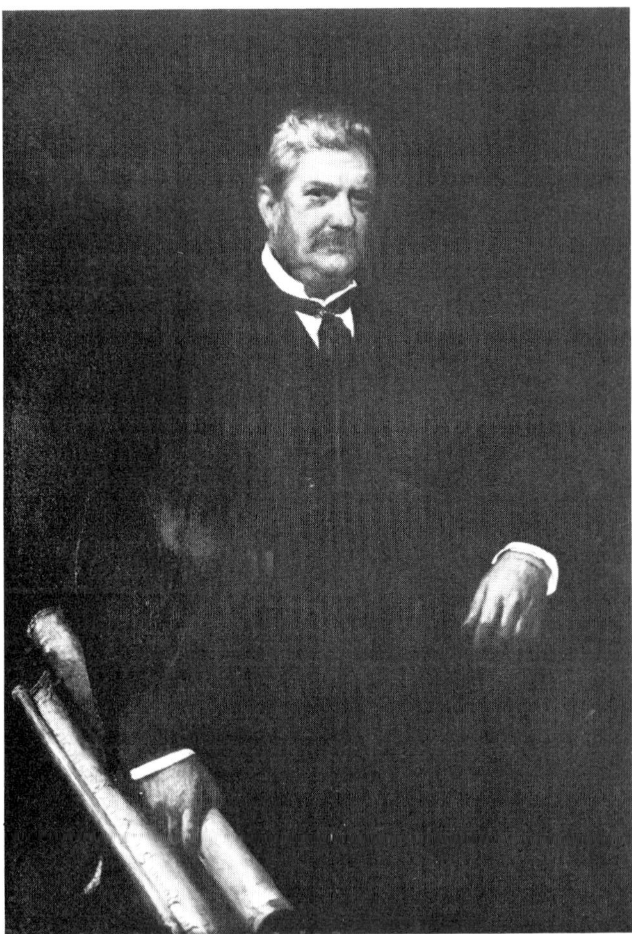

The hon. Ashley Eden, Deputy Governor of Bengal, 1883.

address. Eden must have been an interesting subject. Born in 1831, he was the third son of the 3rd Lord Auckland, Bishop of Bath and Wells. He started his official career in India as an Assistant Magistrate, but his outspokenness and contempt for the conventional led to severe criticism. He was an impartial Magistrate, but openly friendly with the Indians, whom he did not hesitate to side with, if there was any doubt, against the British Government. In 1863–4, while he was Secretary to the Governor of Bengal, he was sent on a hazardous

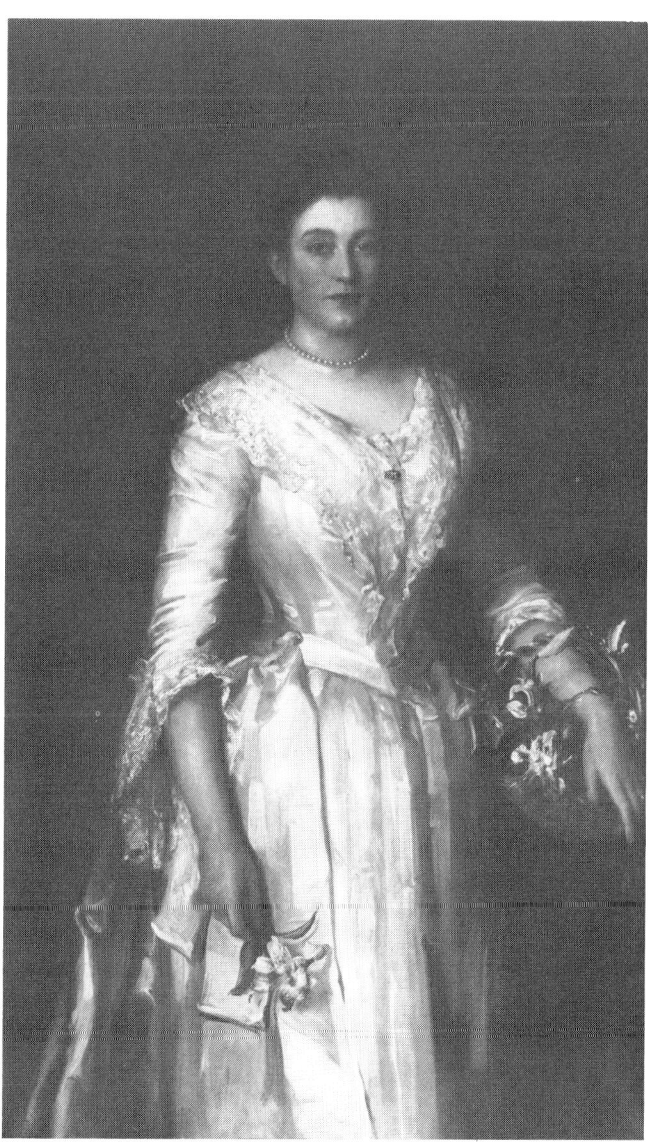

Jessie Lawrence (Lady Trevethin) *circa* 1882.

journey on foot over high mountainous passes to Bhutan, to try to force a treaty on the ruler and persuade him to hand back British territory illegally annexed. On arrival he found himself in such danger that he was forced to sign a treaty too favourable to Bhutan, for which he was again much criticised. However, he was a popular and successful Lieutenant Governor, reforming the financial system, the indigo farming, and the administration of the schools and hospitals.[112]

At Glasgow Walker exhibited the portrait of the late Colonel Mure, M.P. for Renfrew. It was a popular Victorian custom to paint an obituary portrait, and this was sometimes done from a death mask. For the Walker children this meant that their father's studio was not without its terrors, for his son Jolliffe vividly remembered stumbling upon the death mask of a Mr. Myers in his father's paint store room, and being horrified by the few real hairs he found on it. From that time on the children evolved a game, in which the words 'Mr. Myers' meant 'scatter'.

Walker still painted the occasional watercolour, and in 1883 sat on the council of the Dudley Art Gallery. Besides Severn (who was the founder-member) there were thirty-seven other council members, among them W. Q. Orchardson, Henry Moore and Ruskin. Walker's son Jolliffe, records in his memoirs, (which are, on the whole, remarkably accurate) that Ruskin considered his father to be the best portrait painter of his generation, though this exciting remark has not been traced in any of Ruskin's writings! The year after sitting on the Council, Walker painted portraits of Severn's two children, Cecil and Helen Christian, in exchange for a watercolour Severn had given him.

After a very successful period from 1875 to 1883, Walker seems to have arrived at a levelling off in his career: he exhibited only one painting at the Academy in 1884, and none in 1885. Despite Leighton's help and encouragement, he was no nearer being elected an Academician like his friend Ouless, who had become a full member of the Academy in 1880. Although he had a better year in 1886, exhibiting five paintings in the Summer Exhibition, (among them a portrait of Ouless' daughter Evelyn) he made a big decision: to venture across the Atlantic to paint in America. He collected together a portfolio of his work, said goodbye to Fanny (who was expecting their tenth child) and set sail for New York.

CHAPTER SEVEN

THE NEW WORLD

John Hanson Walker sailed for America some time in the late summer or early autumn of 1886. The New York Directory for 1886–7 lists Walker, John H., painter at h.336E, 53rd Street for that year only.[113] Walker had no personal links with the city, although Fanny's brother Ronald, an engineer, had been there several times, and her eldest brother, Walter, was just emigrating to Montana. It was now twenty five years since the Civil War had split the country in two,

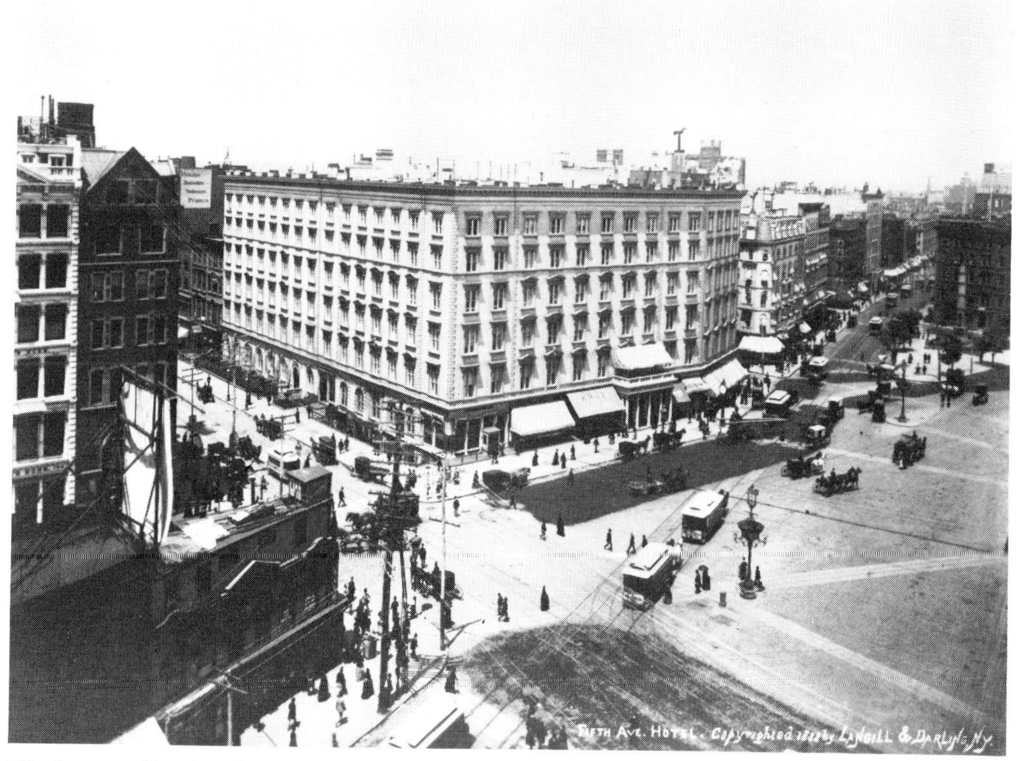

5th Avenue Hotel and 5th Avenue *1888*

and New York was growing rapidly, although Fifth Avenue was still hardly more than a double line of low brown-stone houses, of an unambitious uniformity.

There was a New York élite, almost an aristocracy, who modelled themselves on the British gentry. Gentlemen did not work except for the few who interested themselves in banking, law or government. There were no men's clubs as yet, and so they married young, and their wives gave themselves up to child-bearing, spoke softly and took care to be ornamental but not outré. Although they travelled to Europe, they were shy and tentative when confronted with the arts, were suspicious of artists or writers, and preferred, in conversation, to keep their subject to practicalities. Money and sex were never discussed, and ladies were not supposed even to think about them. Edith Wharton, who describes this era of New York Society so vividly in her autobiography *A Backward Glance* says 'their value lay in upholding two standards of importance in any community, that of education and good manners, and of scrupulous probity in business and private affairs. New York has always been a commercial community, . . . and the merits and defects of its citizens were those of a mercantile middle class. The first duty of such a class was to maintain a strict standard of uprighteousness in affairs'. . .[114]

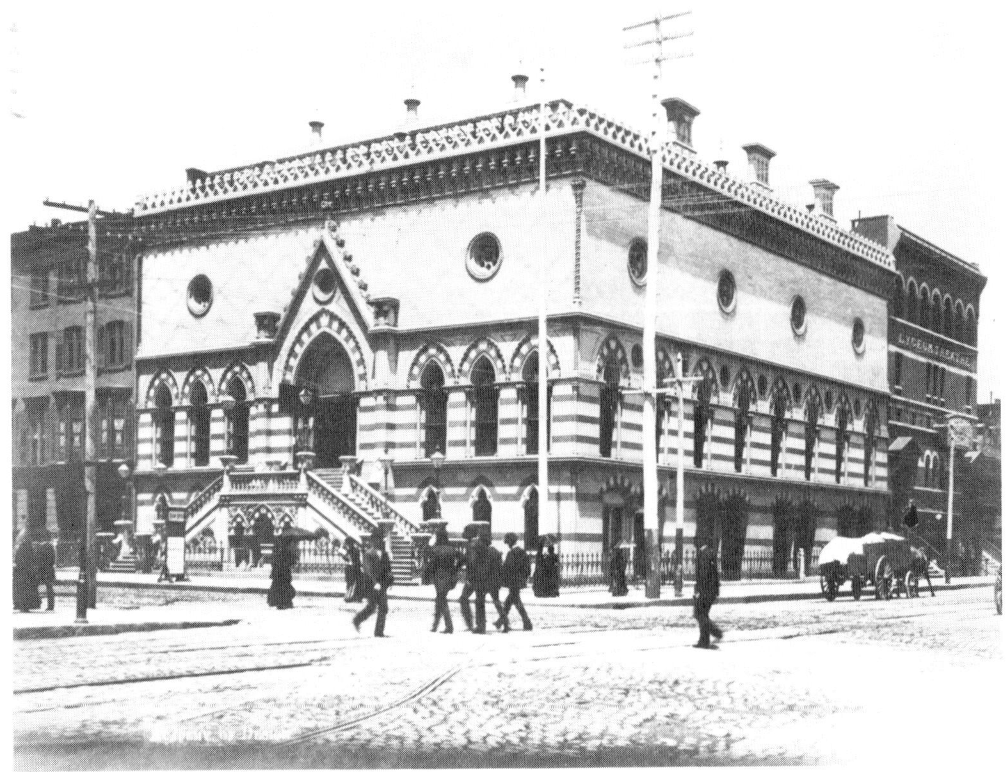

The National Academy of Design at 23rd St. and 4th Avenue, *circa 1888.*

Society had a clear code of manners, and respect for 'good' taste – it was unpretentious and wore its opulence quietly. These people had dark cedar panelling inside their houses, and decorations and stained glass by Tiffany, La Farge and St. Gaudens.

Impinging on the old elite was a new set, those who had made vast fortunes from railroads, coal or steel: the Vanderbilts, Astors and Whitneys, who lived flamboyantly. The Vanderbilts had a huge French chateau style home in the heart of New York, while Andrew Carnegie a decade later announced he intended to build 'the most modest, plainest house in New York' and ended up with a sixty-four room mansion![115]

The patrons of art like Morgan, Frick and Mellon went to Paris and London in search of pictures. In Paris a patron could visit all the greatest studios without an introduction; by the end of the century they had Duveen to supply them with paintings prised from aristocratic walls in England. The young American artists went to Paris to be trained in the ateliers, and were not felt to have made their mark unless they had been to Europe. The State encouraged architects but not artists. In consequence, there was an opening for a London portrait painter to fill their place and Walker would undoubtedly have arrived with a certain cachet.

The last letter from Leighton to Walker was written to him while he was in America. It was written from Leighton House, and dated February 12, 1887: 'Dear Johnnie (the spelling is Leighton's) I was very glad to get your letter giving so very satisfactory an account of yourself and your dealings. I had already heard of your prosperity in a general way from Nan, who came to see me before starting, but who told me how lonely you felt. It must have been a great joy to you to see her again, and it will be still greater when you see the (fourteen?) youngsters about you once more; you will, like everybody who crosses the water, bring back a very pleasant recollection of American kindness and hospitality, and, I am glad to think, also a good pocketful of money. I hope it will bring you luck here. I am glad that Mr. Marquand has made you welcome in his house, which I understand is very beautiful. I know his Vandyke well; it belonged to an acquaintance of mine, Lord Methuen, who has a number of beautiful things at Corsham. It is one of the finest I know, and stands quite in the front rank of Vandykes. The Turner also I know, a rare favourite of mine. But of the Rembrandt I know nothing. I am glad, too, you thought my ceiling looked well. I hope he has introduced a little gold in the rafters to bind the paintings to the ceiling itself. Give my love to Nan, and believe me, with all good wishes, sincerely yours, Fred Leighton. P.S. Please remember me to the Marquands and to your friends the Osbornes.'[116]

Leighton had shown his painting for the Music Room ceiling at the Royal Academy exhibition the year Johnny left for America. It had a centre panel showing the figures of Mnemosyne, Euterpe and Thalia and two side panels showing the dancing figures of Erato and Terpsichore.

Henry Marquand must have introduced Walker to Henry Fairfield Osborn: both he and Osborn had been brought up in Fairfield, Connecticut. Marquand, at the time Walker visited him, was sixty-seven years old, and had retired from his activities in real estate, railroads and banking to devote himself to being Treasurer of the Metropolitan Museum.

Russell Sturgis said of Marquand that 'He bought like an Italian Prince of the Renaissance' (he had bought the Rembrandt mentioned in Leighton's letter from the Marquess of Lansdowne for $25,000). The Metropolitan benefited from many treasures given to them by Marquand, including collections of glass, ivory carvings, Renaissance iron work and a Della Robbia altar-piece. To him, in large measure, the Museum owed its growth and distinction.[117]

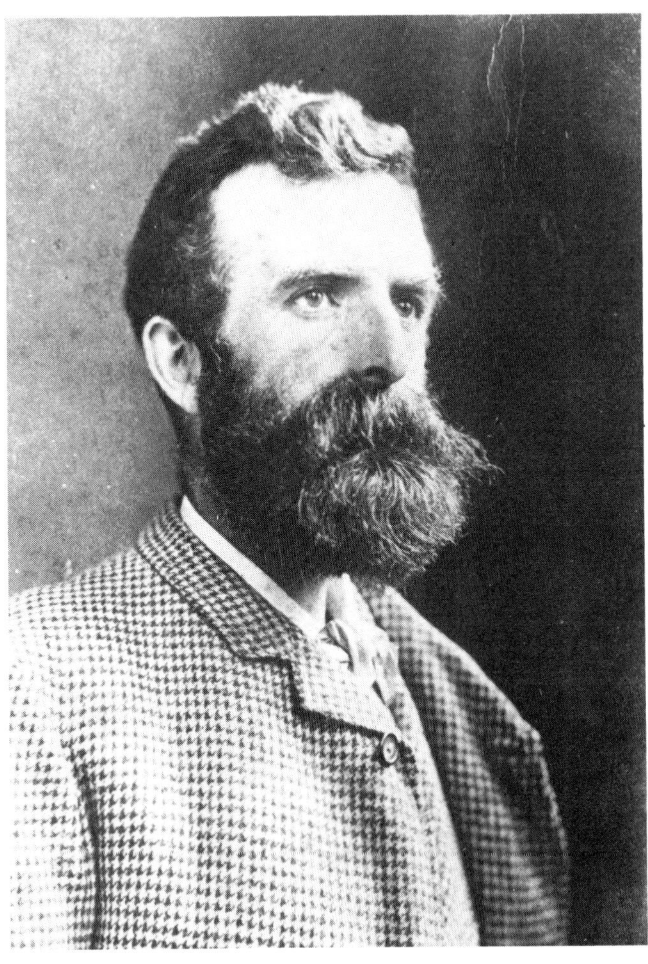

John Hanson Walker photographed in 1887.

When John Singer Sargent (who was American born but brought up in Europe) first visited America to paint portraits in 1887, he was invited by Marquand to Newport, Rhode Island, to paint Marquand's wife Elizabeth. Walker was undoubtedly very lucky that Leighton had given him an introduction to such a grandiose patron of the arts.

Henry Fairfield Osborn was much younger than Marquand: he was only twenty-nine when Walker, who was now forty-two, visited America. Osborn was then Professor of Comparative Anatomy in Princeton: through the popularisation of palaeontology he was to make 'dinosaur' into a household word. In 1881 Fairfield Osborn (as he was always called) had married Lucretia Thatcher, daughter of General Alexander James Perry, of Augusta, Georgia. They had five children and in 1890 Walker was asked to paint their small son, named 'Fairfield' after his father. This portrait was exhibited in the Loan

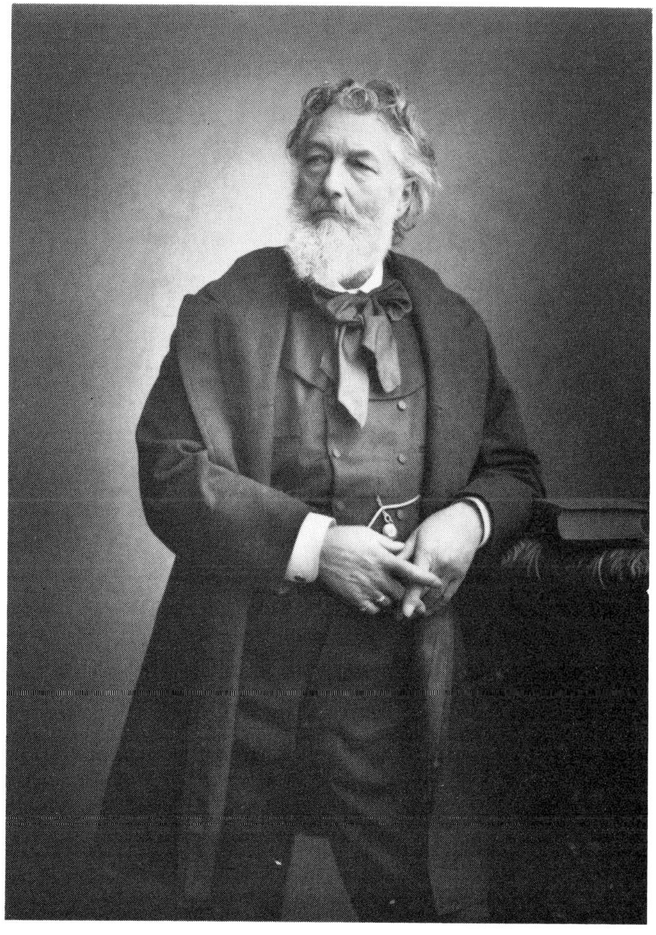

Leighton. Photograph by Walery.

Exhibition of Portraits for the Benefit of the St. John's Guild and the Orthopaedic Hospital at the National Academy of Design in 1895 (no.325). Another Walker portrait of Mrs. Eleanor Duer Wilson was lent to the same exhibition by Henry Fairfield's mother.

According to the *Dictionary of American Biography* Osborn was physically large, with strong, rather heavy but aristocratic features. His demeanour was affable, often enthusiastic, but marked by a strong sense of personal dignity. He was quick to resent brusque treatment or any other affront to this dignity, but he had endless patience and respect for honest disagreement courteously expressed. His own opinions, however, once reached were seldom modified by such disagreement, and he often invited criticism and advice but rarely acted on it! He was fully conscious of his own worth and as frank in statement of it as he was in acknowledging his faults. This serene self-confidence was one of the main elements in his successful leadership complemented by great optimism. His active, restless interest found a thousand tasks both for himself and for all around him, usually practical but occasionally visionary, and he considered any hints of difficulty or impossibility as destructive criticism and therefore inadmissible. This characteristic sometimes invited failure and resentment, but it also sometimes resulted in accomplishing the apparently impossible. A favourite word, constantly repeated in the titles and text of his works and his conversation, was 'creative'. He believed in and worked for creative education, creative evolution, creative administration, and creative living.[118] Mrs Osborn accompanied her husband on many of his scientific expeditions, and was herself a well-known author – among her books was *The Chain of Life* which dealt with evolution.

Walker used to tell his family that it was his misfortune that most of the work he obtained was of prosperous gentlemen, and rarely of beautiful American ladies! It is rather ironic, therefore, that nearly all the portraits that have been traced so far as having been exhibited or sold in America are of the female sex! After the success of his first visit, Walker crossed the Atlantic several times more. In 1891/2 he painted Helen, the third daughter of a Dr. W. W. Seely of Cincinnati. Helen Seely was born in 1879 and so was about thirteen when this portrait was painted. The portrait, which now belongs to her grandson, Mr. Van Hamm Wilshire of Greenwich, Connecticut, was exhibited at the Cincinnati Art Museum in 1892 and again in 1896. Helen's father was Dean of the Faculty in the Medical College of Ohio, having been Professor of Ophthalmology there.[119]

When Walker went to the States in 1891/2 he was accompanied by his daughter May (for if Fanny could not go herself, she always made sure he had a chaperone!) The visit was made memorable to May by a visit to Tiffany's, where she extravagantly bought a dozen silver gilt spoons!

One mystery about Walker's visits to the United States remains to be solved, for it is said that he got many of his best introductions through having painted Elizabeth Mills Reid, the wife of Whitelaw Reid. This was generally known in the family, but has been impossible to verify. Whitelaw Reid was a distinguished journalist, political leader and diplomat who at the end of his life became American Ambassador to London, 1905–12, when he died in office. His wife was born Elizabeth Mills, the heiress daughter of the banker and philanthropist D. O. Mills, who founded Mills college and hospital, San Mateo, California. The Mills' owned a huge estate, 'Millbrae' on the Sacramento Peninsula.

Elizabeth supported her husband in his various roles as Editor-in-Chief and then proprietor of the *New York Tribune*, U.S. Minister to France (1889–92), Republican nominee as Vice-President (1892) and special ambassador to Queen Victoria's Diamond Jubilee, 1897 and again at Edward VII's coronation, 1902. She was, throughout her life, very actively involved in philanthropy and in London became Chairman of the American Red Cross, and

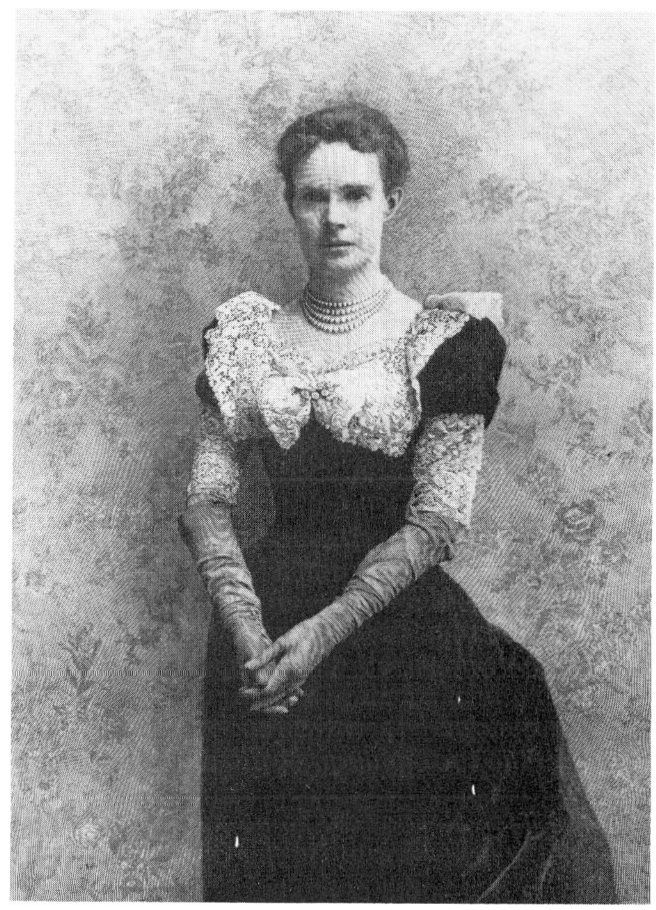

Mrs. Whitelaw Reid. Photograph from *Harper's Weekly, New York* 1892

established the Elizabeth Whitelaw Reid home and club for boys and girls in north-west London, and a working-men's club.

The Whitelaw Reids had many beautiful homes, including Ophir, Purchase, New York. This epitomised the splendour with which the wealthy surrounded themselves: the house was built in the manner of an old-world castle, surrounded by a vast estate, which included a nine-hole golf course. It was filled with paintings, porcelain and furniture of immense value: on the genuine English Tudor panelling hung Van Dykes, Raeburns, and Canalettos, and Louis XV chairs and furniture were to be found in the hall and drawing-room, while the library was furnished with an Italian Renaissance table, antique Jacobean sofa and a portrait by Beechey on the overmantel. In addition, they had their town house on Madison Avenue, New York, where they were leaders of New York society and entertained Edward VII and Queen Alexandra, and virtually all the royal family on various brilliant occasions.[120] The Whitelaw Reid's son, Ogden, married Helen Mills Rogers, of Racine, Wisconsin and their daughter, Jean, married the Earl of Dudley's second son, Major the Hon. Sir John Ward.

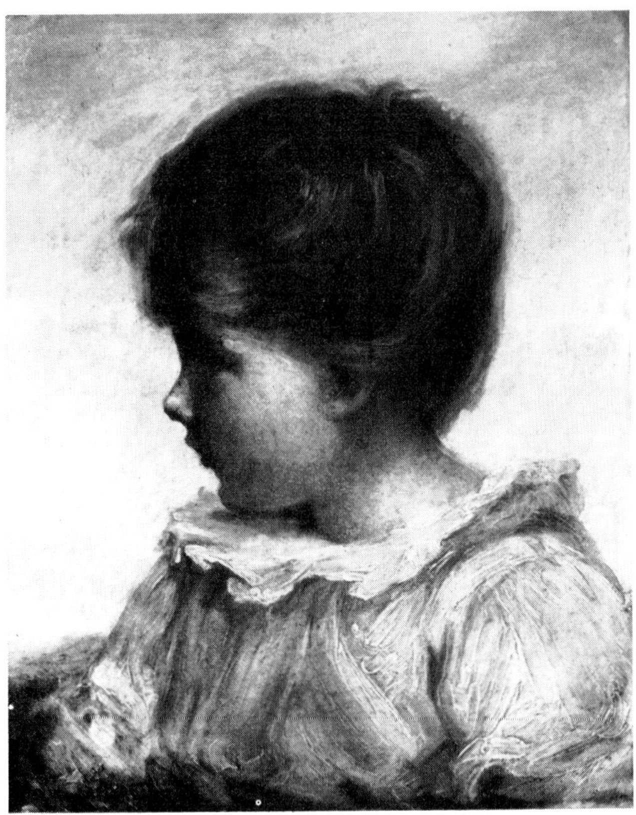

Dorothy Walker, 1884 (*The Age of Happiness*).

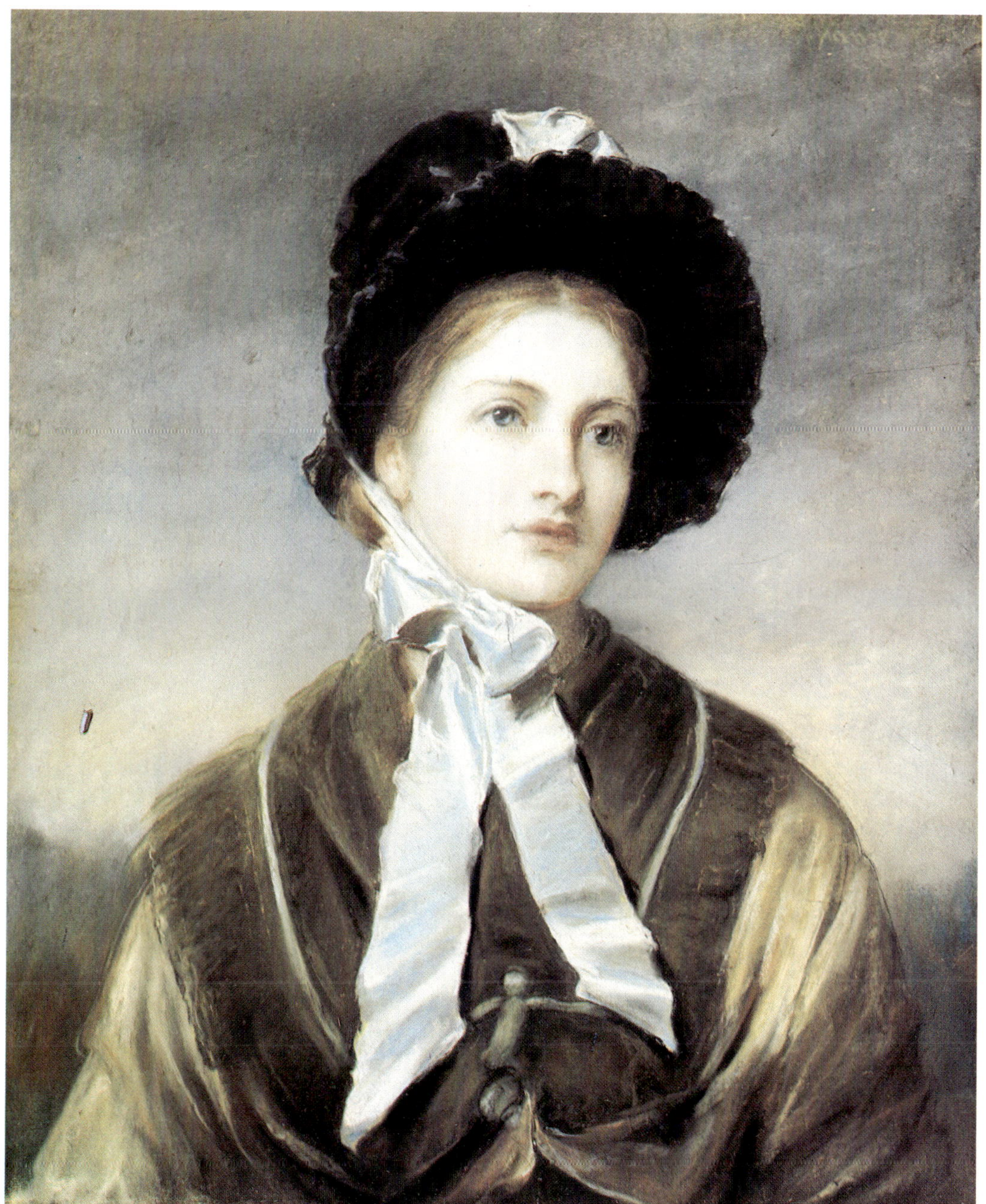

Plate 1. *'Nan'* Whitaker: an engagement pastel painted by John Hanson Walker in *c.* 1866.

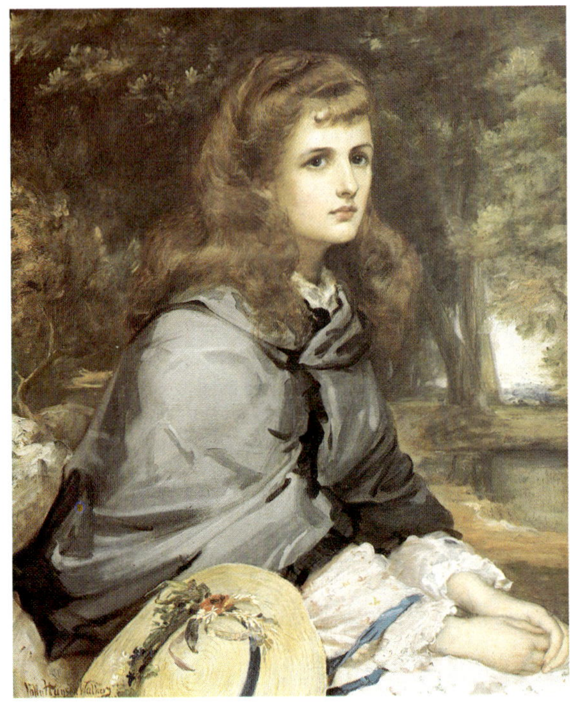

Plate 2. *Mary*, 1873.

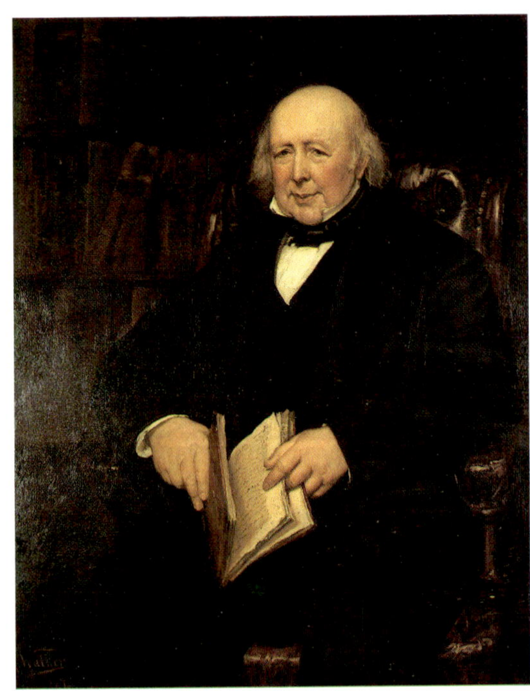

Plate 3. *James Crossley*, Founder and President of the Chetham Society, 1875.

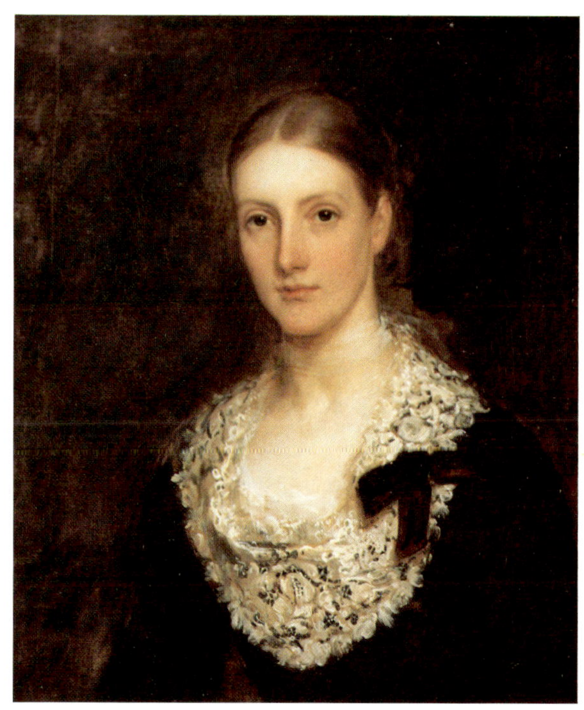

Plate 4. *Mrs. John Hill:* a wedding portrait painted 1879.

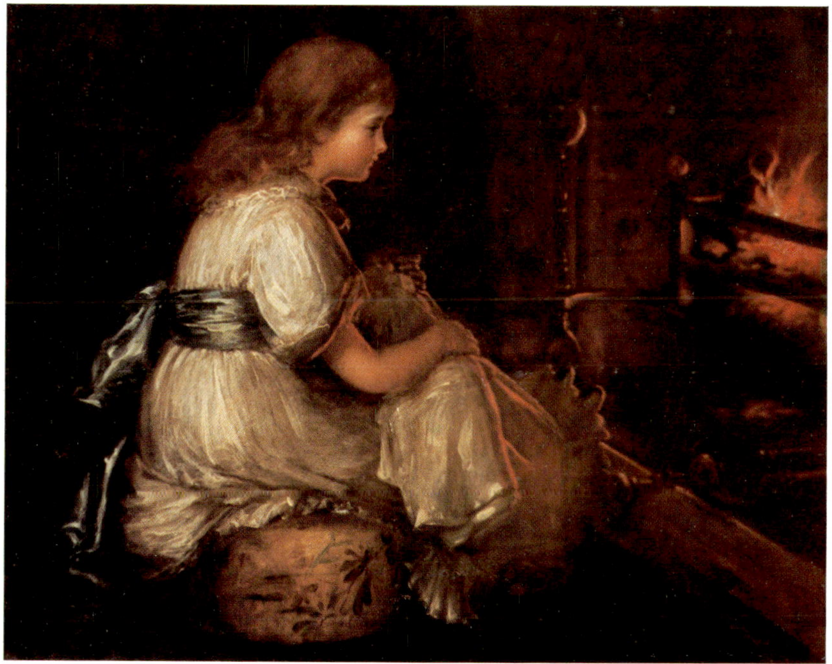

Plate 5. *'Faces in the Fire'*, 1878: the model was the artist's daughter May.

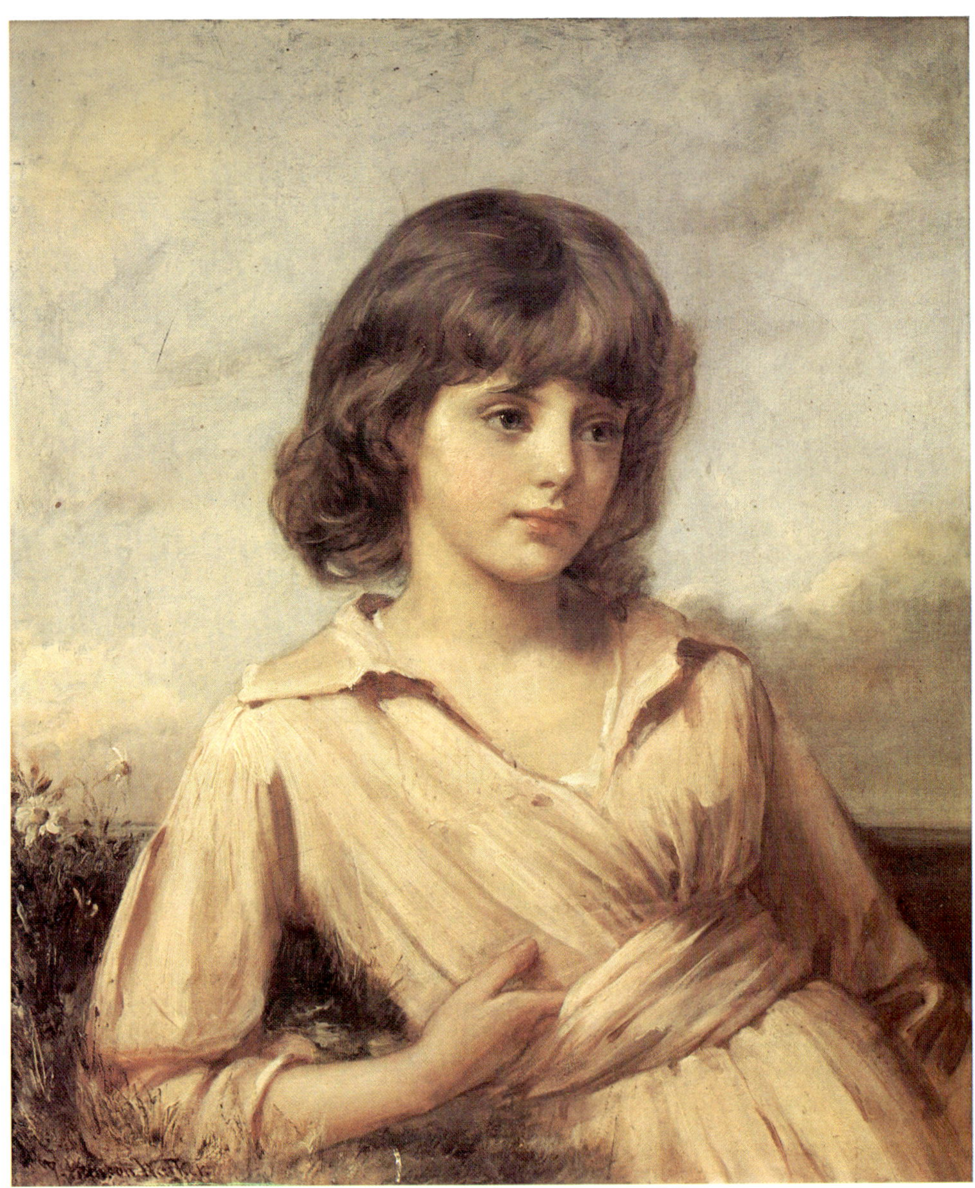

Plate 6. *'Free as the Air'*; exhibited at the Glasgow International Exhibition 1888.

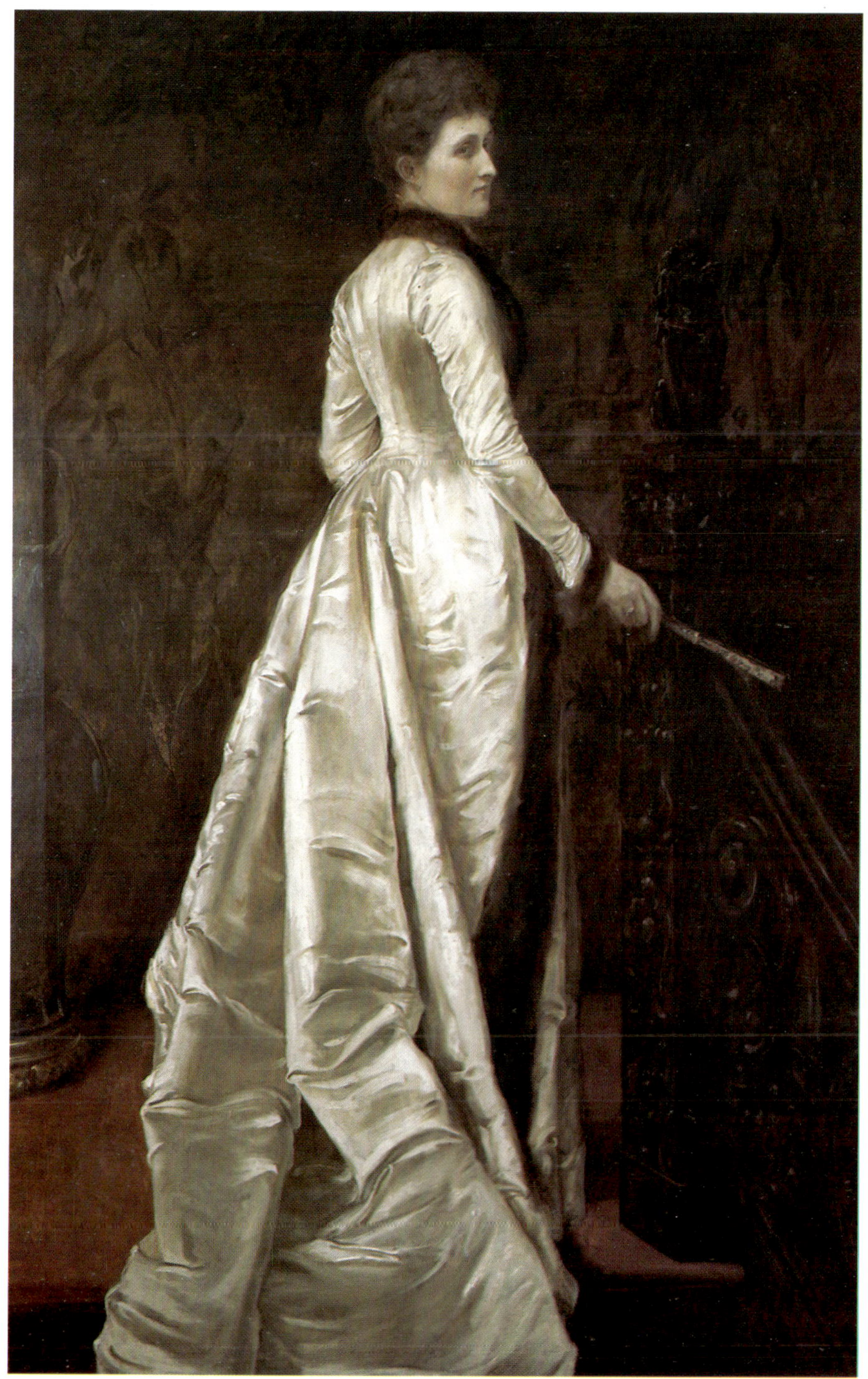

Plate 7. *The Countess of March & Kinrara, circa* 1887.

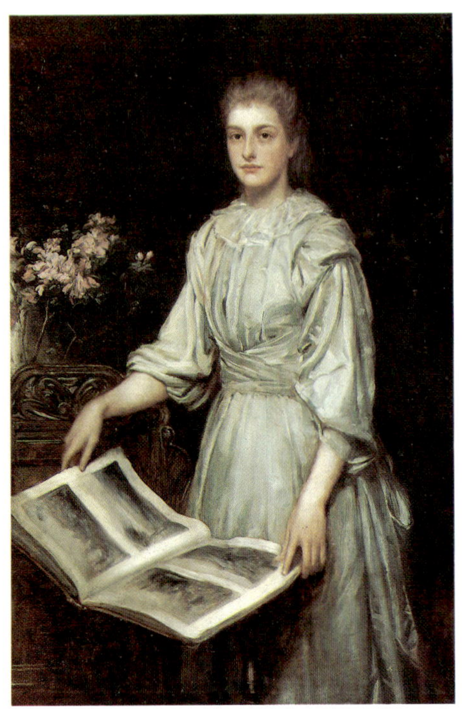

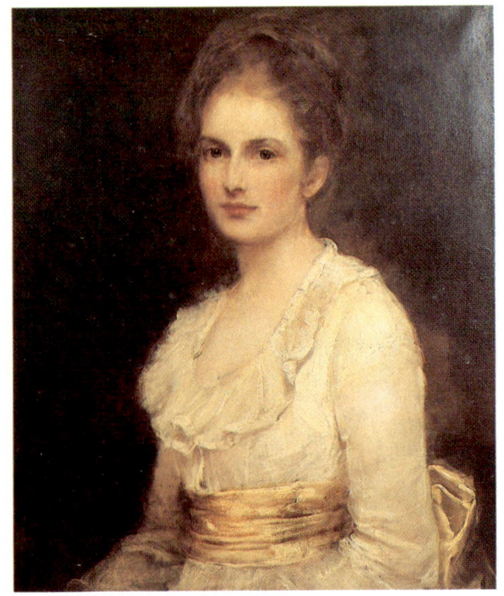

Plate 9. *May Walker*, 1893.

Plate 8. *Elsie Walker, circa* 1892.

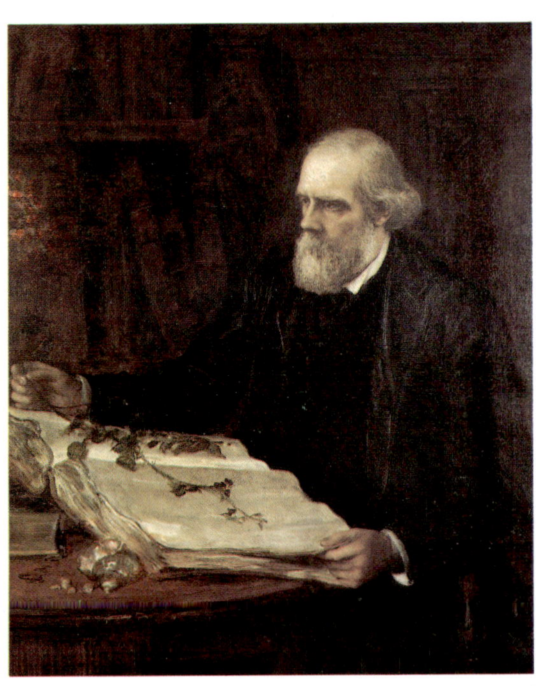

Plate 10. *The late Lord de Tabley*, 1897.

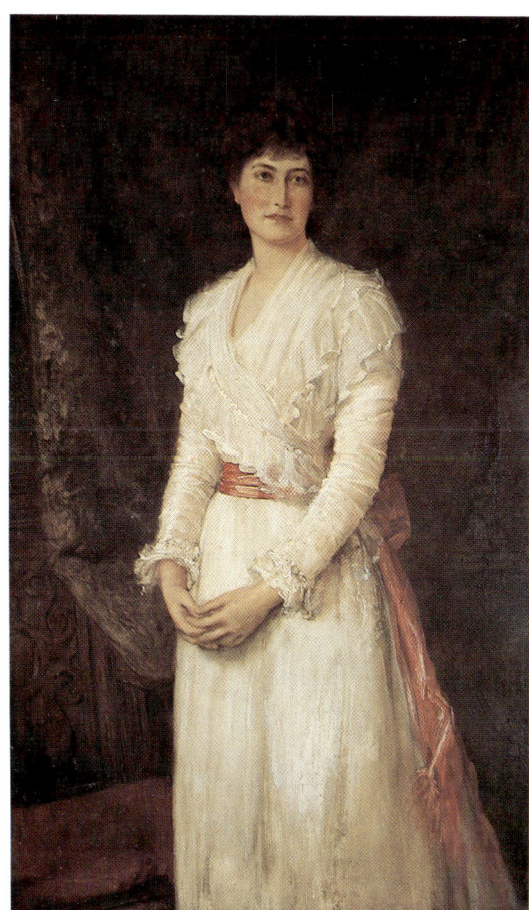

Plate 11. *Bessie Wellesley-Colley*, 1899.

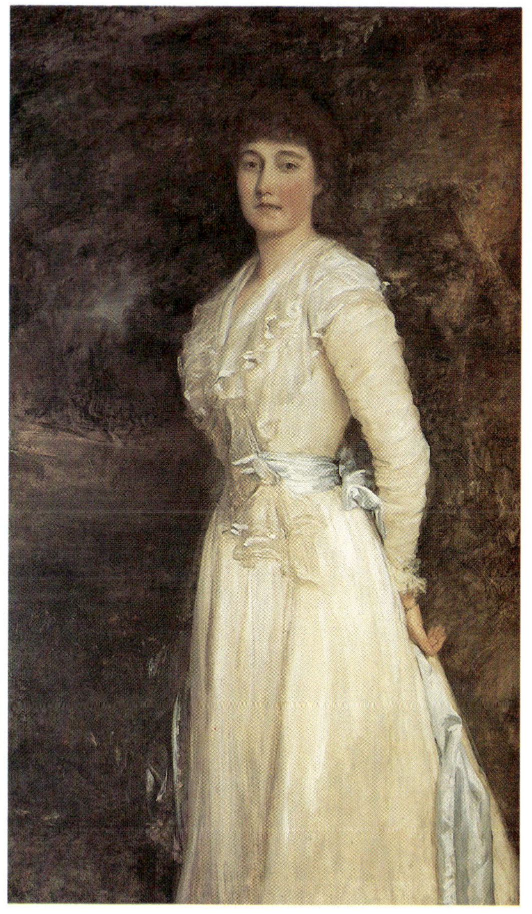

Plate 12. *Mary Wellesley-Colley*, 1899.

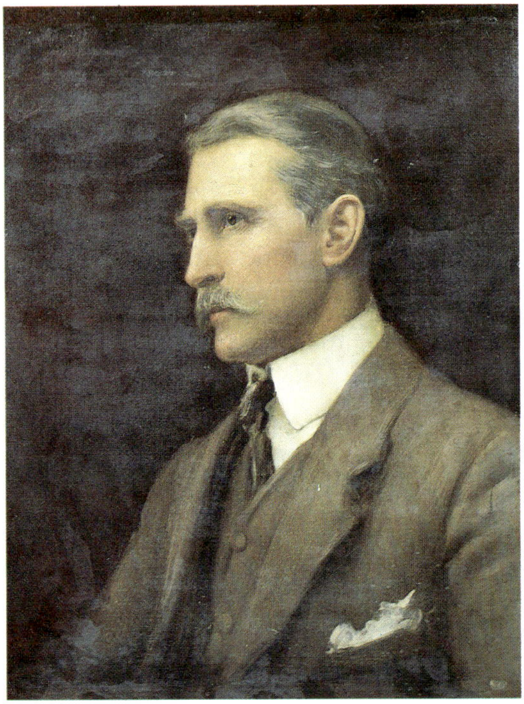

Plate 13. *Robert Mills, c.* 1910.

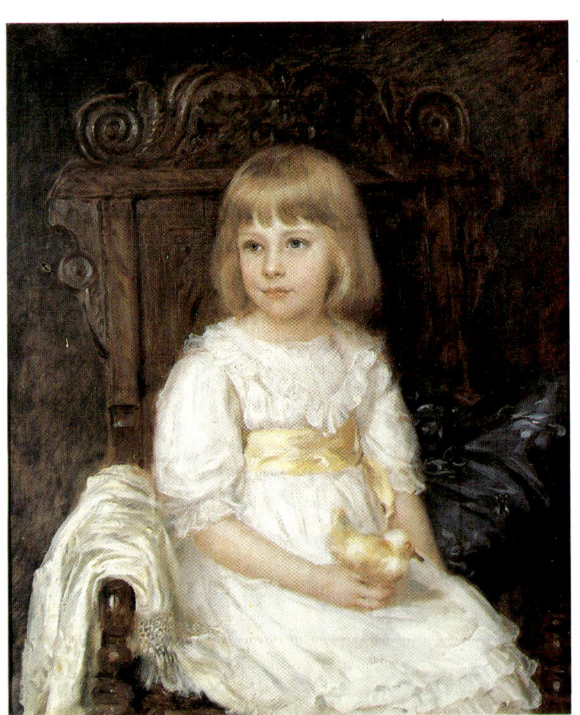

Plate 14. *Diana Mills,* 1919.

Walker took several examples of his work to America when he went for the first time in 1886, among them the portrait he had painted of his four year old daughter Dorothy, which he had called *The Age of Happiness*. It is not certain whether it was some of these portraits, or others which had been imported by dealers, which were auctioned in America in the early years of this century. Between 1903 and 1906 nine paintings of Walker's were put up for sale in New York, nearly all by dealers. They were given luscious descriptions. Walker's *The White Rose* was put up for sale in April 1904 by an American art importer, Blakeslee, and the subject was described thus: 'A sweet-faced young lady, her head gracefully poised in profile with a mass of wavy auburn hair brushed over her ears and gathered in a large bow behind, has fastened a large white rose to her dress over her left breast and the pale yellow petals contrast with the soft white of her dress and the refined flesh colour of her bosom. The head is in relief against a mass of foliage in the background, below which is seen a distant landscape'. As lovely a passage as in any rose catalogue, and an exact description of a Hanson Walker daughter!

As can be seen from Leighton's letter to Johnny, Fanny came to join him on his first trip in 1886, and only just got home again in time to give birth to her tenth and last child. Her husband's success in the new world must have given them courage to face home shores again.

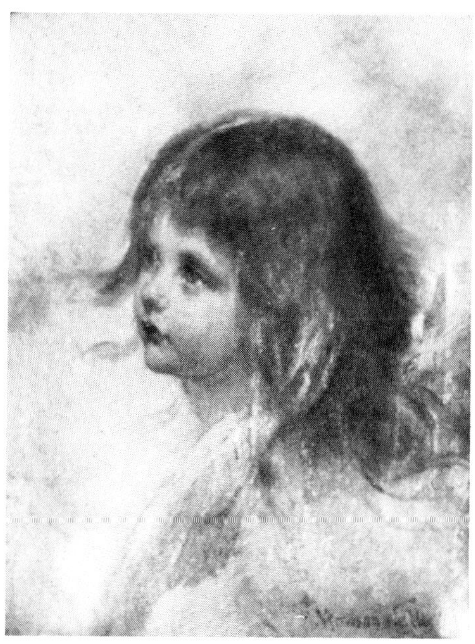

Maud Hanson Walker, 1890.

CHAPTER EIGHT

ARTIST AND DEALER

Fanny gave birth to Maud Walker on May 19, 1887, and the baby is thought to have been named after Maud, the eleven year old daughter of the *Punch* cartoonist, Linley Sambourne. Maud Sambourne later became an artist, and when in 1898 she married Lenny Messel at St. Mary Abbots church, Maud Walker was one of her seven bridesmaids. The Linley Sambournes lived near the Walkers at 18 Stafford Terrace, (now open to the public as Linley Sambourne House) and the two families had a common link in that Linley Sambourne was descended from the famous musical Linleys of Bath, one of whom, Elizabeth Linley had eloped with Sheridan. Acquaintanceship with the Sambournes might originally have been made through Aunt Fanny Unwin, who had links with *Punch* through her pupil John Leech, and whose husband, Ronald McIan was in the same theatrical world as *Punch's* founder, Mark Lemon.

In the years 1887–9 Walker exhibited very little. The most interesting painting of this period would have been *The Rehearsal*, a large subject painting now vanished, which presumably portrayed his own children. The sudden drop in output in England suggests that he again crossed the Atlantic to paint in America.

In 1887 the Grosvenor Gallery had closed, but although this rival of the Royal Academy had vanished, Leighton was having difficulties in that so many well-known painters did not exhibit their works at the Academy. In 1885 he had coaxed Burne-Jones to allow himself to be elected as an Associate, but he exhibited only one painting before he resigned in 1893. Watts, who had been elected an Academician just before Leighton, constantly questioned the wisdom of continuing to be one. In the last two decades of the century rebellion was rooted in a general feeling of antipathy to the Academy – 'That nearly all artists dislike and despise the Royal Academy is a matter of common knowledge' wrote George Moore in 1893.[121]

In 1886 the New English Art Club was founded by a group of artists broadly sympathetic to French Impressionist art and hostile to the Academy: its main members were Philip Wilson Steer and Sickert, (who were exact contemporaries, 1860–1942); others included Tonks, Guthrie and Lavery, and an American, James Jebusa Shannon.[122]

Even Leighton seems to have had private worries over the standard of Academy exhibitions for in 1887 he wrote confidentially to Watts 'there are great gaps . . . Poynter has nothing, Stone little or nothing, Calderon nil, Gilbert not much – Millais (*in strictest confidence*) a dreadfully theatrical and tasteless Hugenot subject'. He continued on a more optimistic note: 'Nevertheless the exhibition will be a distinctly good one – Hook is *splendid* – Holl very fine – Herkomer good – Orchardson admirable – Gregory capital – Henry Moore very fine – Tadema at his best; then there are a good many *capital* works by young outsiders; amongst others a startling but in my opinion *brilliantly* talented picture by *Sargent*'. This picture was *Carnation, Lily, Lily, Rose* (Tate Gallery) and Leighton used his casting vote to secure it for the Chantrey Bequest.[123]

Carnation, Lily, Lily, Rose was painted out of doors in the summer of 1885 and 1886 and shows the two young daughters of Frederick Bernard lighting Chinese lanterns in the twilight of their father's Broadway garden. Sargent had an immense struggle in creating the impression he wanted, but the result was a painting that literally glows with diffused light like a lantern itself. Sargent told a pupil 'Don't concentrate too much on the features, they are only like spots on the apple. Paint the head. Never leave empty spaces, every stroke of the brush should have significance'.[124] Soon Sargent's portraits were to dominate the walls of the Royal Academy: he became the presiding genius of English society portraiture in the last decade of the nineteenth century.

John Hanson Walker appears to have been uninfluenced by any new style of painting, although one can detect a certain loosening of his brush strokes when painting clothes as he grew older. He continued to exhibit two or three paintings each year at the Academy, all of them portraits.

In 1889/90 he visited Lanhydrock in Cornwall to paint two of the sons of Viscount Clifden, 2nd Baron Robartes. Lanhydrock (now National Trust) is a fine seventeenth century house, largely rebuilt after a fire in 1881, and the two portraits hang on the teak staircase. The first portrait is of the Hon. Thomas, Lord Clifden's eldest son, dressed as an Eton schoolboy, and is a very fine example of the artist's work. His younger brother Gerald, a boy of seven or eight, is shown sitting holding an orange,and is dressed in the girlish clothes that young Victorian boys, even at the age of seven or eight, were subjected to. Thomas was killed during the Great War in 1917 and so it was Gerald who succeeded to the title, and it was he who gave Lanhydrock to the National Trust in 1966, just before his own death.

Walker was so good at getting a likeness of his sitters that it is interesting to speculate whether or not he used photography to help, as did so many Victorian artists, including Watts. On January 1, 1873 Watts, writing to Sir Charles Dilke to arrange a portrait sitting, said 'I should be glad if you will bring any good photographs you may have. They help to make one

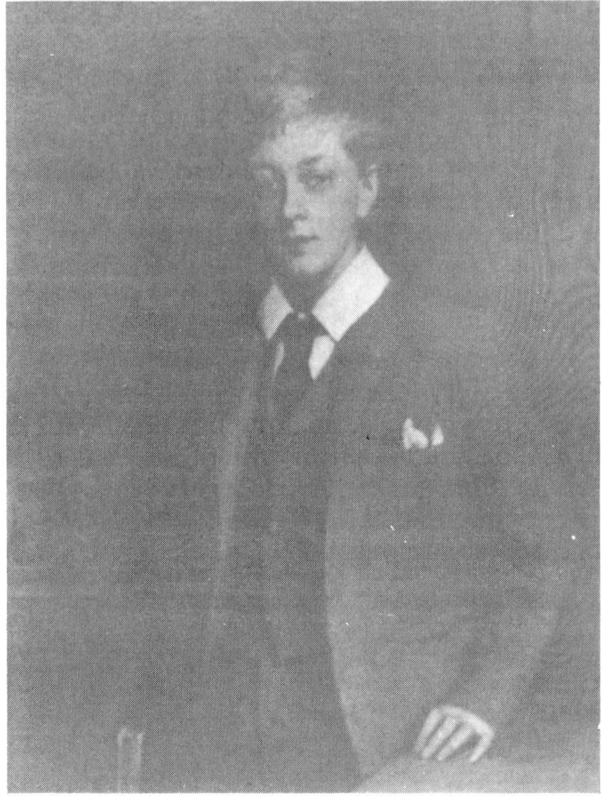

The hon. Thomas Agar-Robartes.

acquainted with peculiarities and shorten the sittings necessary'.[125] By the early 1880s Millais made use of photographs, not to set but to confirm his viewpoint. His second portrait of Gladstone is an instance of this, where a photograph of the identical pose to Gladstone's was taken by Rupert Potter, Beatrix Potter's father. In her Journal Beatrix Potter mentions other instances: she says he used it in *The Idyll* and *Bubbles*. He asked Potter to photograph his little grandson Willie James for *Bubbles* saying he wanted the photo 'just to compare it . . . I hold it in my hand and compare it with the life, and I can see where the drawing's wrong'.[126]

Walker was soon to have a grandchild himself, for his eldest daughter Sissie, a lively, spirited and very beautiful girl was married to a young solicitor, Sydney Pitt, in 1888. The Walkers again moved house in this year, as their lease of Vicarage Gate had expired. They moved a little northwards, to 88 Kensington Park Road, a large house that had been the Rectory of St. Peter's church two doors away.

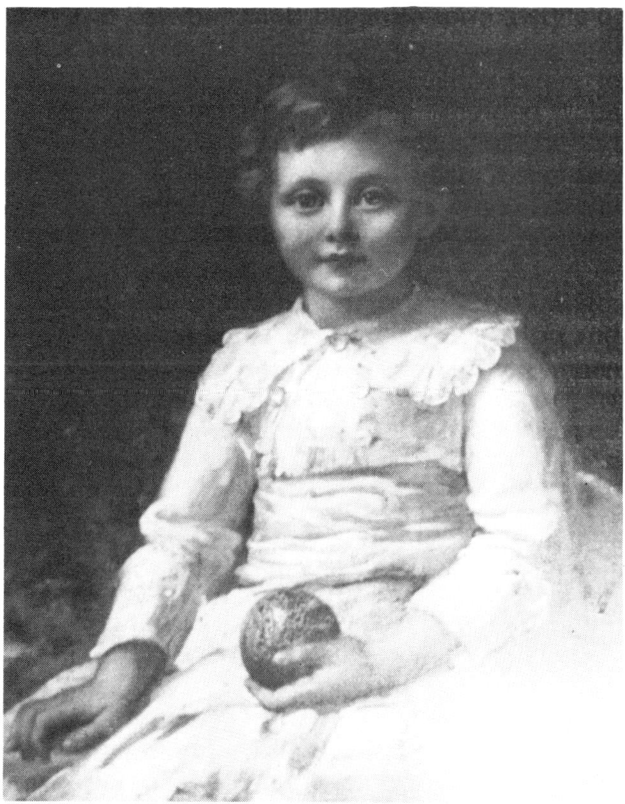

The hon. Gerald Agar-Robartes.

In 1892 Walker exhibited the portrait of *Mrs. Frank St. Clair Grimwood of Manipur, 'wearing the V.C. and dressed in black'* at the Royal Academy (no.976). This must have been one of the most touching commissions he ever received, for Mrs. Grimwood was newly returned from India as a young widow of twenty-four, having been the heroine of a massacre at Manipur the previous year, 1891. Queen Victoria had just decorated her personally at Windsor with the Royal Red Cross for her services to the wounded during the seige of the Residency, 'under trying circumstances': it is the Royal Red Cross she therefore wears rather than the V.C. The portrait, missing when this book was started, was miraculously discovered in Washington, D.C. four days before going to press, by Mr. Robert Stewart, Senior Curator of the Washington National Portrait Gallery! Immediately after her escape from Manipur she set her experiences down most vividly in a book, *My Three Years in Manipur*, published just at the time Walker was painting her.[127]

She describes how Manipur, situated in beautiful mountainous country in remote N.E. India had been the scene of quarrels between the royal princes.

The Maharajah had been ousted from the throne by his two brothers, the eldest of whom had become Regent, and the younger (their particular friend) the deputy ruler or Jubraj. The English decided to make their friend the scapegoat for the affair, and arranged that he should be arrested during a durbar given in honour of a proposed visit by the Chief Commissioner, Mr. Quinton. A telegram was sent, saying that 'a big tiger would shortly be caught in Manipur' – which was intercepted by the Indians, who began to stockpile arms in their palace. By the time Mr. Quinton arrived with two hundred troops, the atmosphere had become tense. The Indians, pleading ill-health, refused to attend the durbar, and after unsuccessful negotiations by Frank Grimwood it was decided to use force. As dawn broke the next day the English attacked, but the Indians counter-attacked, and soon the Residency was under siege. Mrs. Grimwood, under shell-fire, fed and nursed the wounded in the Residency cellar, which had been turned into a rough hospital, helping the doctor single-handed, as all her staff had fled. Late that night her husband set off with the official party in a desperate attempt to

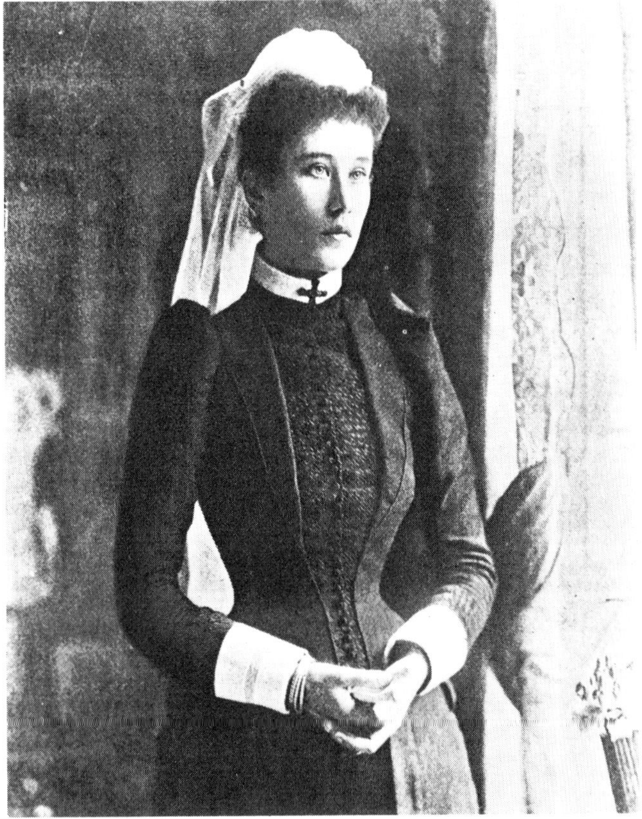

Mrs. Frank St. Clair Grimwood, the heroine of Manipur.

negotiate a truce, and during their absence it was decided that the Residency would have to be abandoned under cover of night. Wounded in the arm and under gunfire, Mrs. Grimwood and the Residency party, accompanied by some of the soldiers, waded through the river surrounding the garden and started a gruelling ascent into the hills, walking by burning sun by day and piercing cold by night for thirty-six hours, until by great good fortune they met a party of Gurkhas, who accompanied them for a further week's walk to safety at Simla. Mrs. Grimwood arrived in Simla to find herself a heroine, but without news of her husband. A week later news came by telegram that Frank Grimwood and his party had been murdered in the palace at Manipur after no terms for a truce had been found. *The Times* of 1891 is full of reports of the Manipur incident, which caused a stir in that it was felt that the British Government had mishandled a delicate situation.

The Academy Exhibition in which Mrs. Grimwood's picture was shown was reviewed for the *Art Journal* by Claude Phillips, the first Keeper of the Wallace Collection. He attacked Leighton, who showed two great circular canvases *The Garden of the Hesperides* and *And the Sea Gave Up its Dead* (Tate Gallery) saying 'We do not count ourselves among the most ardent admirers of Sir Frederick Leighton's *polished* art – so polished that of late years all invigorating elements have well-nigh disappeared'.[128] Although Leighton was now criticised, *And the Sea Gave Up its Dead* had an interesting history as a painting. Its design was originally conceived as a continuation of the scheme for redecorating the dome of St. Pauls Cathedral, the main outlines of which had been provided by Alfred Stevens. Stevens had proposed dividing the dome into eight sections, each section containing circles in which the main figurative elements would be placed. When Leighton's trial cartoon, together with those of other artists, was hung in the dome of the cathedral from the winter of 1884 until the following summer these attracted very little public support and the project was eventually abandoned. Citing the opinion of friends that it was his best design, Leighton offered to paint the work, with the design little altered. This idea was taken up by Sir Henry Tate, who commissioned him to do so, and gave it as his gift to the Tate Gallery. This, therefore was the painting which was exhibited in 1892.[129]

According to *The Magazine of Art* of 1893 there had been a depression in the sale of current painters' work, although the sale of Old Masters was now booming. This may have been the underlying reason why John Hanson Walker eventually became an art dealer as well as a painter, although the venture started initially with his sons. The three eldest Walker boys were presenting problems to their parents. Frederick (Leighton's godson) had had difficulty in passing his medical exams at St. George's Hospital, while Bob, their second boy had contracted tuberculosis, and had to be sent first to France and then California before returning home to study painting with the Newlyn School in Cornwall. John, the third boy, preferred spending his days with the Thames bargees rather than with the insurance broker with whom he was meant to be training in the City. Aunt Fanny Unwin (who was now bedridden and living with the Walkers) came to the rescue; she proposed to set Bob and John up as dealers to sell off part of her collection of china, furniture and pictures which were now stored away in a depository. A gallery was rented off Oxford Street and the two boys (who were joined by the fourth son, Jolliffe, who had failed his entrance examination for the navy) found themselves surrounded by crates of china and pictures about which they knew very little, until their father came to help price and sort them!

The Walker girls were no problem. They were lively, talented, good-looking, and much sought after. In 1895, the year after her brothers were set up in business, May, their second daughter, married Frank Romer, son of Justice Sir Robert Romer and his wife Betty, who was a daughter of Mark Lemon, *Punch's* first editor.

A year later the Walkers were on the move again, leaving Kensington Park Road for 12 Montague St., in Oxford Street, just off Portman Square. Here they would be near an old friend, Walter Ouless, now an extraordinarily successful portrait painter, who lived in Bryanston Square.

The following two years were years of sadness. The Walkers must have known that Leighton was becoming ill: in 1894 he suffered his first attack of angina, and offered to resign as President of the Royal Academy, but was refused. He had to ask Millais, (himself struggling with cancer of the lung) to make his speech at the Academy banquet in his stead: a task Millais gallantly undertook, although he could hardly make himself heard.

On January 1 1896, in the New Year's Honours List, Leighton was created Baron Leighton of Stretton, the first artist to be given a peerage. A few days later he took his sisters to the theatre, and disclosed to them how very ill he was. Early in the morning of Thursday January 23 he woke in great pain and breathless. He waited until 7 a.m. to summon his servant, asking him to fetch the doctor and his two sisters, Mrs Matthews and Mrs Sutherland Orr. They were with him in his monastic little bedroom at Leighton House all day, and the following morning he rallied a little, saying 'Would it not have been a pity if I had had to die just when I was going to paint better'. He then made his brief will leaving his sisters everything, having before that instructed them that on their death they should leave certain legacies, including the £10,000 he wished to leave the Royal Academy. During the afternoon he murmured 'Give my love to all at the Academy' and a few words in German to his sisters, and finally died, attended by his sisters and two of his closest friends, Val Prinsep and Cockerell.[130]

The coffin lay at first in Leighton's studio, surrounded by flowers and his last pictures: it was then removed to lie in state in the Octagon Gallery in the Academy. On the coffin was a wreath from Queen Victoria, who had bought his first Academy painting: it simply said 'A mark of respect from Victoria R.I.' It was accompanied by a wreath from the Prince and Princess of Wales, with whom he had often stayed at Sandringham. With the flowers on the coffin were placed his palette and brushes and his many orders and decorations.

John and Fanny Hanson Walker must have been present at the funeral service in St. Paul's, which was regal in its dignity. On Monday, February 3, a sunny winter's day, the funeral cortège left Burlington House for St. Paul's preceded by a detachment from the Artist's Rifles which regiment Leighton had commanded from 1876 to 1883. The route to the Cathedral was lined with dense silent crowds. As the cortège advanced into the cathedral, the peal of silver trumpets was played, and the solemn notes of Chopin's Funeral March. The Archbishop of York presided at the service, which was exceptionally fine musically. The Royal Family, the German Emperor and the King of the Belgians were represented. Purcell's setting of 'Thou knowest, Lord, the secret of our hearts' was played as the coffin was lowered into the crypt from under the central dome. At this moment Millais, the only artist, (although so near his own end) to be a pall-bearer, stepped forward to place the Queen's wreath on it. Thus was buried the Prince of the Victorian art establishment, the kindest of friends, a figure of towering importance, but an increasingly isolated man, who died without leaving any school to follow him.[131] There were, however, many who would say, like Johnny, 'He was the truest friend I ever had'.[132]

One of his oldest and most intimate friends, Professor Costa, with whom he spent his last holiday in the autumn before he died, summed up his life thus: 'Leighton solved certain problems which appeared insoluble. For instance, he combined a life at high pressure with the most exquisite politeness – truth with poetry, an iron will with the tenderness of a mother's heart, high aims with a practical life and with the worship of beauty, the ardour of which was only equalled by its purity'.[133]

In 1897 a memorial exhibition of Leighton's work was held at the Royal Academy, to which John Hanson Walker lent the chalk portrait drawing of his own head, drawn by Leighton in 1861 (exhibited as no. 218) and illustrated in Alice Corkran's biography of Leighton, and the wedding portrait of 'Nan' (exhibited as no. 95). The Queen lent *Portrait of John Hanson Walker, Esq.* – the painting now known by the name by which it was first exhibited: *Duett*. The review of the exhibition in the *Art Journal* said that the visitors to it would be astonished by its variety, and the variations and changes it showed in Leighton's style, the result of a careful process of 'thinking out' in which he had changed his style systematically but gradually.[134] The exhibition was attended by 50,000 visitors, and had to be kept open for an extra half hour on the last day. Nearly all Leighton's major works were exhibited.

On 28 February 1896 George Aitchison (Leighton's friend who built Leighton House), wrote a letter to the Royal Academy mourning his death and describing him as 'the most brilliant personality that this century has yet seen' and mentioned that he felt that Leighton House should be preserved intact, although he did not like, having built it himself, to urge this

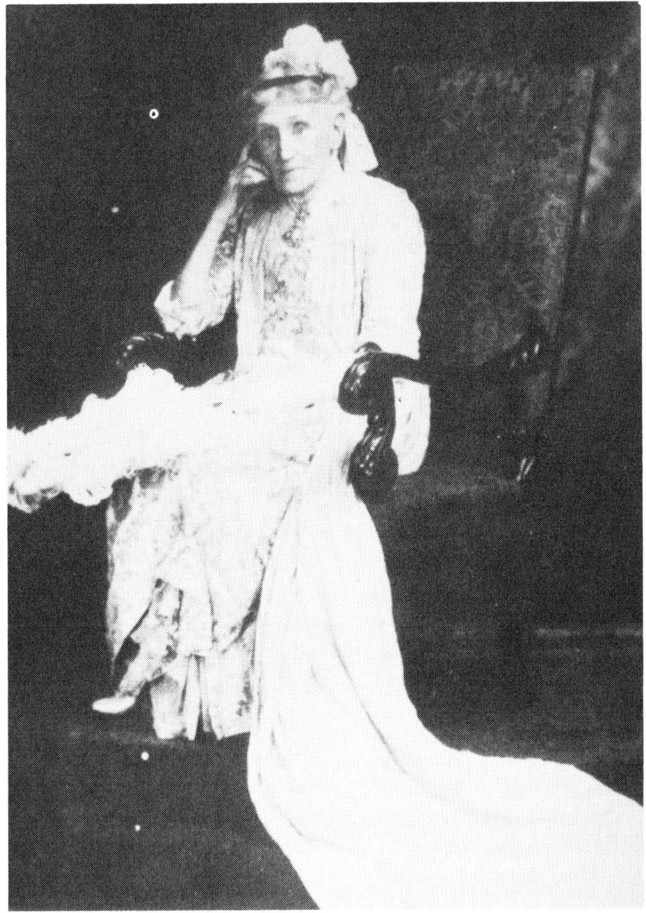

Mrs. Russell Barrington.

personally.[135] With Mrs. Russell Barrington as the Secretary and moving spirit, a committee was formed with the object of making the house and its treasures a centre for art in Kensington. Leighton's sisters, Mrs. Matthews and Mrs. Sutherland Orr, gave up the ground lease which had 66 years to run and assigned it to the committee. The committee arranged concerts, lectures and readings to take place in the house, and friends and admirers of Leighton added to its treasures, among them the Prince of Wales, who gave his study for *Summer Slumbers*. *A Crowded Scene in Florence* which was put up for sale for the Museum to buy as part of the Fine Arts group, was bought and given by John Hanson Walker (no price is recorded). This was a preliminary study for *Preparing for a Festa* (LH 832) and is full of interest and movement. *Preparing for a Festa* was itself a watercolour of a romantic quattrocento scene decked out as a fifteenth century altar-piece, which Leighton had painted in 1851.

1896 was a year of deaths: George Richmond died on March 19 aged 86 (his son was to do the mosaics in St. Paul's Cathedral), and William Morris (the pre-Raphaelite and leader of the Arts and Crafts Movement) and George du Maurier, the brilliant *Punch* cartoonist both died as well. In February Millais was elected President of the Royal Academy to succeed Leighton, but was probably too ill to enjoy Holman Hunt's congratulations on the fact that he had 'gone a letter higher – from P.R.B. to P.R.A.'[136] He died on August 13, and was buried in St. Paul's Cathedral. 'By his death', wrote the *Art Journal*, 'British Art has lost one of the greatest leaders it ever had'.[137]

It is interesting to note that after Leighton's death John Hanson Walker's list of grand patrons dies away dramatically and it must be presumed, although it is impossible to prove, that Walker was, even to the end of Leighton's life, dependent on him to a certain extent for recommendation as a portraitist. Even after death his influence lingered on, for in 1897 he exhibited an interesting portrait at the Royal Academy entitled *The Late Lord de Tabley*. (no. 304). This portrait was painted posthumously, probably for Lord de Tabley's sister, Eleanor, Lady Leighton.

It shows John Byrne Leicester (the 3rd and last Baron de Tabley, 1835–95) in his library, examining botanical specimens. De Tabley (who never marrried) was a good minor poet, who first published his poems under the pseudonym 'George Preston'. He was also a numismatist. He was a near neighbour of the Egertons at Tatton Park, and in 1868 had unsuccessfully contested mid-Cheshire for the Liberals. Like Tatton, Tabley House had a magnificent collection of paintings acquired by Sir John Leicester, the 5th Baronet, (1762–1827) who was created Lord de Tabley in 1826. Despite going on the Grand Tour, de Tabley had made no acquisitions abroad, and unlike his neigbour collected only the work of English artists. With the exception of Wilkie and Constable he patronised every major native painter of the period, especially Turner, who stayed at the house and painted it in 1808. The collection had been offered to the nation in 1823 but declined, and so collecting was resumed, but on a more modest scale.

The following year was an equally unhappy one for the Walkers, for on April 7, 1897 Aunt Fanny Unwin, who had played such a major role in their lives, died. She had lived to be eighty-six and had outlived the memory of all she had done in her earlier years as Principal of the first Female School of Design and one of the best women painters of her generation, so she appears to have had no obituary. She had always intimated to the Walkers that she would provide for them at her death, and had urged them to enjoy life instead of trying to put money aside. However, towards the end of her life she came under strong pressure from another member of the family to change her mind about this, and before anything had been resolved she had a stroke and died intestate. To John and Fanny Walker (who had been looking after her regularly during her bedridden years) this came as a tremendous blow, for the small amount of money that would eventually come to them would be minimal compared to what they had believed they would inherit. Their life-style became, for a while at least, curtailed, and it was an event which left a deep impression upon their children.

Perhaps it was this blow, and the fact that his society patrons were now flocking in other directions, that persuaded Walker to go into the art market on his own account, as his father and his own boys (now retired!) had done before him. His first recorded sale at Christie's was on December 10th, 1898 when he sold *River Scene* by Richard Wilson for eleven guineas. Two days later he sold another four paintings, including Sir John Phillips' *Portrait of Sir J. E. Millais, P.R.A. as a Highland Page aged 13* and two of his own. In June he again sold a painting of his own *The Trysting Place* which he had exhibited at Manchester in 1893 for £84, and for which he now received only nine guineas.

During the '90s Walker was also engaged on some ambitious portraiture, particularly on a painting showing his three elder daughters, Sissie, May and Elsie, who by the time the painting was finished and exhibited at the Royal

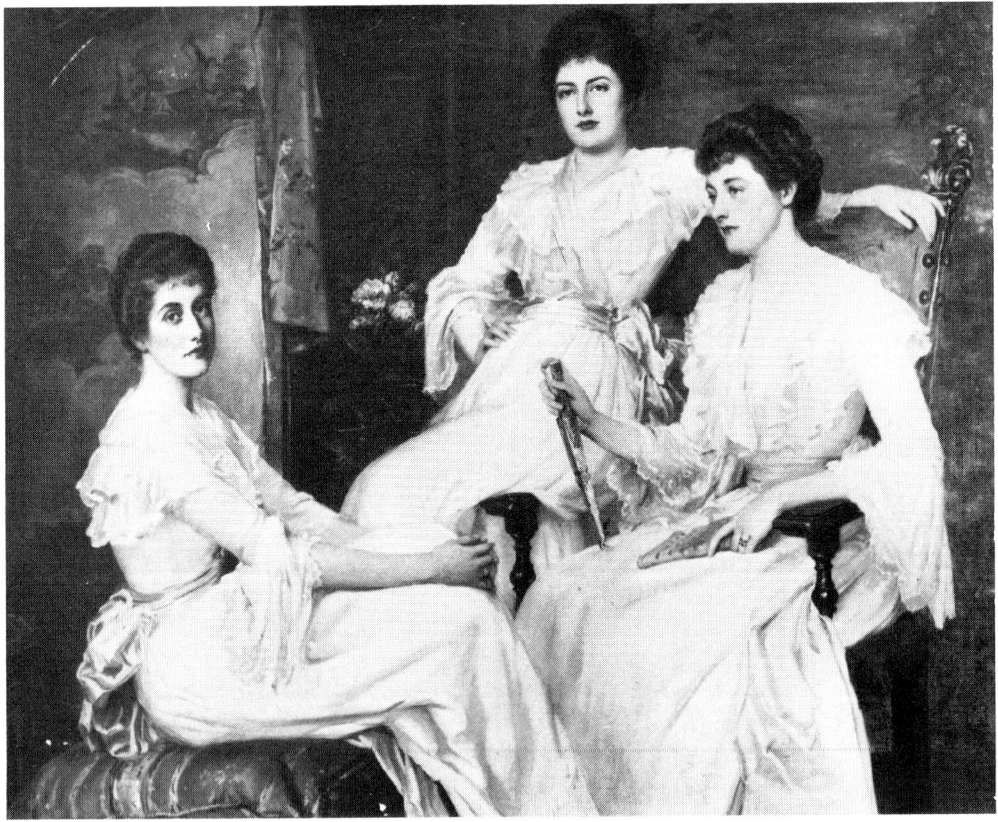

Sisters (The Three Graces) Mrs. Mills, Mrs. Romer and Mrs Pitt.

Academy of 1899 (no. 124) had all married. The painting has similarities with Millais' *Hearts are Trumps* of 1872 which Millais had painted in response to a challenge to equal Reynolds' *Three Ladies Waldegrave as the Three Graces* which had been acknowledged as a triumph of virtuoso technique and a high-point of his fashionable portrait painting. In Walker's *Sisters* (which was always nicknamed 'The Three Graces') the Walker girls, instead of playing cards are shown posed in a conversation group round his model's chair. As in Millais's painting two of the girls look directly at the viewer, while the third (Sissie in this case) is lost in her own thoughts. Forming the background on the left in each painting is a beautiful screen, and each sister is dressed like the other.

The painting took at least four years to complete, and May (the central figure) who had been married soon after it was started was indignant with her father for showing her with no ring on her finger! Elsie (the figure on the left) had been married the year before the painting was completed to Robert Mills,

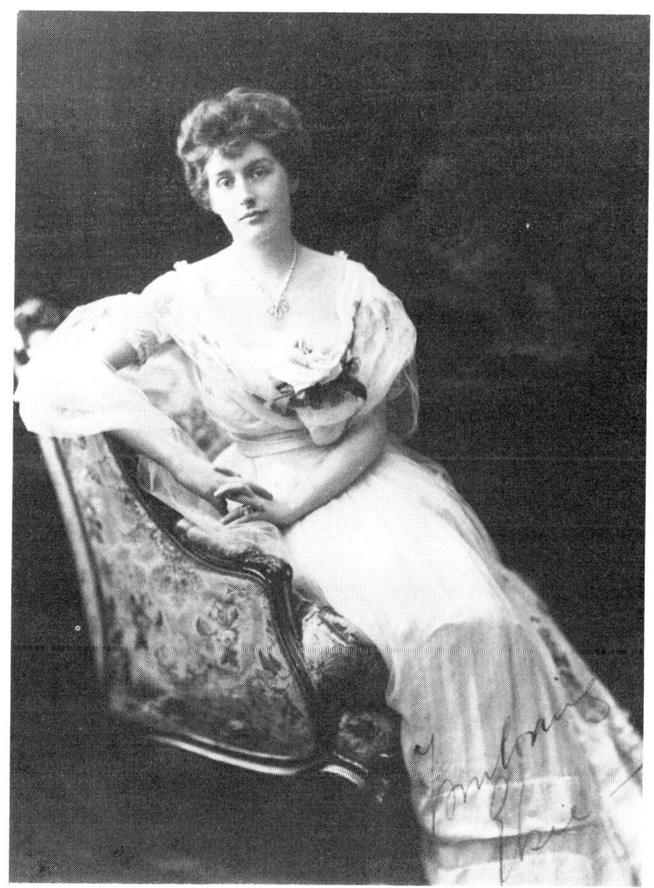

Elsie Walker, an engagement photograph.

an Englishman who had a textile printing business in France. A romantic story is told about their engagement, for Robert had seen the portrait of Elsie which her father had exhibited at the Academy in 1895 (no. 778) and had fallen in love with it. He found out Walker's address, and visited him, hoping to persuade him to sell the painting. Walker refused, so Robert had no alternative but to marry the sitter herself! The screen to the left of the painting is a beautiful Japanese one, from the early Edo period. A story is told about this too. It originally belonged, it seems, to a sitter in San Francisco whom Walker was painting. He was so taken with the screen (which presented a challenge to the painter because of the gold leaf and the intricacies of the design) that he asked the owner whether he could have it in lieu of his fee. Unfortunately although this is a well-known family story, the name of the sitter is not remembered!

The same year as *Sisters* was shown at the Royal Academy Walker showed a large pair of portraits of the two daughters of Philip Wellesley-Colley. Each girl is shown three-quarter length and the differing characters of the two girls, who are otherwise alike to look at and dressed in identical dresses, are cleverly conveyed by the portraits. Mary, the elder daughter, and the Colleys' second child (who never married) is shown with a woodland background,

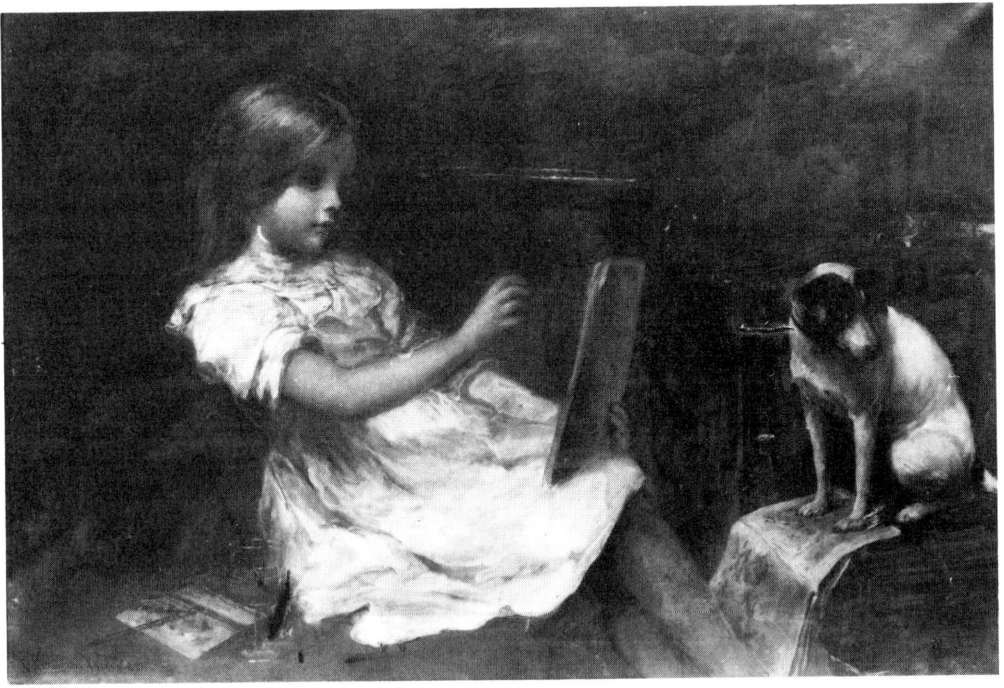

A Shy Sitter, 1899.

posed in an independant attitude, with her hands behind her back. She was then aged eighteen, and she became a very good rider. Bessie Colley, aged sixteen in the portrait, stands in a more demure attitude, her hands clasped in front of her. She was the Colleys' fourth child and married the third son of Sir Acquin Martin, a multi-millionaire who lived in India and had made his money in engineering and jute. The Colleys (who were a leading Roman Catholic family), were related to the Duke of Wellington through the Earl of Mornington and were family friends of the Walkers. The paintings are very typical of Walker's style. The faces with their good flesh tones are very carefully finished, while the frills of their dresses are painted in true Leightonesque style: almost as if Walker was now thinking deeply of all that Leighton had taught him in his youth.

In 1897 Queen Victoria celebrated her Diamond Jubilee, at last throwing aside the mourning she had worn for so many years for Prince Albert and donning a beautiful miniature crown especially made so as not to be too weighty for her ageing head. London was *en fête* and enlivened by the sight of Indian Rajahs and princes driving by in golden jewelled breastplates and turbans.

To mark the Jubilee a huge 'Victorian Era' exhibition was organised, divided between Earl's Court and the Crystal Palace. This was a culmination of a series of exhibitions which had been held at Earl's Court in the late '80s and '90s: there had been an American exhibition followed by French, German, Italian and Indian ones. Earl's Court had taken the place of Cremorne Gardens: the grounds were well laid-out and illuminated, and people could stroll about and listen to the band. Besides art the exibition included sections on Women's Work, Inventions, Sports, Music and Drama. J. M. McWhirter was Chairman of the Exhibition Committee, and others involved on it were Thomas Brock, J. C. Horsley, W. Q. Orchardson, Solomon J. Solomon, and several other famous artists.

Walker must have felt proud to be asked to exhibit the portrait he had shown of Leighton in the 1877 Academy, for also exhibiting were Sir Edward Poynter, Sir John Gilbert, Alma-Tadema and J. B. Burgess. There were also newcomers like John Lavery, who was to create the prototype for the variety of society portrait that became so popular in the Edwardian period.

Unfortunately the exhibition did not please everyone. The *Art Journal* said it could be described in one word – 'bad'. The reviewer thought that the exhibition (which purported to show the works of artists who had lived in Victoria's reign) was a very inadequate one and 'in no sense represented the best of modern British Art'. The few paintings that there were had been badly hung in galleries which were insufficiently lighted.[138]

By now the 'Naughty Nineties' were drawing to a close, and it is often thought that a sort of *fin de siècle* miasma of gloom surrounded the art world. This was not entirely true. Many of the established Victorian artists were still doing fine work, and in the late 1880s and early 1890s one last follower of the imaginative tradition of Rossetti and Burne-Jones appeared. This was Aubrey Beardsley who, in his brief life which ended when he died of tuberculosis in 1898, carved out a short but glittering career as a draughtsman. He drew both the imaginative literary mythological and medieval world, and the world around him, which he portrayed with an eye which was akin to that of a cartoonist.[139] Leighton had patronised Beardsley, offering him five pounds to produce a drawing for him on any subject he liked. In return Beardsley asked Leighton to contribute two drawings to the first number of the *Yellow Book* and he was subsequently rather startled to find himself among the avant-garde![140]

Sargent was at his very height as a portrait painter in the '90s, and William Orpen, who was to succeed him as one of London's principal portrait painters when Sargent gave up taking commissions in portraiture was also beginning to exhibit, as was Augustus John.

With the advent of a new international *nouveau riche* the demand for the sort of Victorian portraits painted for rooms with dark-patterned wallpapers, heavy mahogany furniture and plush or velvet curtains died away. For Walker, who had been schooled in the steps of Leighton and Watts, the aim would still be to follow the principles of his teachers. Watts had said 'a portrait should have in it something of the monumental: it is a summary of the life of a person, not the record of an accidental position or arrangement of light and shadows'.[141]

'Victorian artists had considered themselves as superior tradesmen', says Jeremy Maas in his *Victorian Painters,* 'who painted subjects more or less to order, or in a way that was expected of them. By the close of the century, the painter, no less dependent on his work for a living, had become "modern" in that he was an individual whose works were valid as an expression of his own artistic personality, independent of capricious patronage.[142]

The last quarter of the nineteenth century had seen much movement in the art world: including the first Impressionist Exhibition, followed by the Post-Impressionists. In 1899 Freud published his *Interpretation of Dreams,* a work which was to be of major importance in the years to come for painters like the Surrealists. The 1890s saw a period of changing values which must in many ways have distressed those painters who had, like Walker, been trained in the rigid Victorian school of art.

The old century having slipped away, Wilfred Blunt wrote in his diary on the last day of 1900: 'And so, poor wicked Nineteenth Century, Farewell!' Just over three weeks later Queen Victoria died of a stroke, having reigned for sixty-three years, and the great Victorian age was at an end.[143]

CHAPTER NINE

INTO THE EDWARDIAN ERA

An impression of purple and black, immense silent crowds, muffled drums, a solemn procession led by the Queen's cream coloured horses, is what Estella Canziani, Lousia Starr's daughter, recalls of Queen Victoria's funeral procession. This solemnity did not last long, and soon Edwardian England was in full swing, with gargantuan dinner parties, balls, and weekend parties of near feudal splendour in the country. The rich were waited on by an army of

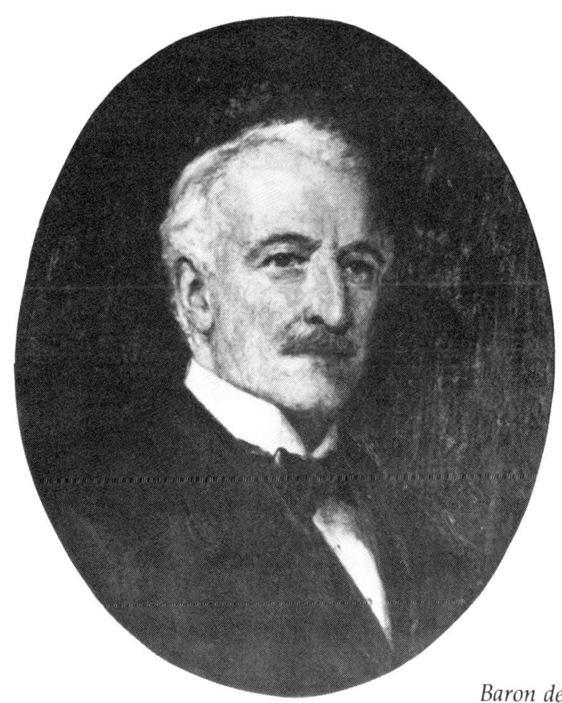

Baron de Ferrieres 1900

domestics who were often overcrowded and underpaid. Even when the Walkers were young and struggling they had been able to afford two 'living in' domestics. There was little income tax, – it was paid by under a million people at the beginning of the century, and it is doubtful whether Walker paid any at all.[144] John and Fanny Hanson Walker were able to live comfortably, and had many friends. Old photograph albums show them taking part in houseparties and family holidays with such friends as the Quilters, Gilchrists and Moncrieffs, (whose family of seven Walker painted twice over, and who had been their neighbours in Vicarage Gate).

In 1900 Hanson Walker had an interesting commission – this was to paint Baron de Ferrieres, a resident of Cheltenham. The Baron, of Belgian and French Huguenot ancestry, gave Cheltenham a gift of £1,000 towards the building of a public art gallery, and presented the town with forty-three paintings for it, mainly of the Dutch and Belgian school. The gallery was opened on October 26, 1899 and it was then that it was decided to commission Walker to paint an oval portrait of de Ferrieres, which would be hung over the entrance to the room in the gallery which contained his collection. De Ferrieres stood as Liberal Member of Parliament for Chel-

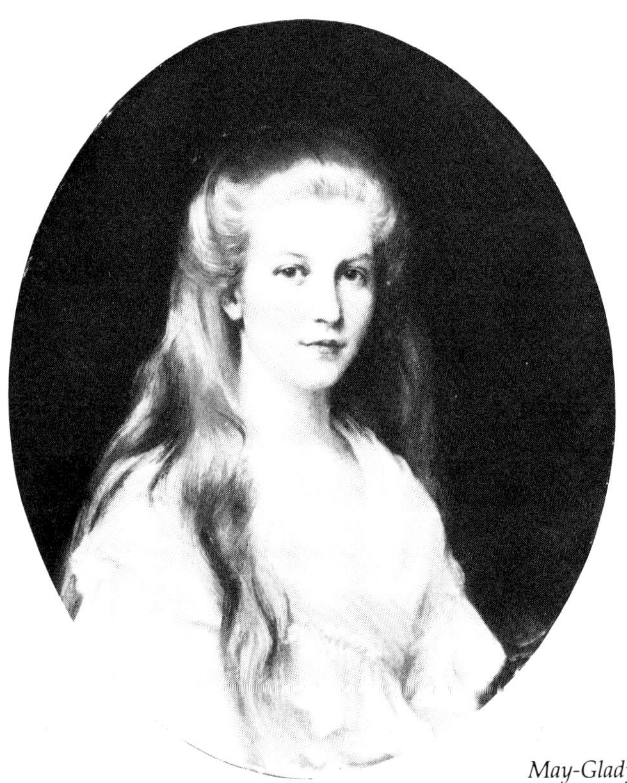

May-Gladys Moncrieff 1906.

tenham from 1880 to 1885, and so it is to be supposed that Walker was recommended to him by a parliamentary friend from those days. From 1875 onwards Walker had painted more than a dozen Members of Parliament from both Conservative and Liberal parties. Walker's portrait of de Ferrieres still hangs in the Cheltenham Art Gallery in Clarence Street.

Walker was next approached to do some copy work for Herbert Spencer: he seems to have been a difficult person to work for, for like Queen Victoria he wanted a portrait of himself copied for the lowest price obtainable! He was therefore in two minds as to whether or not to employ Walker. Neither could he decide which of his two portraits to have copied, an early one by Burgess painted in 1872 (now in the National Portrait Gallery, cat. no.1358) or one recently completed of him by Herkomer. By 1900 Spencer was eighty and had only three more years to live. Early in life he had trained as an engineer, but

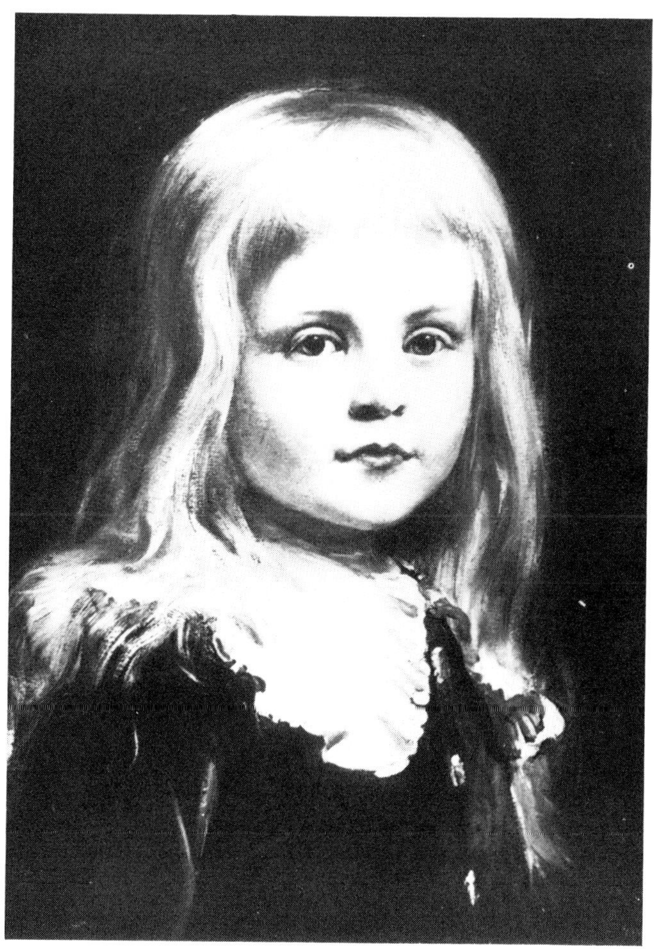

Duncan-Campbell Moncrieff
1898.

soon gave up this profession to devote himself to philosophical study and writing. He was the founder of evolutionary philosophy. Spencer has been diversely judged, and Carlyle called him 'the most immeasurable ass in Christendom!'[145]

Two letters exist covering this commission: the first, dated October 30 1900 written from 5 Percival Terrace, Brighton, reads 'Dear Sir, Within a few hours after writing to you yesterday I received a letter which has again changed my intention. I therefore resume the proposed arrangement with you, and accept your terms – sixty guineas for the copy of the portrait by J. B. Burgess. If you will say about what time you will commence work upon it I will have it packed up and sent to you'. It seems as if Spencer was becoming confused, for there is a second letter, dated January 9, 1901 from the same address, which reads, 'My dear Sir, As both Mrs. Courtney and Mrs. Reed have seen Burgess' portrait and given me their opinion respecting its merits in comparison with that of Herkomer, there is no reason for delay in returning the original back and with it sending the copy. You will, I presume, pack them both in the case used for sending the original. I will, on receipt, forward you a cheque in payment'.[146] Walker's copy of Spencer's portrait was bequeathed to the City of Derby Art Gallery in 1908 by a Mr. Spencer (no address recorded).

In 1901 Walker again became very active in the art market. On February 18 he sold lots 11–18 at Christie's. (Until 1910 Christie's dominated the London art sales). Included for sale by Walker was a Rembrandt *Still Life* and a panel scene from *The Pirate* by William Dyce. On March 30 he sold four of his own paintings (the top price gained being £50 for his painting *The Rehearsal*). More sales followed on April 3, 13 and 22, when he sold more of his own paintings and others by Girtin, Wilson, Tintoretto and Poussin. This activity was a prelude to moving to a new house, 20 Victoria Road, in 1902. Victoria Road is just south of Kensington High Street and was very near, therefore, to Kensington Gardens and his earlier home at Vicarage Gate.

John Hanson Walker lent three of the ten paintings he owned by Leighton to the opening of the Whitechapel Art Gallery in 1901. These were *Mosque in Algiers*, *A Spanish Landscape* and the wedding portrait of Fanny. The gallery had been the brain-child of Canon Barnett who with his wife Henrietta was the social innovator who founded Toynbee Hall in the deprived East End of London. This settlement, to be run by Oxford and Cambridge graduates, was named in memory of Toynbee, who had preached the gospel in bridging the gap between the classes by encouraging the educated to live and work among the poor. Barnett felt that an art gallery could give a quality of life to those who lived in such dismal conditions, so he founded it next to his first free library and very near Toynbee Hall.

In 1903–5 Walker exhibited nothing at the Royal Academy, and painted very little. His small output at this time must have been influenced by the illness and death of his two eldest sons, Frederick and Robert (Bob). Frederick had become, after initial difficulties over his medical examinations, a fully qualified and successful surgeon. He was encouraged to take up medicine by his godfather, Leighton, who had apparently always nursed a feeling of guilt, believing his own father would have preferred him to be a doctor rather than an artist. Despite Frederick Walker's love of hunting and open-air life, he was unfortunate in contracting tuberculosis and this caused his death at the early age of thirty-three. He left behind a wife and two small daughters, still in their infancy. Within a few months the babies were orphaned when their mother, Connie, died shortly after her husband. Although Connie's brother, the Rev. Aubrey Leake made himself responsible for the girls, they came for part of every summer to stay with their Walker grandparents.

In 1905 tuberculosis claimed the Walker's second son, Bob. He had suffered from the disease since his twenties, and neither an open-air life chicken farming nor travel to Canada and California could cure it. He was artistic, and spent some time painting with the Newlyn School in Cornwall. At the end of

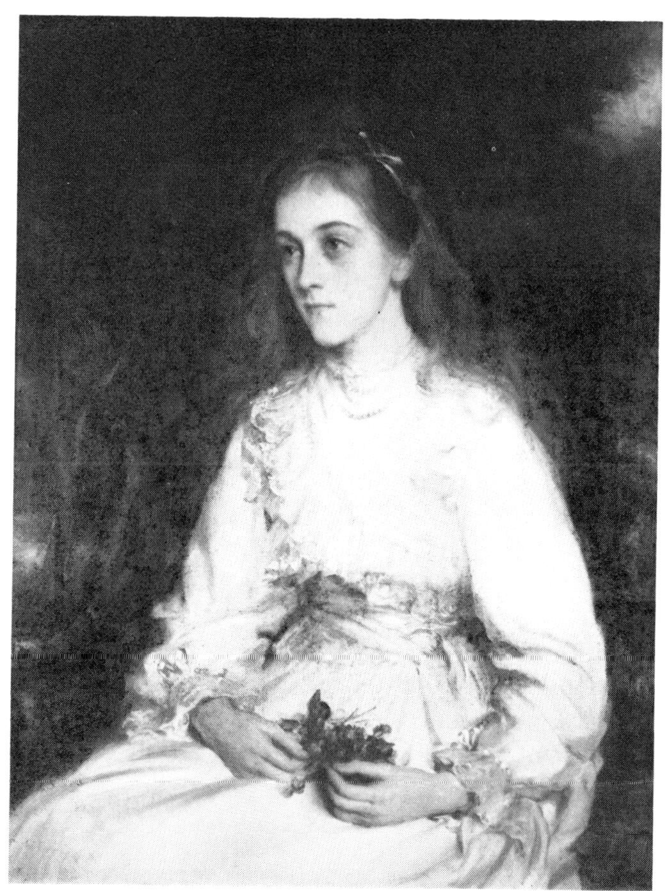

Marjorie McCorquodale 1901.

his life he was cared for by a much-loved sister of Fanny Walker's 'Aunt Mill' (Millicent Whitaker), at Wareham, Dorset and when he died he was buried there in the churchyard of St. Mary's.

Despite the sadness of this period, and the fact that Walker painted very little, he produced a very fine portrait in 1903 of an elderly woman (as yet, sadly, unidentified). It is a very good character-study of a keen intellect and an indomitable spirit. The effect has been achieved by the clarity given to the eyes, and the simplicity of the treatment of the sitter's black and white clothes, relieved by the red pendant hanging from the neck and the red bow of her white mob cap.

Throughout this time Walker's friendship with Ouless continued, as a card addressed to him by the latter and sent to Victoria Road indicates: 'I hope to call tomorrow afternoon – I have long intended doing so, but have been very busy'.[147] In 1905 Walker exhibited the portrait of Ouless' third daughter Margaret at the Walker Art Gallery, Liverpool, having painted her two elder sisters, Kitty and Evelyn in 1885 and 1886.

Walker grandchildren were proliferating, and portraits were painted of them, too: Betty, Nancy and Susan Romer, and Elsie Pitt. Meanwhile Dorothy, their ninth child was engaged to be married to James Stansfeld, and Walker painted his two youngest daughters to celebrate this.

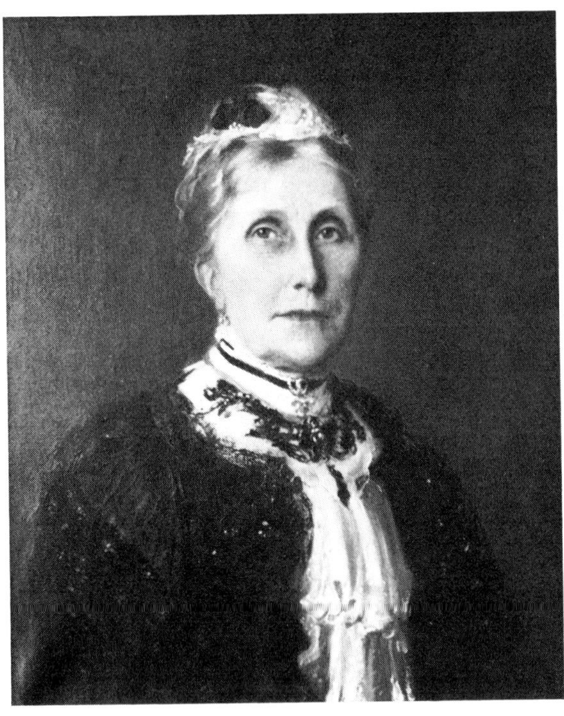

Unknown Lady 1903.

As in *Sisters* (the portrait of his three elder daughters) the girls sit in the artist's model's chair, and Dorothy has her arm round Maud's shoulders. The girls are dressed alike, in white voile dresses with blue sashes. This painting demonstrates that Walker was beginning in these years to apply his paint less thickly, and the effect is a much flatter finish.

It is possible that Walker was still visiting New York between 1900 and 1909. If so, he would have seen the first skyscrapers going up, and very large houses being built with the coming of great wealth to the city. There was a keen interest in acquiring works of art, and leading picture dealers from London and Paris were seizing the opportunity to open branches as fast as they could and to educate their new clientèle by organising loan exhibitions of paintings. Several of Walker's portrait studies of heads were auctioned in New York at this period. They were nearly all of women or young girls, and were still lusciously described in the catalogues. *An English Maiden* was thus described as 'The life-size head and shoulders of an auburn-haired young English girl with the delicate complexion and translucent skin which is often found with hair of this colour. With her head slightly inclined toward the right shoulder she looks straight at the spectator with calm eyes and a sweet and modest

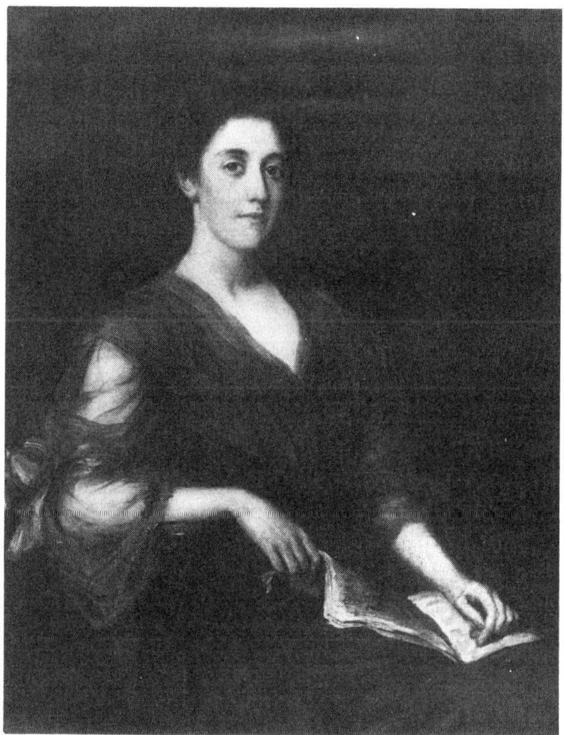

Margaret, Daughter of W.W. Ouless, Esq., R.A. 1905.

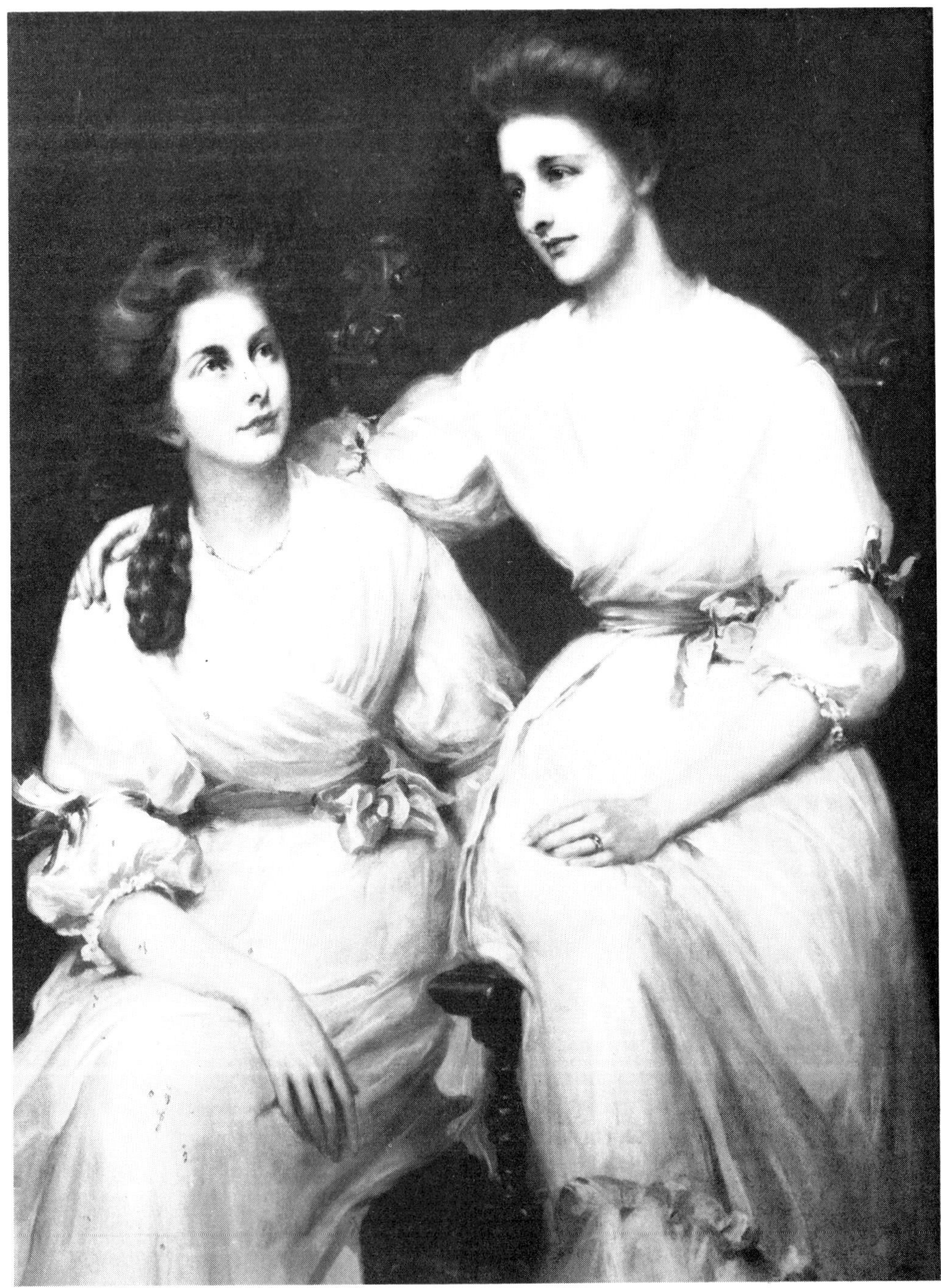

Mrs. James Stansfeld and Sister, 1904.

expression. She wears a low-cut white dress, with a white diaphanous scarf or wrap thrown over her shoulders'. These Walker paintings were sold for between $100 and $500 ($500 is roughly equivalent to £4,000 in today's terms). Decorative studies of heads had always been much in demand by the public, and even Leighton in his day had painted many of these 'bread and butter' studies. From 1907 Walker began to exhibit an increased number of paintings in England, and this may be a pointer to the fact that he ceased to cross the Atlantic after that date.

In 1904 Watts (who according to Walker's son Jolliffe and Spanton gave Walker some instruction in painting) died. This grand old man of Victorian art had lived to his eighty-eighth year, and was working to the last. He had twice been offered a baronetcy by Gladstone, but had refused it each time.

In the year of Watts' death, Alice Corkran, a friend of Leighton's and a writer and artist in the 'aesthetic' school published the first small biography of Leighton. It makes fascinating reading, for it contains first hand accounts of conversations she must have had with Walker, in which he describes his friendship with Leighton from the time the latter asked him to model for him up to an account of how Leighton came to paint his wedding portrait of 'Nan', roughly covering the years 1858–67. In her book Alice Corkran includes the beautiful study made by Leighton of Johnny's head in 1861, which Walker lent to the Leighton exhibition of 1897 and which is now owned by a descendant of the Whitakers.

Alice Corkran's biography was followed by two which were published in 1906: *Lord Leighton of Stretton* by Edgcumbe Staley, and Mrs. Russell Barrington's *The Life, Letters and Work of Frederic Leighton* which was published in two large volumes. For the latter, Hanson Walker lent Mrs. Barrington most of the thirty or so letters which Leighton had written to him, and which were kindly lent again to the present writer by Walker's grand-daughter, Mrs. Pamela Smith, and great-grandson, James Stansfeld, forming the basis of this account.

Mrs. Russell Barrington (who had published her *Reminscences of Watts* the previous year), presents a mine of information on Leighton and her work contains many letters to him written by Henry Greville (Walker's first patron) and others. Unfortunately, after her death her daughter burnt many of the letters still in her possession, feeling them to be too revealing.

Mrs. Russell Barrington had been a friend of Leighton and Watts for many years, and therefore knew them extremely well. When Watts remarried in 1886 she continued to visit his studio informally as she had always done in the past, coming and going so freely that she caused Mary Watts intense annoyance. Five years after their marriage Mary, unable to bear Emilie Russell Barrington's continual presence in the house any longer, removed Watts to Linnerslease, at Compton in Surrey. When Emilie's biography of Watts was published in 1905 Mary took hold of a copy and scribbled the words 'poisonous snake' over the author's name on the flyleaf! At Linnerslease she commemorated Watts' death in 1904 in her own way, by building a Mortuary Chapel to him, with the Watts Gallery beside it.[148]

In 1905 an Impressionist Exhibition had been held at the Grafton Galleries in London. This had been well attended, but very few paintings had been sold. John Hanson Walker asked his son Jolliffe to visit the exhibition with him, but according to Jolliffe's *Memoirs* his father felt 'disgusted, and not a bit impressed'. While it is sad that Walker, unlike his master Leighton, was unable to see good in what was then considered *avant-garde* art, it is understandable, and Louisa Starr Canziani summed up the attitude of their generation in a speech she made at the Lyceum Club on May 25, 1907 about the 'Impressionist' School of Painting. Asked if the painting pleased her she replied 'I can't endure much of the work that belongs to it. I love impressionism when good; but I find cheap imitation of it intolerable; in fact such work seems to me an insult to art. The way some people paint nowadays is merely nothing but a subterfuge, a means to hide ignorance. Half of them know nothing whatever about drawing. That is what makes Whistler and Sargent stand out from among the crowd of their imitators like giants in a land

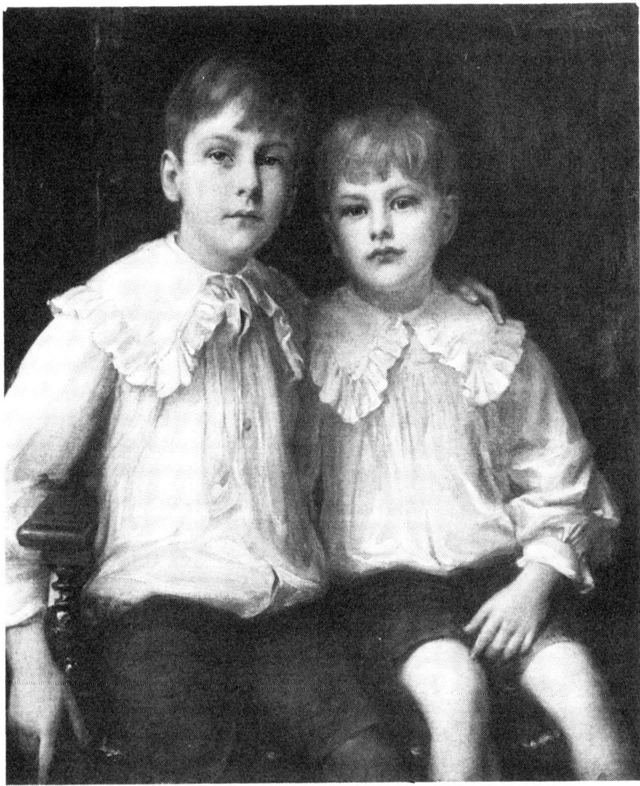

Breynton and Jack Mills, 1907.

of pygmies. In their work is knowledge! Look at their early productions, the exactness of them, the infinite care with which everything is rendered. It is Truth!'[149]

As he had done before other moves, Walker sold paintings again at Christie's in 1905, the year in which he was buying his new house. On May 6 1905 he sold an early Flemish *Madonna and Child* for 180 guineas, approximately £7,500 in 1986. Two years later he sold a further four paintings including *A Mountainous Landscape* by Murillo and Van Dyck's *Two Children of Charles I*. These did not go for high prices (£50 for the Van Dyck) and so it is to be supposed that they were not well authenticated, for in Edwardian times very high prices were paid for old masters. In 1906 The National Art Collections Fund (founded in 1903) bought Velasquez' *Rokeby Venus* for £45,000 (equal to £1.7m in 1986) and in 1912 Duveen paid 21,200 guineas at Christie's for *Mrs. Hay* by Raeburn from the Charles Wertheimer Collection, (in today's terms £800,000).[150]

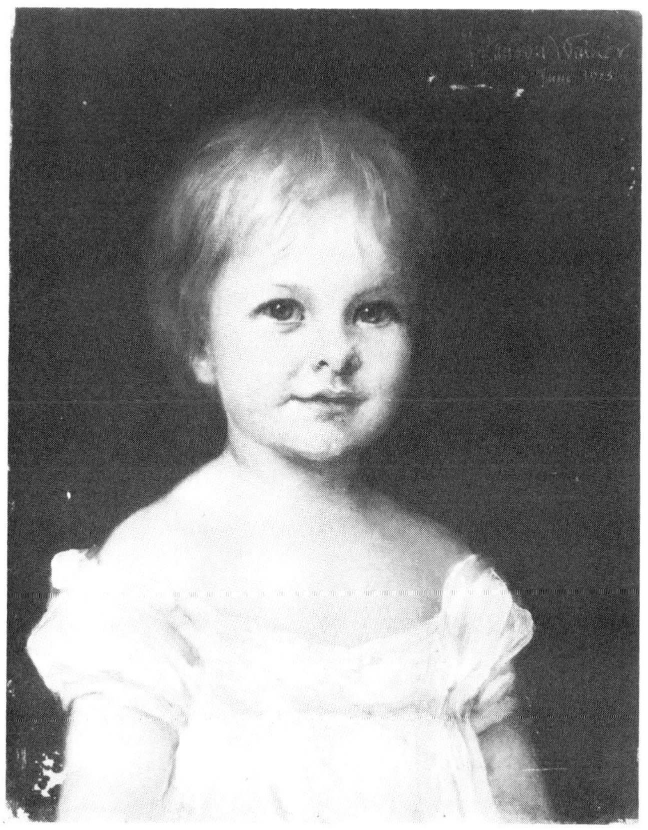

Diana Mills, 1915.

Although he was busy in the saleroom, Walker had not given up painting: between 1905 and 1911 he exhibited seven paintings at the Royal Academy, all of them portraits, although unfortunately only five of them are named. Of these, four are of relations: his grandsons Breynton and Jack Mills and his grand-daughter Nancy Romer, his own daughter Maud, and a 'Mrs. John Hanson Walker' who could have been his wife or daughter-in-law. The only named portrait which is not one of the family is of *Mrs. Crichton-Stuart* (no. 719). Mrs. Crichton-Stuart is shown wearing a dark jacket with a heather-coloured dress under it, and Walker also painted her husband, Patrick James Crichton-Stuart, who was a Captain in the Grenadier Guards, wearing Scottish clothes, including a lace jabot and doublet. The two portraits make a charming pair.

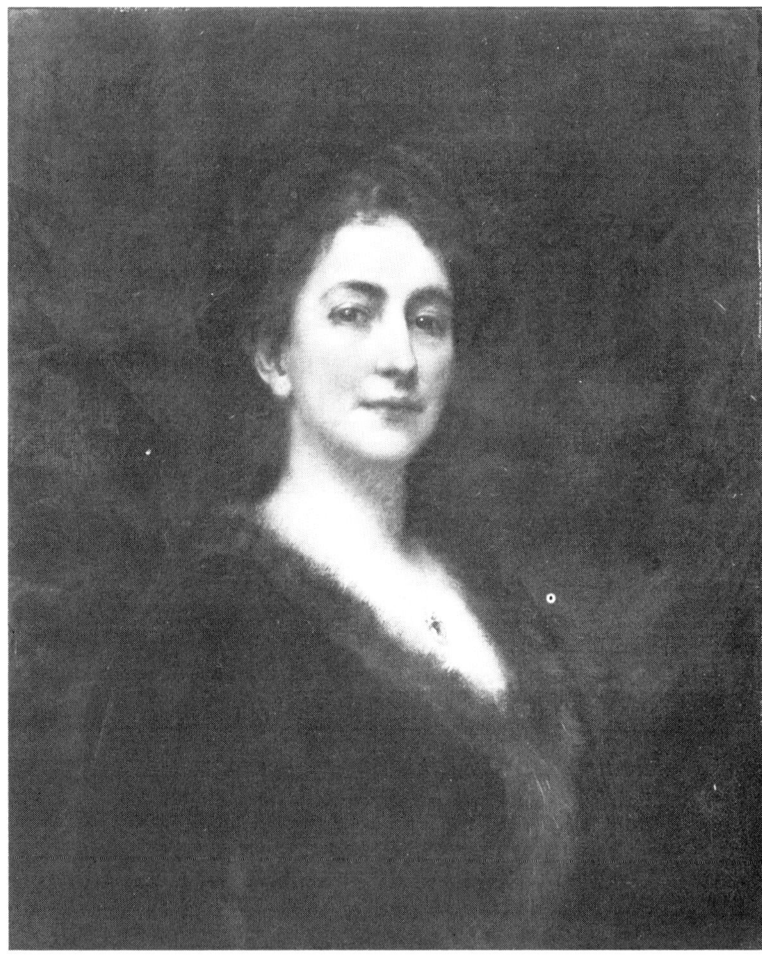

Mrs. Crichton-Stuart
1911.

Mrs. Crichton-Stuart, (who was the daughter of the Hon. J. C. Phillipo, M. D. of Jamaica) had been married before: her first husband, who died in 1897, was the Hon. Arthur St. Aubyn, son of the 1st Lord St. Levan of St. Michael's Mount, Cornwall. She was very petite, and her husband, who had been injured in a riding accident in the army was rather delicate. The artist has brought these two points out and contrasted them well.

The two early portraits that Leighton had painted of Johnny were destined to travel. *Rustic Music* went to India, to form part of the collection of the Nawab of Nawanger, and in 1911 *Duett* was lent by King George V to the International Fine Arts Exhibition in Rome, where it was shown under its alternative title *Johnny Walker* (no. 50). In the same room hung *The Earl of*

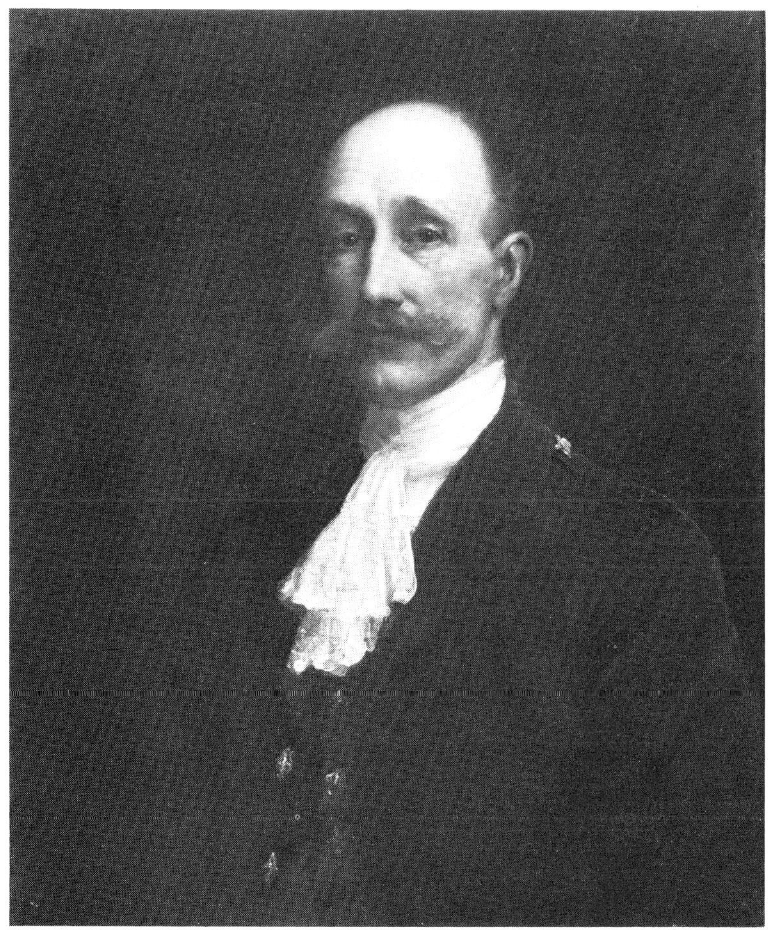

Patrick James Crichton-Stuart 1911.

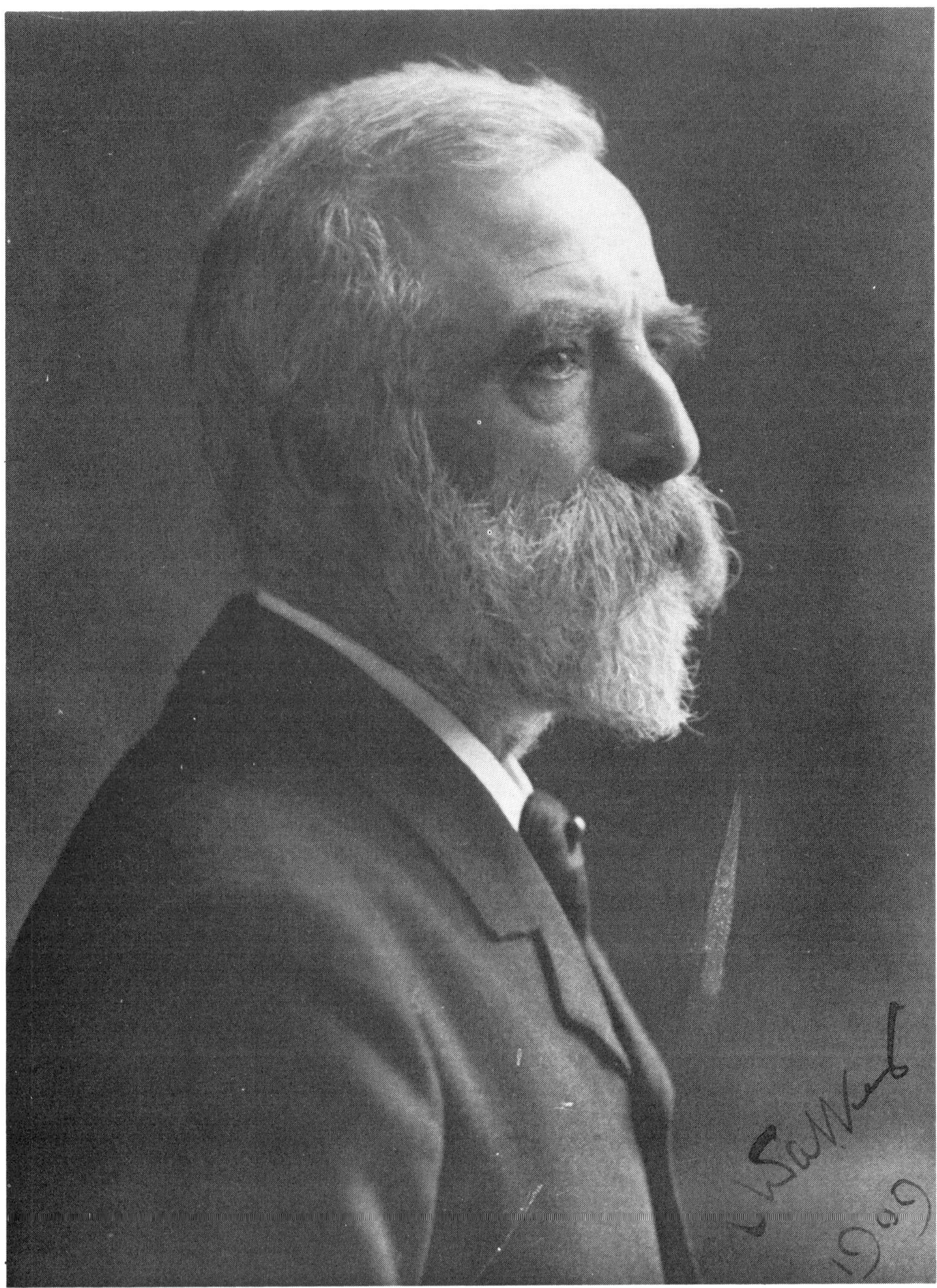

John Hanson Walker photographed in 1909.

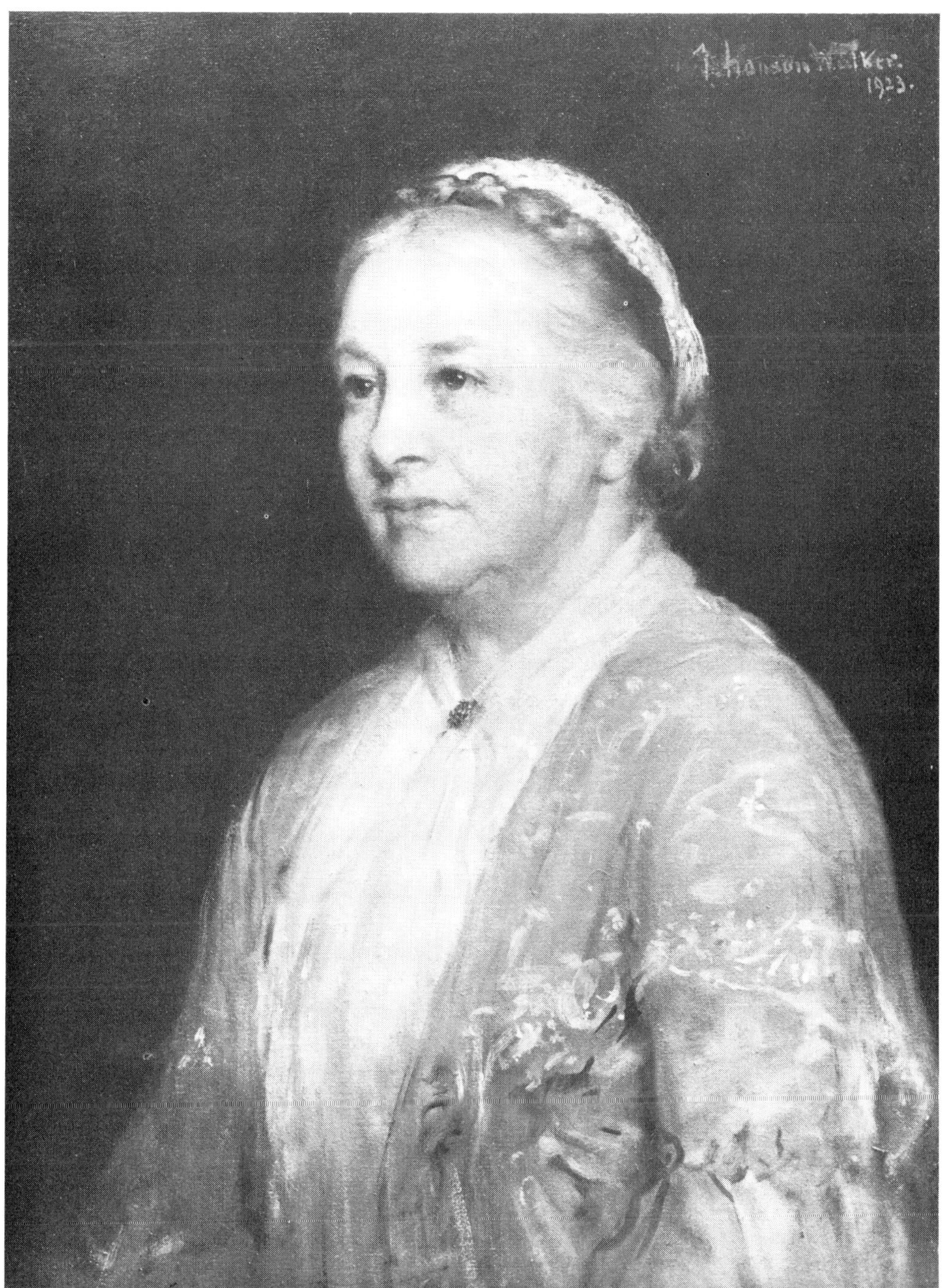

Fanny Hanson Walker, 1923.

Beaconsfield (Disraeli) by Millais, *Love and Death* by Watts and the *Return of Persephone* which Leighton had painted in the early 1890s.

John Hanson Walker (now aged sixty-seven) moved to his last London home in 1912. This time he moved southwards to Chelsea, always a haunt for artists. 2, Queen's Elm Square was a newly-built black and white mock Tudor house in a small crescent just off Old Church Street, Chelsea. This house is well remembered by his grandchildren who visited him there. One of them, Susan Romer (now Mrs. Palmer) lived nearby. She had her portrait painted by her grandfather, and was also often called in to sit for him in the clothes his other child sitters were to be painted in, to save them the trouble! For his grandson Giles Mills, who stayed at the house on his way to prep. school from his home in France, the memory was of the combined smell of Pears soap and turps. in his grandfather's studio (a smell which also extended to his grandfather's beard!) He also remembered his grandfather whistling, something he often did as he painted. By this time Walker had snow white hair, which set off his fresh complexion and blue eyes. He had become a little

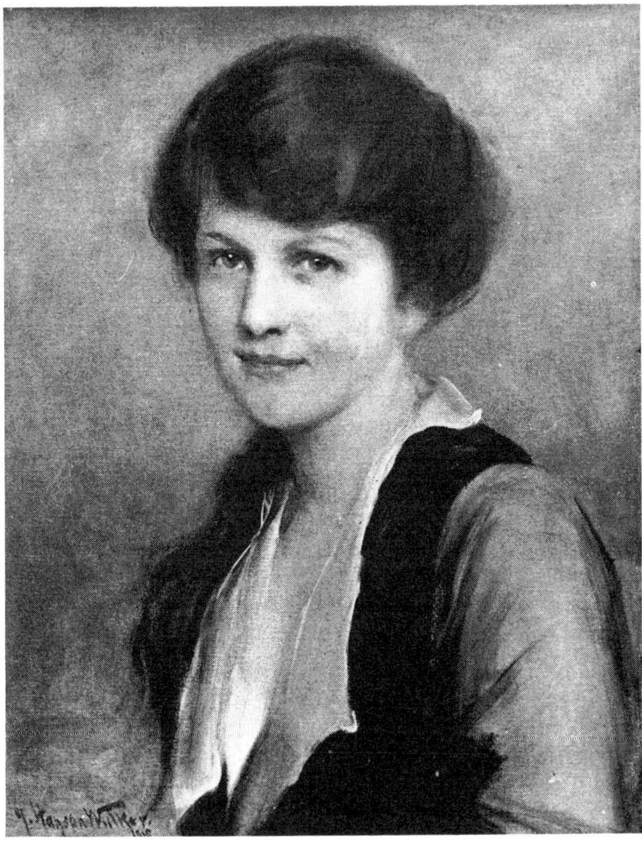

Elsie Pitt, 1915.

deaf, and would put his hand up to his ear in order to listen to what was said to him. He was willing to play interminable card games, and was given to the childish practical joking so much beloved by Victorian artists like Alma-Tadema. On one occasion Giles Mills recalls seeing Walker feeding sparrows with crumbs soaked in brandy and water; however, this may have been for a practical reason. Estella Canziani relates how Leighton, when he painted *Summer Slumbers* in the 1890s needed to make studies of sleeping pigeons. In order to get them quiescent, he fed them with bread soaked in brandy and water, so that after wobbling round in a tipsy state they finally sank to sleep.[151] In 1912 Walker exhibited his *Girl Feeding Pigeons* at the Derby City Art Gallery (no. 157) and so may have resorted to the same expedient!

Fanny seems to have been a more remote character than her husband. The hard work involved in looking after an artist and a large family seem to have taken their toll, and she appears to have become rather an austere person. Her relatives found her manner grand, although (unlike her husband) she kept her Somersetshire accent to the end. Her grandchildren remember her as a

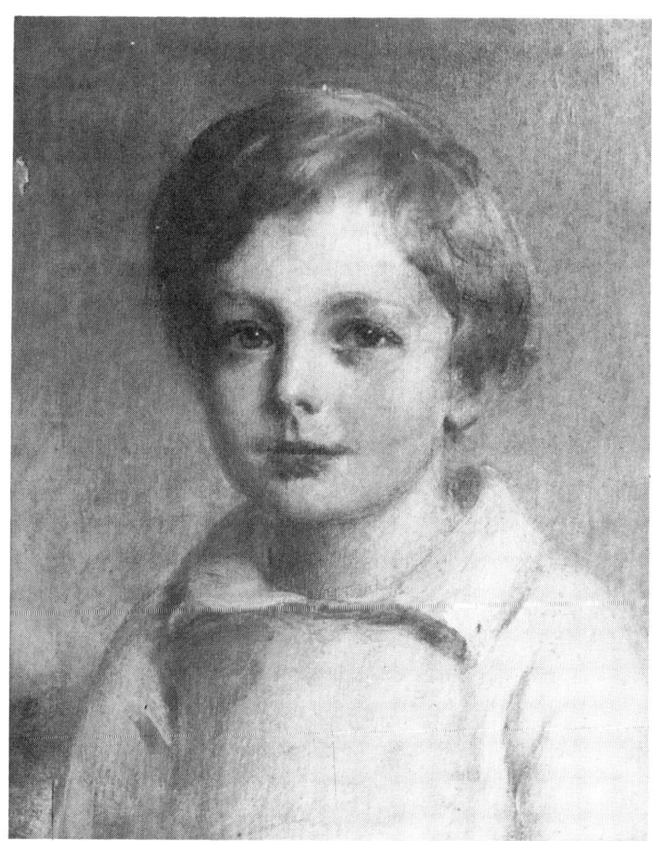

Tony Stansfeld, 1917.

good story-teller. She had a jealous temperment, so that when she and Johnny were together she appeared to dominate him – as a result he was rather timid when with her. Fanny's father had been unworldly, and Johnny was generous to a fault, so it was she who looked after their finances, and ran the household so that her husband could be entirely free to paint. It is interesting that when Leighton's sister, Augusta Matthews, died in 1919 and as arranged with him made several bequests, she left a 'small oil sketch of Donegal' to Johnny, but £100 to a 'Mrs. H. Walker'.

An undated letter from Dean Inge (the 'gloomy' Dean of St. Paul's from 1911 to 1934 who was a distant relative of Fanny's) to Walker indicates that Walker was still interested in trying to attract an illustrious sitter, for Inge writes 'Dear Mr. Walker, It is a great honour that you propose to do me. But I am afraid I do not wish to be painted, I agree too entirely with the good man who said "which man do you wish to paint? One is not finished yet, and the other is not

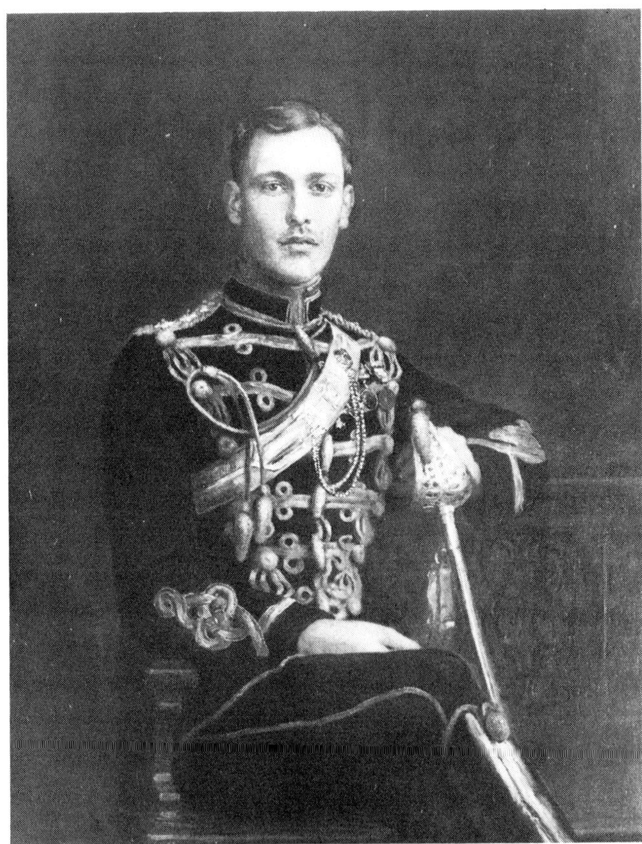

'Ted' Davidson M.C.: killed in the retreat from Mons, April, 1918.

worth painting" And I could only show the one that is not worth painting. Very many thanks all the same. Yours sincerely, W. R. Inge'.

By this time (1912–14) Walker was exhibiting four or five paintings annually, and in each of those years he had one painting in the Royal Academy. He was still selling at Christie's and in 1912 sold fifteen paintings in three different sales in March. Among these were drawings by Rowlandson (*The Studio and Architectural drawings in pen and sepia*), and *A landscape with Cottages* by Gainsborough. He also sold four of his own paintings, of which *Sweet Simplicity* and *Artemis* each made 15 guineas, equal to about £570 for each painting today. On June 10 1912 he sold *The Garden of a Palace* by Fragonard for 280 guineas, roughly equivalent to £10,500 in 1986.[152]

With the outbreak of war in 1914 a whole way of life came to an end, and flamboyant society painting was extinguished. The Walkers remained in London during the war, and it is remembered that Walker, ever an eager experimenter, took the pulses of his fellow shelterers from the air raids to find out what effect the excitement had on them. As the war drew to a close,

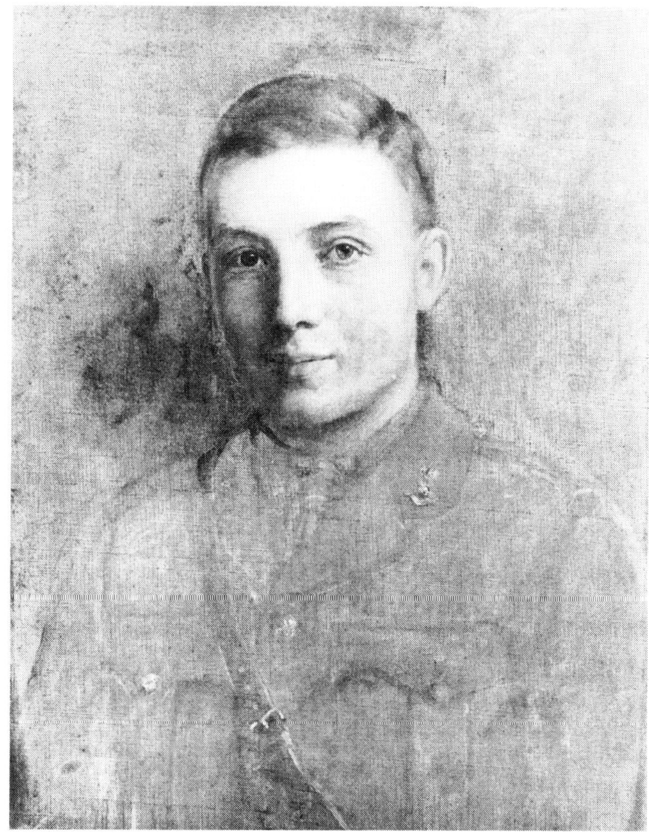

'Billy' Mills, killed in action Ypres Salient, 1917 aged 19.

relatives who had lost sons in the fighting asked for a portrait to remember them by, and Walker painted two such portraits: one was of 'Billy' Mills, (a relative by marriage) and another of 'Ted' Davidson. Both were young men who were killed towards the end of the war, and would otherwise have had distinguished careers in front of them. These portraits were painted posthumously from photographs.

In 1918 Walker exhibited his last painting at the Royal Academy: *Ursula, daughter of Charles Reiss, Esq.* (no. 490). In all he exhibited 75 works at the Academy from 1867 to 1918 compared with his friend Blake-Wirgman's 86 and Ouless' 183. (Blake-Wirgman lived 1848–1925, and Ouless 1848–1933).

After the war Walker used pastel quite frequently and very successfully, having exhibited pictures in that medium from time to time throughout his career. His pastel portrait of his daughter Sissie Pitt, dated 1920, is a good example. He continued as well to paint portraits of his grandchildren, who found him a demanding artist who required a well-held pose in 1921! He painted an excellent likeness of Mrs. Hurst of Horsham Park, another relative by marriage. A descendant of Mrs. Hurst recalls that while painting his subject at Horsham Park Walker met her near neighbour, Mrs. Ossario, who

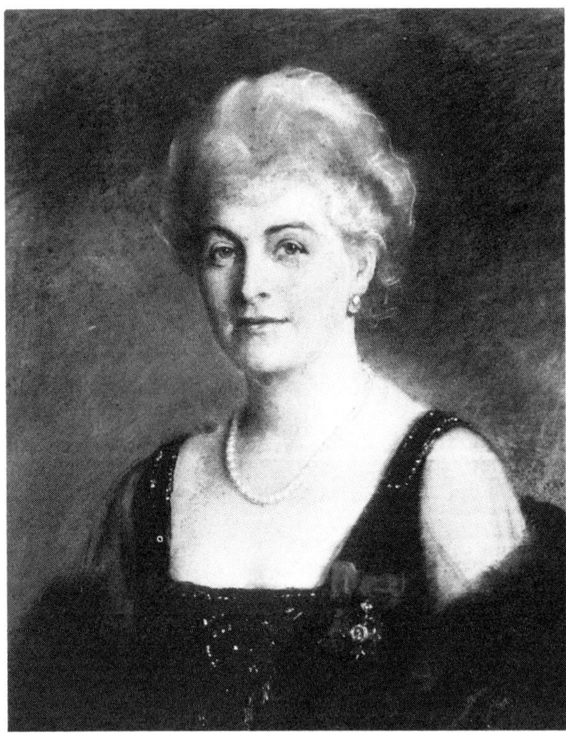

'Sissie' Pitt, (Pastel, circa 1920).

was a great friend, and who had been the model for Millais' *Cherry Ripe* as a little girl. Edie Ramage (as she then was) had amused Millais, for she used to come to his studio accompanied by her mother, who was so shy and nervous that the little girl did all the social honours, and even occasionally answered for her when necessary![153] Needless to say, Walker and Madame Ossario found a great deal in common, and much to reminisce about.

In 1923 two of Walker's elder grandchildren married, and both weddings must have given him pleasure and pride. His grandson Hewitt Pitt married Amice, the daughter of Millais' eldest son Everett, and his grand-daughter Elsie Pitt married 'Kit' Woolner (later Major General Christopher Woolner), the grandson of the pre-Raphaelite sculptor Woolner.

In 1923 John Hanson Walker painted a portrait of his wife; this is, sadly, untraced, and only a photograph exists of it. In it Fanny is shown three-quarter face with her hair braided on top of her head. The back of her head is covered by a little lace cap. Although she is remembered as a rather formidable old lady, the portrait is lovingly painted, and Fanny is shown with a sparkle of humour in her eyes. In the early spring of 1924, Fanny, who was now seventy-nine, became unwell and in order for her to get some sea air, the Walkers took rooms at Boscombe, near Bournemouth. Their eldest daughter

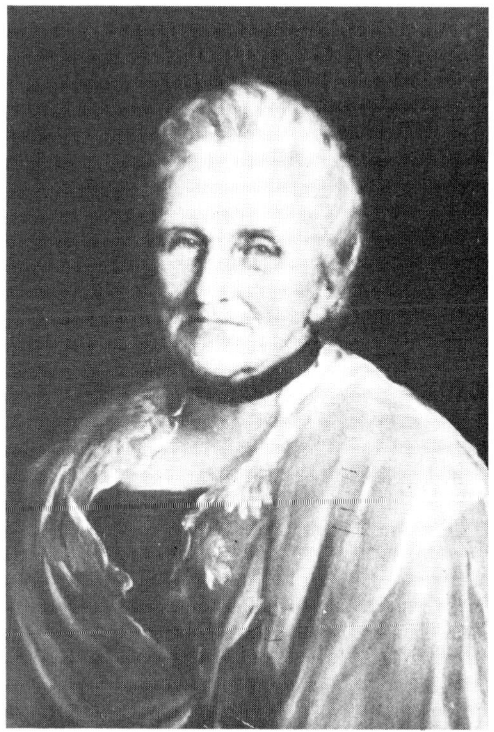

Mrs. Hurst, 1921.

Sissie joined them. On March 4 Fanny caught influenza, and by March 10 she was dead. She was buried at Wareham, Dorset in the same grave as her second son, Bob, who had died nineteen years earlier.

In his memoirs Jolliffe Walker, the Walker's fourth son, describes how with Fanny's death his father was left a very helpless and lonely man, for he had become accustomed to have everything done for him by her. In re-arranging his life, his thoughts turned to Leighton House, and he wrote on April 29, 1924 to Mrs. Russell Barrington to offer her the portrait Leighton had, at some time, given him of Dr. Leighton, his father. He wrote 'Dear Mrs. Russell Barrington, I fear there is no space available at Leighton House for another canvas measuring 30″ × 25″. I have a very fine head of Dr. Leighton, painted by my dear old friend and Master, which really ought to be placed in a prominent position there. Several weeks ago I had the terrible misfortune of losing my dear Wife, so now my house no. 2 Queen's Elm Square will either have to be let furnished or the contents scattered to the winds shortly. A south west wind I will pray for to waft the canvas to its proper resting place, if a good light could be found for it. My daughter Mrs. Frank Romer said she thought she saw you at Christie's a few weeks ago looking remarkably well, I am glad to hear. With kind regards, Yours sincerely, J. Hanson Walker'.

A week later he wrote a further letter from his son Churton's home, the Cordons, Chalfont St. Peter: 'Dear Mrs. Russell Barrington, I must apologise for not answering your kind letter of sympathy before, my plea being that I have been on the move nearly ever since I received it. Immediately the contents of my house are beginning to be dispersed I shall have much pleasure in sending Dr. Leighton's portrait up to Leighton House where I am sure you will manage to find a suitable place and light for it. It was painted at Frankfurt-on-Main and is signed F. Leighton 1849 when our dear old friend was 19. Quite a wonderful performance! When I get a little settled I will with much pleasure come up and see you. *The* picture I treasure most of the 10 I have by my old Master is the portrait he gave me of my dear wife as a wedding present – a truly noble gift! G. F. Watts said it was the best thing he had ever seen painted by his old friend. *That* I should much like to go to the National Gallery where it will be seen by many thousands every year, and also I hope help to stem the tide of that rapidly onward rush of the crude, wretched, vulgar "Bolshie" school which is influencing in the most poisonous manner the youngsters who are beginning their art career. Just look at nine tenths of the works of the R.A. or at least half! simply awful and contrast it with the exhibitions of 25 years ago, when there were two splendid leaders – Leighton and Millais. With kindest regards and many thanks – trusting that Guy and his wife are well. Yours sincerely, J. Hanson Walker'.[154] Hanson Walker's gift of the portrait of Dr. Leighton can be seen hanging today in Leighton House (no. 371)

The 'Bolshie School of painting' that so upset Walker could have been the Vorticists, (painters like Wyndham Lewis, who combined Cubism and

Futurism) or the German Expressionists (the Bauhaus had been founded in 1919). In 1924, the year of Fanny's death, Surrealism was founded in Paris with the aim of reviving imaginative art.

On November 24, 1924 Walker had a final large sale of paintings at Christie's, including Rowlandson's *A Pedlar* and a *River Scene* by Turner. Among the last lots were three of his own paintings, the proceeds of which (8 guineas in all) were to go to the Artist's General Benevolent Institution, an organisation which had been founded by Millais, together with Philip Hardwick, in 1871 and of which his friend Ouless was Secretary for many years.

Towards the end of 1924 John Hanson Walker, who still felt the loss of Fanny keenly, was coaxed by his son Jolliffe to come with him on a tour of Italy. They started from Territet, near Geneva, where Walker had been staying for a while with his sixth child, Elsie. Their trip is described by Jolliffe in his memoirs. He felt how touching it was that at last his father should be going to see the works of art he had studied all his life, but never before

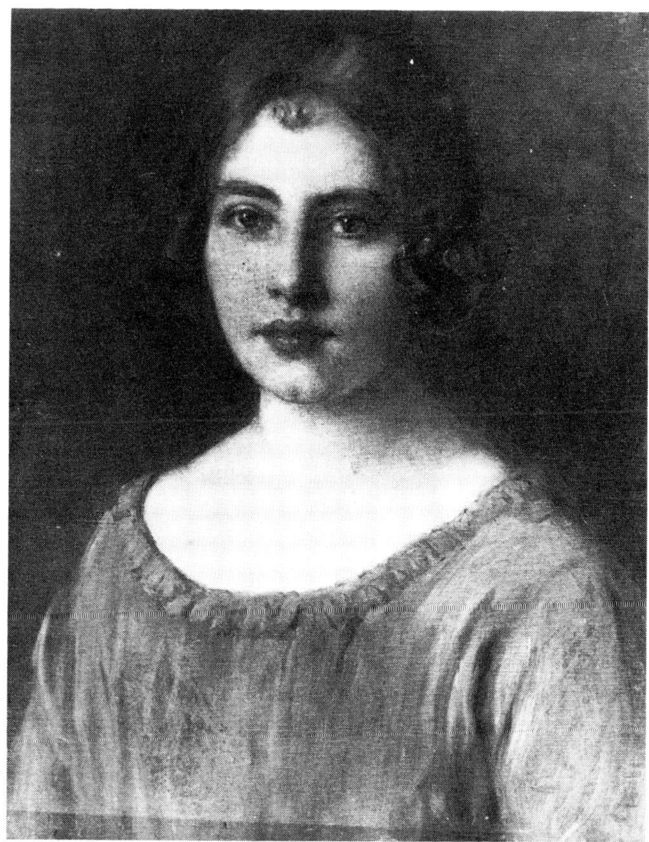

Philippa Savery, 1924.

been able to visit. From Switzerland they went to Genoa, and were in Citivecchia for Christmas. Then followed Rome, with visits to the Vatican, St Peter's and all the churches. Several weeks were spent at a *pension* in Naples, where Walker automatically began to hunt for the 'treasures' he continually searched for in England: he was always on the look-out for undiscovered masterpieces! His grandson, Tony Stansfeld, himself a Professor of Art, recalls that his grandfather in fact bought only one thing on his tour – a little sepia drawing of a Venetian canal. Walker had a way of picking up something he liked, saying 'That's clever!'

Jolliffe came to know his father much better as a result of the trip (he had always been busy in his studio when he was at home as a child). One day he was touched to discover that his father regretted having, in the past, patched up damaged paintings for restorers, because he now felt it to have been fraudulent. This illustrates that this was yet another way Walker made money to keep his family going, and fortunately Jolliffe was able to reassure his father on this point.

The journey was continued by Amalfi, Capri, Palermo and Sicily (where they found Messina in ruins after an earthquake), and finished with visits to Florence and Venice.

After returning from Italy Walker went to live for a while with his daughter Dorothy Stansfeld at Wittersham, in Kent. Later he paid a visit to his brother William's widow, Annie, who lived at Whitstable with her daughter Fay and son-in-law, Arthur Grundy. On August 4 1925 John Hanson Walker married Annie. He was eighty-one years of age, and she was sixty-four. She was born Annie Saxty, and from the marriage certificate it is known that her father was a numismatist. William, like his brother, had been a portraitist. He was eight years younger than John – otherwise little is known about him. In marrying his sister-in-law Walker was following the example of other artists like Holman Hunt, but the family deeply resented the marriage. A coolness sprang up among them towards 'Tanny' Walker, which means that knowledge about this period of the artist's life becomes rather sketchy. This coolness may be reflected by the fact that when Annie's daughter Fay Grundy died (a widow) in 1964 aged 78, she ordered in her will that any portraits left in her house at the date of her death should be burnt.

It is known that although Walker's hands became arthritic he continued to paint the small sketches of flowers and fruit that had occupied him as he grew older and painted fewer portraits. His grand-daughter, Pamela Lidderdale (Mrs. Smith), remembers that as a child she asked him to paint her little terrier 'Patch'. Sitting with Patch on her knees she watched fascinated as her grandfather prepared a piece of brown wrapping paper as a canvas by sealing it with white of egg, then with his paintbrush gripped together between his two shaky third fingers started to paint with his hands clasped together. The picture was very quickly completed, with very few strokes, but each exactly where it should be, which seemed magical to her. The painting was framed,

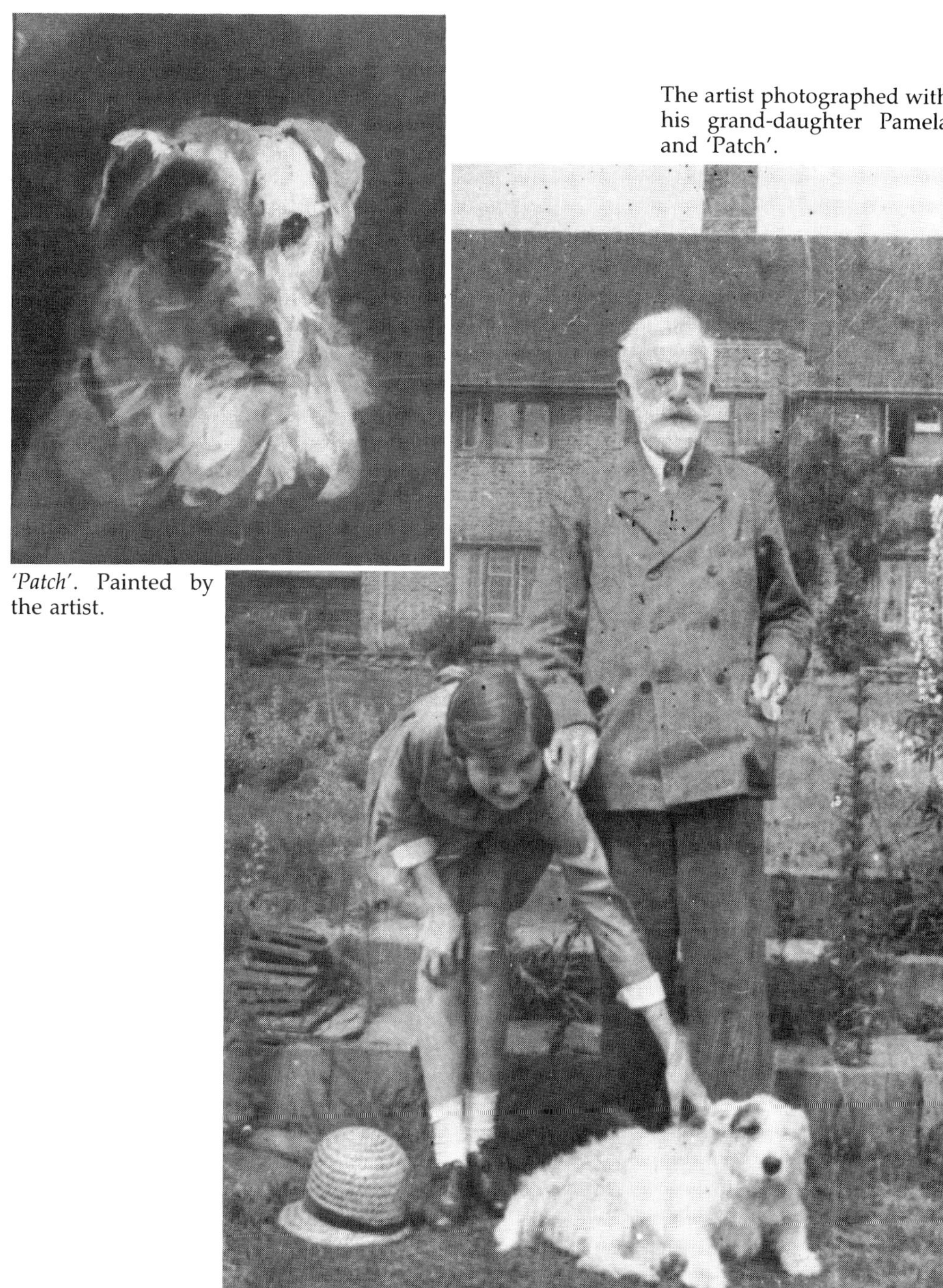

'*Patch*'. Painted by the artist.

The artist photographed with his grand-daughter Pamela and 'Patch'.

and still exists today. Walker also overcame his disability of shaking hands by having his palette attached to a thick rod, the padded end of which could be rested on the canvas, and thus support the weight for the hand which used it.

By a wonderfully apt coincidence, the last recorded memory we have of Walker is a visit paid him at Cintra, Tankerton, Kent (where he and his wife still lived with the Grundys) by the mother of the present curator of Leighton House, Stephen Jones! As a child, Mrs. Jones (then Joyce Marler), lived next door to the Walkers. She recalls that Walker was ill in bed with pneumonia one day, and her mother sent her round with her brother with a basket of good things for him. The sight of his long white beard, stretched out on the coverlet, made a deep impression on her. Each child was given a small painting by Walker as a reward for their visit, and it is delightful to think that her small painting of apples now belongs to her son, who is so actively involved in keeping the memory of Leighton alive.

John Hanson Walker died in his ninetieth year, on November 13 1933 at Tankerton. He was buried at Wareham, Dorset in the same grave as his first wife Fanny, and their son Bob.

Leighton's protégé and pupil never became an Academician, and by the end of his life his paintings were being sold for a price which barely covered the frame (a trend, fortunately, which is being reversed today). He kept his zeal and energy which had so impressed Leighton to the end, walking the twelve miles to Canterbury just before he died.

David Piper, in his book *The English Face* says 'even the most wretchedly executed portrait has generally some value, offering something that words cannot. Even the most incompetent or most mannered artist has had as starting point a unique face; the body may be more often or not a symbol or a clothes horse . . . but some attempt must have been made to catch the individuality of a face, each one unique'.[155] Walker had a particular talent for faces and the personalities expressed. W. S. Spanton, in his book *An Art Student and his Teachers in the Sixties* gives a neat and apt summary of Walker's achievements: 'John Hanson Walker, the friend and pupil of Leighton and Watts . . . had a long and honourable career as a portrait painter'.[156]

ANCESTRY OF JOHN HANSON WALKER

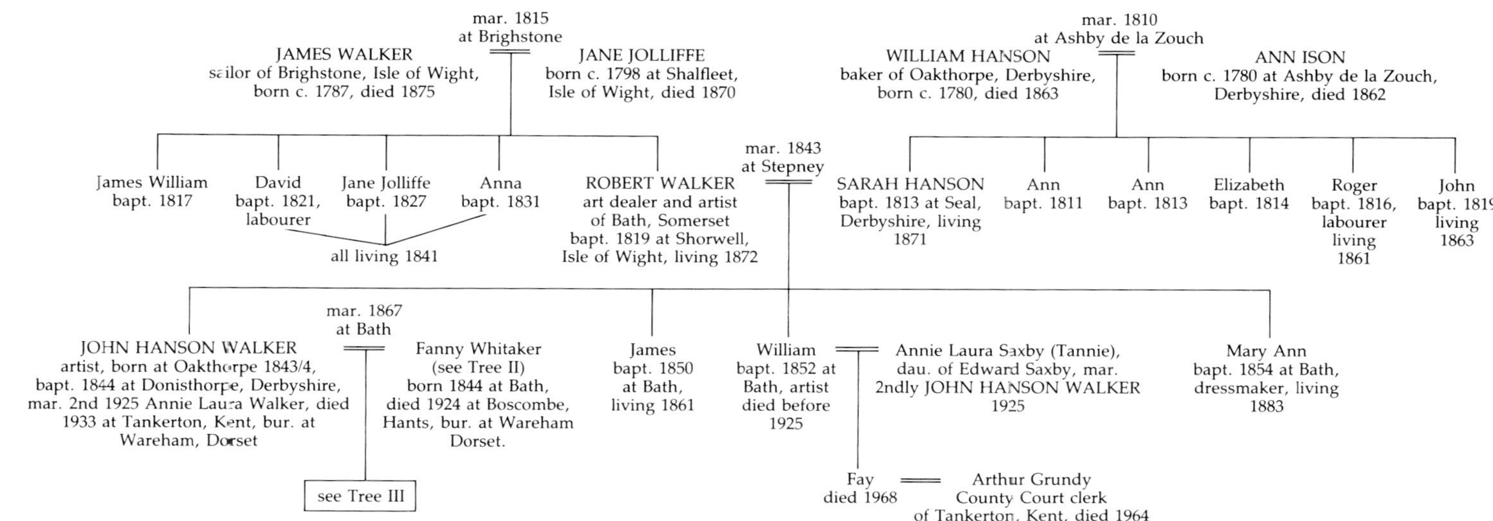

Tree II

ANCESTRY OF FANNY WALKER

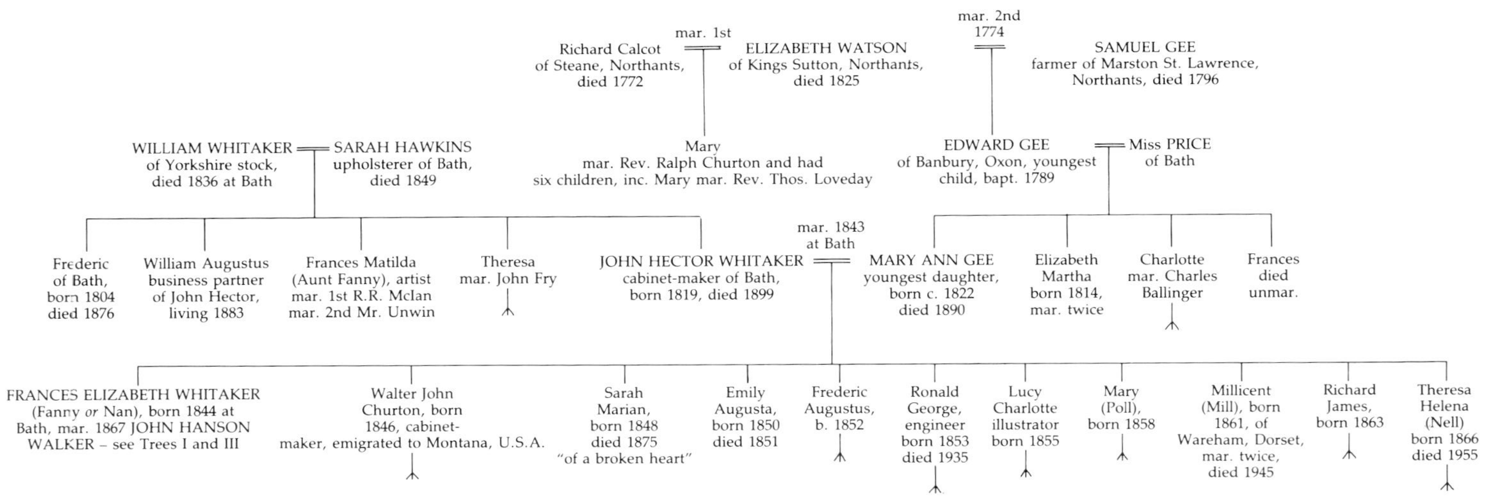

Richard Calcot
of Steane, Northants,
died 1772

mar. 1st

ELIZABETH WATSON
of Kings Sutton, Northants,
died 1825

mar. 2nd
1774

SAMUEL GEE
farmer of Marston St. Lawrence,
Northants, died 1796

WILLIAM WHITAKER
of Yorkshire stock,
died 1836 at Bath

SARAH HAWKINS
upholsterer of Bath,
died 1849

Mary
mar. Rev. Ralph Churton and had
six children, inc. Mary mar. Rev. Thos. Loveday

EDWARD GEE
of Banbury, Oxon, youngest
child, bapt. 1789

Miss PRICE
of Bath

Frederic
of Bath,
born 1804
died 1876

William Augustus
business partner
of John Hector,
living 1883

Frances Matilda
(Aunt Fanny), artist
mar. 1st R.R. McIan
mar. 2nd Mr. Unwin

Theresa
mar. John Fry

JOHN HECTOR WHITAKER
cabinet-maker of Bath,
born 1819, died 1899

mar. 1843
at Bath

MARY ANN GEE
youngest daughter,
born c. 1822
died 1890

Elizabeth
Martha
born 1814,
mar. twice

Charlotte
mar. Charles
Ballinger

Frances
died
unmar.

FRANCES ELIZABETH WHITAKER
(Fanny *or* Nan), born 1844 at
Bath, mar. 1867 JOHN HANSON
WALKER – see Trees I and III

Walter John
Churton, born
1846, cabinet-
maker, emigrated to Montana, U.S.A.

Sarah
Marian,
born 1848
died 1875
"of a broken heart"

Emily
Augusta,
born 1850
died 1851

Frederic
Augustus,
b. 1852

Ronald
George,
engineer
born 1853
died 1935

Lucy
Charlotte
illustrator
born 1855

Mary
(Poll),
born 1858

Millicent
(Mill), born
1861, of
Wareham, Dorset,
mar. twice,
died 1945

Richard
James,
born 1863

Theresa
Helena
(Nell)
born 1866
died 1955

Tree III

JOHN HANSON WALKER (1843/4–1933) – see Tree I
= FRANCES ELIZABETH WHITAKER (1844–1924) – see Trees I and II

- **Frederick Hanson Robert John Unwin**, b. 1868, surgeon, mar. Constance Leake d. c. 1900
  1. Marjorie
  2. Dorothy
- **Robert** b. 1869 studied painting at Newlyn, d. 1905
- **Fanny Sarah Marian (*Sissie*)** b. 1870, mar. 1888 Sidney Pitt, solicitor d. 1948
  1. Hewitt, mar. (1)Amice Millais (2)Alethea Dew and had issue
  2. St. John
  3. Elsie (*Anne*) mar. Major-Gen C.G. Woolner and had issue.
- **May** b. 1872, mar. 1895 Frank Romer, osteopath d. 1931
  1. Betty, mar J.H.L. Macdonald and had issue
  2. Nancy
  3. Susan, mar. George Palmer
- **John Hanson** b. 1874 painter and sculptor, mar. c. 1925 Margaret Armitage (third of four wives) d. 1946
  - Diana, mar. John Bray (and two sons by first wife)
- **Elsie** b. 1876, mar. 1898 Robert Mills, textile manufacturer and racehorse owner, d. 1967
  1. Breynton, mar. Esther Hurst and had issue.
  2. Jack
  3. Giles, mar. Marianne Soulier and had issue.
  4. Diana, mar. John Barstow and had issue.
- **Jolliffe** b. 1877 actor, painter, planter and involved with Toc H, mar. Edith Faithful d. c. 1950
  - Jolliffe
- **Churton** b. 1879 planter, mar. May Coombe, d. c. 1966
  - Cynthia (adopted)
- **Dorothy** b. 1882, mar. c. 1904 James Stansfeld landowner d. 1969
  1. Elizabeth, mar. Kenneth Burt and had issue.
  2. Wyon, mar. Lorna Fraser and had issue
  3. Anthony
- **Maud Hanson (*Jill*)** b. 1887, mar. 1916 Jock Lidderdale, RNAS and RAF, d. 1983
  - Pamela, mar. James Gellately Smith and had issue.

CATALOGUE OF PAINTINGS

B	Royal Society of Artists, Birmingham	P	Royal Society of Portrait Painters
D	Dudley Gallery, London	RA	Royal Academy
G	Grosvenor Gallery, London	RBA	Royal Society of British Artists, Suffolk Street, London
GI	Glasgow Institute of the Fine Arts	RHA	Royal Hibernian Academy
IPOC	Institute of Painters in Oil Colours	ROI	Royal Institute of Oil Painters
L	Walker Art Gallery, Liverpool (until 1871 Liverpool Museum)	RP	Royal Society of Portrait Painters
M	Manchester City Art Gallery	RSA	Royal Scottish Academy
NG	New Gallery, London	AAG	Atkinson Art Gallery, Southport, Lancashire

The title is followed by details of size in inches and centimetres, and all works are presumed to be oil on canvas, panel or board, unless otherwise stated. Signature, inscriptions and date are given where known. Where the date is unknown, the paintings have been listed chronologically from when they were first exhibited or appeared in the saleroom.

The artist painted many small studies of flowers and fruit, and these are so numerous that they have not been listed.

The catalogue cannot claim to be comprehensive, but lists all the paintings traced by the compiler. A large number of works remain untraced, but many have come to light in recent years, and it is hoped will continue to do so.

Landscape

Oil on wood. 5 × 9 (12.9 × 23 cms) 1864
Prov: By descent to Mrs. Alexander Lindsay, the artist's great granddaughter. Inscribed on back 'Painted by John Hanson Walker aged 20'.

'Nan' Whitaker

Pastel. 26×22 (66.2 × 56 cms) *c.* 1866
Prov: Elsie Mills (née Walker), daughter of the sitter; Mrs. Barstow, her daughter

The artist is thought to have made this pastel of Fanny Whitaker while they were engaged, and by family tradition it was painted in Leighton's studio. (Colour Plate 1)

Old Farm, nr. Stickwill, Edenbridge, Kent

Oil on wood, 8 × 12 (20.5 × 30.5 cms) *c.* 1866
Prov: Dorothy Stansfeld (née Walker), daughter of the artist; Mrs Burt, her daughter.

Girl with a Red Cloak

Two versions exist:
a) 16½ × 13½ (42 × 34.5 cms)
b) 17½ × 13½ (44.5 × 34.5 cms) both probably painted *c.* 1867

Version a)
Prov: By descent to James Henshaw, through his mother Mary Willis (née Whitaker) Plate.

Version b)
Prov: By descent to Molly Henshaw; Mrs. Moore, her daughter.

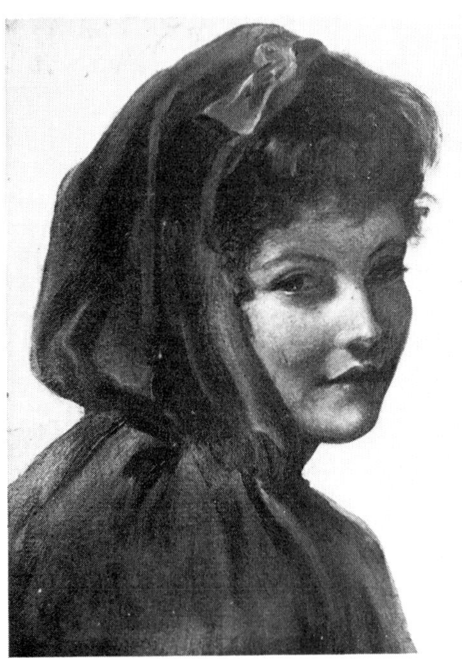

Girl with a Red Cloak (c.1867)

Study of a Head

Prov: Untraced
Exh. RBA, 1867 (141) £20

Ophelia

Prov: Untraced
Exh. RBA, 1868 (84) £2

Frederick Walker

27½ × 23½ (70 × 59.5 cms). Painted *c.* 1869
Prov: Miss Marjorie Walker, daughter of the sitter.

The subject, Frederick Walker, the artist's eldest son, was born in 1868.

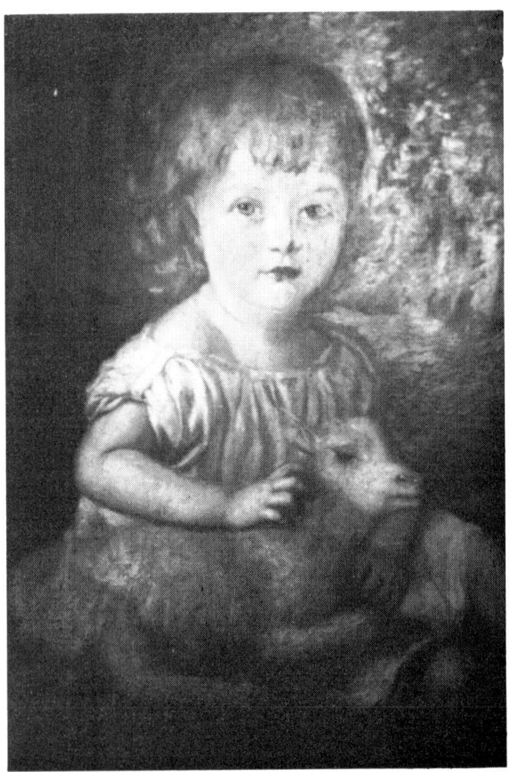

Frederick Walker (1869)

Springtime

Prov: Untraced
Exh. RBA, 1869 (13) £25

Napping

Prov: Untraced
Exh. RBA, 1869 (115) 10 gns.

The Novel

Prov: Untraced
Exh. RBA, 1869 (366) 6 gns.

Freshness of Morn

Prov: Untraced
Exh. D, 1870 (243) 7 gns.

Snowdrops

Prov: Untraced
Exh. RBA, 1870 (441) 12 gns.

The Blonde

Prov: Untraced
Exh. RBA, 1870 (632) 8 gns.

A Brunette

21 × 17 (54 × 44.5 cms)
Prov: Sold by the artist at Christie's January 23, 1925; (lot no 154) bt. Sampson (4 gns)

Theresa Helena Whitaker

15½ × 12½ (39.5 × 31.7 cms) Painted 1870
Prov: Sitter, to her sister, Mary Whitaker (Poll); Miss Philippa Savery, sitter's daughter.

Theresa Helena 'Nell' (1866–1955) was the eleventh child of John Hector Whitaker, and therefore the artist's sister-in-law. She married Robert Stephenson Bailey Savery.

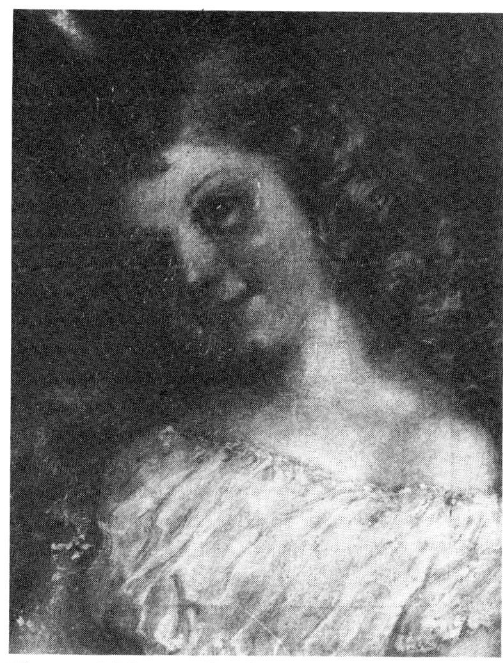

Theresa Helena Whitaker (1870)

Contemplation

14½ × 11½ (37 × 29.2 cms)
Prov: Sold Christie's May 1, 1931 (lot 31) from collection of Malcolm Aird, Woolton, Newbury; bt. by the artist.
Exh. D (Winter Exh.) 1871 (112) 2 gns.

Spring Flowers

Prov: Untraced
Exh. RBA, 1871 (Winter Exh.) (170) 5 gns.

An Old Roman Encampment at English Combe, nr. Bath

Prov: Untraced
Exh. RBA 1871 (Winter Exh.) (4) 7 gns.

Sarah Marion Whitaker

21½ × 17½ (54.5 × 44.5 cms) *c.* 1872
Prov: Mary Willis (née Whitaker); Margery Rowland; James Henshaw.

Sarah Marion, (1848–75) 9th child of John Hector Whitaker, is said to have died of a broken heart, October 2, 1875 because she was refused leave to marry her first cousin. (Plate p. 40)

Dolly Varden

Watercolour
Prov: Untraced
Exh. D, 1872 (Watercolour Exh.) (34), RHA, 1872 (164) 8 gns.

John Hector Whitaker

Oval. 27 × 20 (68.5 × 51.3 cms) Painted *c.* 1872
Prov: By descent to Commander John Whitaker

Miss Philippa Savery owns an identical copy

John Hector Whitaker (1819–1899) was the father of the artist's wife Fanny. He was a Bath cabinet maker. See Whitaker family tree. (Plate p. 34)

Greek Girl

Prov: Untraced
Exh. D, (Winter Exh.) 1872 (218) £55

An Old English Lass

Prov: Untraced
Exh. D, (Winter Exh.) 1872 (367) £25

An Old Somersetshire Lane

Prov: Untraced
Exh. RBA, 1872 (405) 10 gns.

A Florentine

Prov: Untraced
Exh. RBA, 1872 (71) 7 gns.

Returning from Market

Prov: Untraced
Exh. RBA (Winter Exh.) 1872 (346) £15

Idol Worship

Prov: Untraced
Exh. RA, 1872 (458) £126; L (Autumn Exh.) 1872 (347) £126

'La Tarantella'

23½ × 19½ (59.7 × 49.5 cms)
Prov: Sold as 'La Tarantella' Christie's May 3, 1935 (lot 99); bt. Fenton £5.15.6d. The Spanish background and size suggest this may be the painting sold Sotheby's February 7, 1978 (lot 160) £250 as 'A Tall Story'; Sold Bonham's, April 1978.

The model for this painting was probably the artist's son Frederick, born January 4 1868. See Walker family tree. (Plate p. 46)

Neapolitan Fruit Seller

30 × 25 (76.2 × 63.7 cms)
Prov: Presented 1910 to the Victoria Art Gallery, Bath by the Rev. T. P. Methuen. Exhibited as 'Italian Fruit Seller'.
Exh. RBA, 1873 (183) £73; L, 1875 (185); Bath Graphic Society, 1885 as 'Italian Fruit Seller'. (Plate p. 49)

Sketch from Nature

Prov: Untraced
Exh. RBA, 1873 (113) £5.6s.

Undisturbed

Prov: Untraced
Exh. RBA, 1873 (496) £25

A Beggar Boy

Prov: Untraced
Exh. RBA, 1873 (184) £46

Preparing for a Scrape

Prov: Untraced
Exh. RBA, 1873 (305) £15 gns.

Luck

Prov: Untraced
Exh. RA 1873 (32)

'The Catechist'

Prov: Untraced
Exh. RA 1873 (621); L (Autumn Exh.) 1873 (210) £84

The Dawn of Peace

Prov: Untraced
Exh. M, 1873 (400) £50

Ariadne

Oval: 29½ × 22½ (75 × 57 cms) s. & d. 1873
Prov: Sold Christie's, August 6, 1915 bt. Scott (lot 116) £2.12.6d

Rustic Cottage, Essex

Prov: Untraced
Exh. D, (Winter Exh.) 1873, (37)

Medora: The Corsair's Bride

Prov: Untraced
Exh. D, 1873 (297) £52.10s

This painting is sub-titled, 'She all that day had passed
In watching all that Hope proclaimed a mast'

Evening

Prov: Untraced
Exh. D, 1873 (391) 10 gns.

Farmyard nr. Walton-on-the-Naze

Prov: Untraced
Exh. D, 1873 (371) 7 gns.

Study of a Girl's Head

Watercolour
Prov: Untraced
Exh. D, 1873 (Watercolour Exh.) (409) 7 gns

A Portrait

Prov: Untraced
Exh. RA, 1874 (478)

Essie

Prov: Untraced
Exh. RA, 1874 (729) L (Autumn Exh.) 1876 (293)

Essie was the daughter of W. Compton Smith, Esq. see 1882

Devotion

Prov: Untraced
Exh. RBA, 1874 (250) £55

Tired Out

Prov: Untraced
Exh. RBA, 1873 £40; L (Autumn Exh.) (209) £25

Sketch of Honfleur

Prov: Untraced
Exh. RBA, 1874 (292) £5

Quay at Honfleur

Prov: Untraced
Exh. RBA, 1874 (299) £5

'Mary'

23¼ × 19¼ (59 × 49 cms) s. & d. 1873
Prov: Sold Christie's February 22, 1985 (lot 146) as 'Far Away Thoughts' A.W. Gamble; bt. R. & J. Jones (£750); Lady Morse
Exh. RA, 1874 (40) as 'Mary'

It is believed that this is a portrait of the artist's sister, Mary (born 1855). She was a dressmaker by profession. (Colour Plate 2)

Sarah Walker

Prov: Untraced

Only a photograph, in the possession of Mrs. Burt, exists of this painting of the artist's mother, painted *c.* 1874. On the back is inscribed: 'Mrs. Robert Walker, née Hanson, of Ammerdown, Somerset, painted by her son'. (Plate p. 35)

Lady of the Court of Charles II

24 × 20 (61 × 51 cms) Signed. Painted 1874 (?)
Prov: Auctioned Sotheby's December 17, 1986 (lot 177) £850 bt. N. G. Mills

The painting is inscribed with the title on the back of the stretcher.

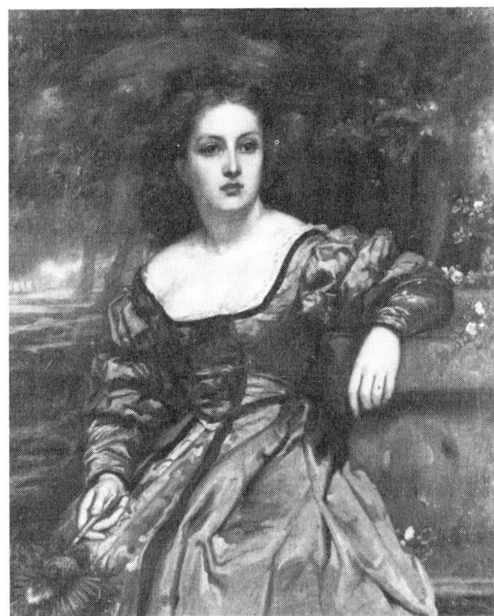

Lady of the Court of Charles II

Diana

Prov: Untraced
Exh. M, 1874 (416) £20; RBA, 1875 (561) £20

Geraldine

Prov: Untraced
Exh. M, 1874 (580)

'Tête a Tête'

Prov: Untraced
Exh. L (Autumn Exh.) 1874, (83) £155

Preparing for a Festival

63 × 34 (164 × 86.4 cms)
Prov: Sold by the artist Christie's March 30, 1901 (lot 76) as 'Preparing for *the* Festival'; bt. Smith £14 14
Exh. RBA 1874/5 (62) £105; RHA, 1877 (7); M, 1878 (149) £105

Fanny Hanson Walker

26 × 22¼ (66.2 × 57.2 cms) Painted *c.* 1874
Prov: By descent to Miss Marjorie Hanson Walker, the sitter's grand-daughter.

Profile, head and shoulders. The sitter wears a brown dress with a low square-cut neck edged with cream muslin. Her hair is drawn up on the nape of her neck.

Frances Elizabeth Hanson Walker (née Whitaker) 1844–1924 was the artist's first wife. See Whitaker family tree.

The Lord Egerton of Tatton

50 × 40 (127 × 101.5 cms) Signed. Painted 1874
Prov: Bequeathed to the National Trust with Tatton Park, Cheshire 1958 by Maurice, 4th Baron Egerton of Tatton.
Exh. M, 1875 (108)

A photograph of this, and the following three paintings are in a portfolio of photographs at Tatton Park, and photographs of these, rather than of the paintings themselves, are in the Witt Library.

William Tatton, 1st Lord Egerton, (1806–83) was M.P. for North Cheshire for 26 years. He was an active politician, and in 1859 was created Baron Egerton of Tatton by the Whig Prime Minister, Lord Palmerston. In 1830 he married Lady Charlotte Loftus (1811–71) the eldest daughter of the 2nd Marquess of Ely; noted for her sharp tongue, she was nicknamed 'Tatty'! Their eldest son Wilbraham Egerton, was the 1st Earl. (q.v.) (Plate p. 52)

Wilbraham Egerton

Prov: Formerly at Tatton Park, present whereabouts unknown. Painted 1874

Wilbraham Egerton, (1832–1909) succeeded his father the 1st Lord (q.v.) in 1883. He followed his father as M.P. for North Cheshire, 1858–68, subsequently sitting for mid-Cheshire. He was created Earl Egerton of Tatton and Viscount Salford in 1887. In 1857 he married Lady Mary Sarah, eldest daughter of the 2nd Earl Amherst, and they had an only daughter, Gertrude, (q.v.). Wilbraham Egerton played a prominent part in furthering the Manchester Ship Canal project, 1887–94. An authority on weapons, he wrote the catalogue of arms and armour for the old East India Museum, S. Kensington, London. Tatton, in his early years, was a scene of lavish hospitality, but he later became more of a recluse. He had no male heir, and on his death the earldom became extinct, the barony passing to his younger brother, Alan de Tatton Egerton, M.P. for Knutsford. (Plate p. 53)

Lady Mary Egerton

24 × 21 (61 × 53.5 cms) Painted 1874. Signed.
Prov: Bequeathed to the National Trust with Tatton Park, Cheshire 1958 by Maurice, 4th Baron Egerton of Tatton.

Lady Mary, eldest daughter of the 2nd Earl

Amherst, married Wilbraham Egerton in 1857, and their only daughter, Gertrude Lucia, was born 1861. Lady Mary worked for the Primrose League and the Red Cross. She died in 1892, and her husband married secondly Alice, Duchess of Buckingham and Chandos. (Plate p. 52)

The Hon. Gertrude Egerton

25 × 21 (63.5 × 53.5 cms) s. & d. 1874
Prov: The sitter to her daughter, The Lady Elizabeth Matheson; Fiona Kendall, her grand-daughter

Plaque on frame is inscribed 'Gertrude Lucia Egerton, Countess of Albemarle only child of 1st Earl Egerton of Tatton Hanson Walker.' Gertrude Lucia was born January 9 1861 and so was fourteen at the time her portrait was painted. In 1881 she married Arnold Keppel, the 8th Earl of Albemarle. (Plate p. 53)

'Five O'Clock P.M.'

35 × 27 (89 × 69.2 cms)
Prov: Sold by the artist Christie's April 13, 1901 as 'Five O'Clock Tea' (lot 105); bt. Cassell, 10 gns.
Exh. RA, 1875 (394); M, 1876 (250) £50; GI, 1876 (440) £50

'Fond Memory brings the Light of Other Days around Me'.

Prov: Untraced
Exh. GI, 1875 (498)

This is a quote from Thomas Moore's 'Oft in the Stilly Night'.

A Portrait

Prov: Untraced
Exh. RBA, 1875 (548)

Cora

Prov: Untraced
Exh. RBA, 1875 (244) £25

James Crossley

49½ × 39½ (175 × 100.5 cms) s. & d. 1875
Prov: Chetham Library, Manchester
Exh. M, 1876 (856)

James Crossley (1800–1883), President of the Chetham Society, was born in Halifax, and aged seventeen was articled to Mr. Thomas Ainsworth, Solicitor, father of the writer Harrison Ainsworth. Although a partner in the firm of Ainsworth, Crossley and Sudlow until he retired in 1860, Crossley found time to contribute to *Blackwood* and many other journals, becoming a figure of importance in the literary circles of Manchester. The Chetham Society 'for the publication of the Historical and Literary Remains connected with the counties of Lancaster and Cheshire' was founded at his house in 1843, and he became its President five years later: coupled with his own huge library, it was his main interest in life. Vol. 96 of the Chetham Society makes it clear that this was a subscription portrait painted for the Governors of Chetham's Library in recognition of James Crossley's valuable contribution to literature. (Colour Plate 3)

Thomas Jones

23½ × 19¼ (59.7 × 49 cms) s. & d. 1875
Prov: Chetham Library, Manchester.

Thomas Jones (1810–75) was Librarian of the Chetham Society 1845–75, and died, on November 29, 1875 having devoted his life to the library, shortly after this portrait was painted. (The library owns Walker's letter of condolence on his death). Jones was shy and modest, but was highly regarded, and even Engels wrote of him with some fondness. The portrait was painted with spare subscription money donated for James Crossley's. (q.v.) (Plate p. 55)

Medora

Prov: Untraced
Exh. RBA, 1875 (Winter Exh.) (164) £40

The painting is sub-titled 'and many a restless hour outstretched each star. And morning came, and still thou wert afar'.

Scylla

Prov: Untraced
Exh. L (Autumn Exh.) 1876, (48) £31.10s; GI, 1881 (93) £52.10s.

'Shall I, or shall I not?'

Prov: Untraced
Exh. RBA, 1876 (71) £25; M, 1879 (14) £26.5s.

Sir Harry Mainwaring, Bt.

Prov: Untraced
Exh. RA, 1876 (1313); M, 1876 (862) as 'Portrait of the late Sir Harry Mainwaring'.

This portrait was presented by the Magistrates of the County of Chester. Sir Harry Mainwaring (1804–75) was born at Peover Hall, Cheshire, which his family had inhabited since they came to England with William the Conqueror. He ran his estate as an agriculturist on the old lines. He was an active magistrate, presiding over the county quarter sessions for many years. E. G. Salisbury, in his *Border County Worthies* records that 'A magnificent testimonial was presented to Sir Harry in 1875 through the hands of the Lord Lieutenant of the County' and the portrait may have been painted to accompany this. The Mainwarings were related to the Egertons of Tatton Park.

Rather Shy

Prov: Untraced
Exh. L, 1876 (224) £42; RHA, 1877 (134) £30

An Awkward Recognition

Prov: Untraced
Exh. RBA, 1876 (252) £35

The First Step of the Ladder

Prov: Untraced
Exh. RBA, 1876 (334) £35

The Late Lord Lyttleton

Prov: Untraced
Exh. RA, 1876 (438)

George William Lyttleton, 4th Baron Frankley (1817–1876) was Lord Lieutenant of Worcestershire and Principal of Queen's College, Birmingham. He lived at Hagley Park, Stourbridge, Wilts.

The Late Mrs. Penfold

Prov: Untraced
Exh. RA, 1876 (490)

The Bubble Company

71 × 92 (180.4 × 223.4 cms) Signed with monogram of artist's initials
Prov: Sold Motcombe Galleries, 1963, bt. Newman & Cooling; sold by Colonel Harbottle Phillips March 15, 1982 (lot 186) (£3,000), bt. Wharfedale Galleries, Yorks; Bourne Galleries, Reigate; Mitsukoshi (UK) Ltd; K. Takenaka, President, Dai-Ichi Securities Ltd., Tokyo. (Cover Plate)

Exh. GI, 1877 (160) £85; L (Autumn Exh.), 1877 (41) £85

The subjects in this painting are three elder children of the artist. The boy is either Fred or Bob, the artist's first or second son; the girl on the left his eldest daughter, 'Sissie', and on the right his second daughter, May. The frame of the painting is inscribed '"Bubble Company" John H. Walker'. Illustrated on book cover.

Hope

Prov: Untraced
Exh. RBA, 1877 (334) £20

'Our Father'

Prov: Untraced
Exh. RBA, 1877 (209) £21

'With Flowering Wreaths Arrayed, Bears Her Pure Offering to the Heavenly Maid'

Prov: Untraced
Exh. RBA, 1877 (Winter Exh.) (417) £52

A Portrait

Prov: Untraced
Exh. M, 1877 (930)

The Rev. Sir George Cornewall, Bt.

Prov. Richard Chester-Master, Esq
Exh. RA, 1877 (952)

The Rev. Sir George Cornewall (1833–1908) lived at Moccas Court, Hereford and was Rector of Moccas 1861–1908. He was a County Councillor, Trustee of the British Museum, and representative for Herefordshire at the Royal College of Music.

May Walker

Oval: 13½ × 12 (34.5 × 30.5 cms) Painted *c.* 1877
Prov: May Romer (née Walker); Mrs. Palmer, her daughter.

May Walker (1872–1932) was the artist's second daughter. See Walker family tree.

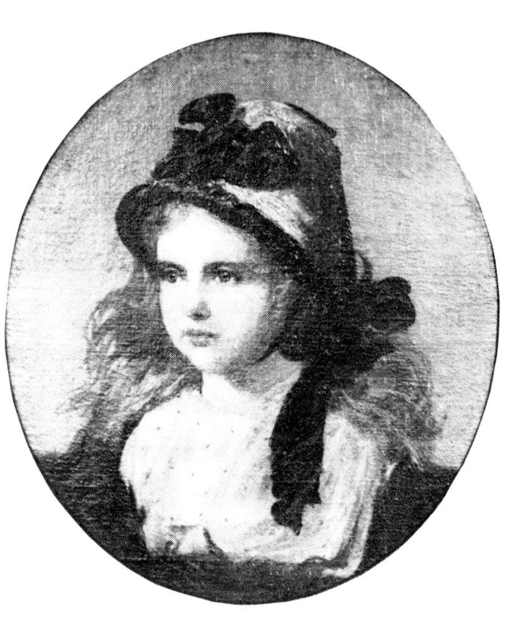

May Walker (1877)

Frederic Leighton

Prov: Untraced
Exh. RA, 1877 (342); L, 1880 (608); GI, 1881 (248); Oldham Loan Exh. (lent by the artist) 1883 (129); RP, 1894 (13); Victorian Era Exh. Earl's Court, London (Historical Section Cat.22 p.17) lent by the artist.

In this painting Leighton is recorded as wearing a brown velvet smoking jacket.

Elsie

13 × 11½ (33 × 29.3 cms)
Prov: Mrs. Breynton Mills (the sitter's daughter-in-law); another identical version belongs to Mrs. Barstow, the sitter's daughter.
Exh. RA 1877 (99).

Elsie (1876–1967) was the artist's third daughter. See Walker family tree.

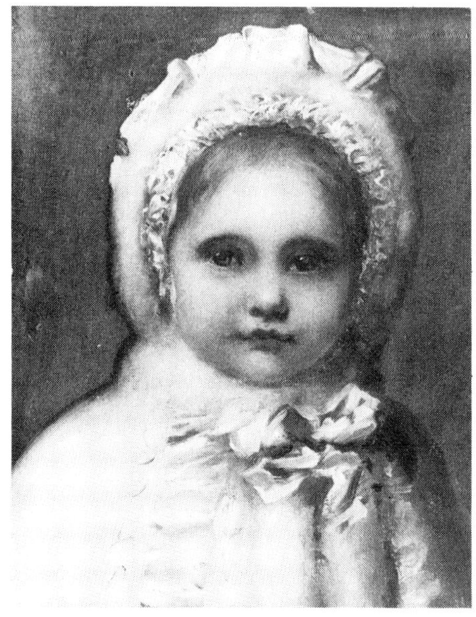

Elsie (1877)

Lucy Gray

Prov: Untraced
Exh. RBA, 1878 (Winter Exh.) (164) £12 12s.

Elmley Park, Worcestershire

Prov: Untraced
Exh. RBA, 1878 (Winter Exh.) (209) £21

Elmley Park, a large stone Elizabethan house, of which the park was laid out by Walter de Beauchamp in 1234, was purchased in 1822 from the Savage family by Colonel Thomas Henry Hastings Davies, M.P. for Worcestershire.

Colonel Davies

32 × 26 (81.3 × 66.2 cms)
Prov: Hugh Davies, great grandson of the sitter
Exh. RA, 1878 (95)

Colonel Henry Fanshawe Davies (1837–1914) was the second son of General Francis John Davies of Danehurst, Sussex, and Elmley Castle. Because his elder brother was killed in action, he left the navy and joined the Grenadier Guards, where he rose to be Lt. General, commanding the Cork District, Ireland (1889–93). He married Ellen Christine, daughter of John Alexander Hankey, of Balcombe Place, Sussex who died 1940 aged 102. This painting was well reviewed in *The Times* of May 4, 1878, and in that year's *Academy Notes*. (Plate p. 59)

Mrs Davies

32 × 26 (81.3 × 66.2 cms)
Prov: Hugh Davies, great-grandson of the sitter

Ellen Christine Davies, (nee Hankey) 1838–1902 was the 2nd daughter of John Alexander Hankey, of Balcombe Place, Sussex. She married Colonel Henry Fanshawe Davies in 1863 and had two sons

This portrait could be the 'Portrait of a Lady' exhibited at the R.A. 1878 (530)

'On Mischief Bent'

Prov: Untraced
Exh. GI, 1878 (394) £31.10s. M, 1878 (706) £31.10s.

Mrs. T. W. Gribble

Prov: Untraced
Exh. RA, 1878 (143)

This, and the following portrait, were described as 'two able portraits' in the year's *Academy Notes*.

Miss Laura Fletcher

Prov: Untraced
Exh. RA, 1878 (148)

This painting was well reviewed in *The Times* of May 4, 1878

Frederick

26 × 22¼ (66 × 56.5 cms)
Prov: Miss Marjorie Walker, daughter of the sitter
Exh. RA, 1878 (491); M, 1878 (251) £31.10s; L, 1878 (284)

The subject, the artist's eldest son, b. 1868, is depicted three-quarter length wearing a dark collarless suit, and has his arms crossed. See Walker family tree. Frederick, born 1868 was aged 9–10 at the time this portrait was painted.

Portrait of a Lady

Prov: Untraced
Exh. RA, 1878 (530)

The Hon. Home Browne

Prov: Untraced
Exh. RA, 1878 (1373)

The Hon. Home Browne was Governor of the Chartered Gas Company.

'Faces in the Fire'

Two versions were painted of this:
a) 30 × 36 (76.2 × 91.5 cms) and
b) 21½ × 25½ (54.5 × 65 cms)

Version a)
Prov: Sold by the artist Christie's, April 13, 1901 (lot 106) bt. Philpot 15 gns. Now in the possession of Mrs. Isabella Findlay.
Exh. L, 1878 (450) £52.10s; M, 1890 (34) £52.10s; GI (Works of Modern Artists) 1910 (12)

Version b)
Prov: Sold Christie's July 16, 1915 (lot 78) bt Witt £5 5s.
Exh. GI, 1879 (192) £36.5s; AAG, 1901 (302)
(Colour Plate 5)

A Study

Prov: Untraced
Exh. RP, 1878 (451) £42

Beechwoods

Prov: Untraced
Exh. L, 1870 (438) £36.10s.

Mrs. John Hill

26 × 23 (66 × 58.5 cms)
Prov: By descent to Kenneth Simonds, Esq., the sitter's grandson.
Exh. RA, 1879 (299)

Amy Hill (née FitzGerald) 1856–1934, married John Hill as his second wife *c.* 1877, and this was her wedding portrait. Her husband was a widower with five children, and Amy was barely older than her eldest step-child when she married. There were four children of the second marriage. (See also Maud and Gwendoline, daughters of Mr. John Hill, 1880). (Colour Plate 4)

Richard Matthews, Esq.

Prov: Untraced
Exh. RA, 1879 (130)

This was a presentation portrait.

Viscountess Sidmouth

41 × 30½ (104.2 × 77.5 cms)
Prov: By descent to the Hon. Christopher John Addington
Exh. RA 1879 (142)

Three-quarter length. Sitter wears a black dress with cream lace edging round neck and sleeves, trimmed black rose. On her head is a lace cap with black bow. She wears drop earrings, and a diamond brooch on a black velvet choker. Plaque on frame inscribed 'Georgiana, wife of 3rd Viscount Sidmouth. Died 1896'.

Georgiana, 3rd Viscountess Sidmouth (1826–1896) was the eldest daughter of the Very Rev. Hon. George Pellew, Dean of Norwich. She married William Wells, 3rd Viscount Sidmouth in 1848 and had three sons and four daughters. She was considered a great beauty. See Viscount Sidmouth, 1880.

Major-General George Willis, C.B.

Prov: Untraced
Exh. RA, 1879 (617)

General Sir George Willis (as he became) (1823–1900) served in many campaigns in Canada and the Crimea. He commanded the 1st Division in the Egyptian Expedition of 1882 at El Magfa, Tel-el-Mahita and Kassassin. He afterwards commanded the Southern District, England (1884–9). He contested Portsmouth for the Conservatives 1892. The artist exhibited a further portrait of General Sir George Willis at the Royal Academy 1883. (q.v.)

Innocence

Prov: Untraced
Exh. B, 1879 (376) 15 gns.

Dorothy, Daughter of E. C. Lees, Esq.

Prov Untraced
Exh. M, 1879 (72)

A Portrait

Prov: Untraced
Exh. RBA, (Winter Exh.) 1879 (392)

Expectancy

Watercolour
Prov: Untraced
Exh. D, 1879 (198) £26.5s

Viscount Sidmouth

41 × 30½ (104.2 × 77.5 cms)
Prov: By descent to the Hon. Christopher John Addington
Exh. RA 1880 (586)

Three-quarter length. Viscount Sidmouth wears a dark frock coat, and holds a stick and gloves.

William Wells, 3rd Viscount Sidmouth (1824–1913) succeeded his father as his eldest surviving son in 1864. He served in the Royal Navy 1837–48, and was Conservative M.P. for Devizes, 1863–4. He married, 1848, Georgiana Susan eldest daughter of the Very Rev. Hon. George Pellew, Dean of Norwich. (q.v. 1879)

The Hon. Lewin Cadogan

Prov: Adele, Countess Cadogan; her paintings were auctioned at her death in the 1960s.
Exh. RA, 1880 (1036)

The hon. Lewin Cadogan (1872–1917) was the son of the 5th Earl Cadogan and his first wife, Beatrix, daughter of the 2nd Earl of Craven.

The 5th Earl, a Conservative, who was M.P. for Bath 1878, held many positions; among them Parliamentary Under-Secretary for War, and Under-Secretary of State for the Colonies. The hon. Lewin Cadogan died, unmarried, in Australia. This portrait once belonged to Adele, Countess Cadogan, on whose death it was left, with her other possessions to be auctioned in aid of the Roman Catholic church.

Lady Sophia Cadogan

Prov: Untraced
Exh. RA, 1880 (84)

Lady Sophie Beatrix Mary, (1874–1937) was the daughter of the 5th Earl Cadogan and his first wife, Beatrix. She married Sir Samuel Scott, the 6th Bt. (who died 1943) and had issue.

Baby Churton

Prov: Untraced
Exh. G, 1880 (113); M, 1880 (252)

Churton, the artist's fifth son, was born 1879. See Walker family tree.

Maud and Gwendoline, Daughters of John S. Hill, Esq.

Prov: By family descent to Dr. Jack Parry
Exh. RA, 1880 (394)

Maud and Gwendoline were John Hill's daughters by his first marriage (see 'Mrs. John Hill' 1879). Maud married Walter Frith, son of the artist William Powell Frith, and Gwendoline married H. Darlington, the rose grower.

Lord Aveland

29 × 31¼ (73.7 × 80 cms)
Prov: Ancaster Collection, Scotland.

The frame is inscribed with the artist's name, and dated 1881.

Gilbert Henry Heathcote-Drummond-Willoughby, 2nd Baron Aveland and 24th Baron Willoughby de Eresby (1830–1910) succeeded his father to the barony in 1867. A Liberal, he spent fifteen years in the House of Commons, as member first for Boston (1852–6) and then Rutland. He continued his parliamentary career from 1867 in the House of Lords, being created Earl of Ancaster in 1892. He was Lord Great Chamberlain as deputy to his mother, the Baroness Willoughby de Eresby. He married, 1863, Lady Evelyn Elizabeth Gordon, 2nd daughter of the 10th Marquess of Huntly. (See also Mary, daughter of Lord Aveland, 1882). (Plate p. 62)

Mrs. Moncrieff

Prov: Untraced
Exh. RA, 1880 (174); RSA, 1881 (397)

Duncan Bowden-Smith, grandson of the sitter, owns a copy, by Spink, of the original.

Harriet-Mary Moncrieff (1850–1907) was the only daughter of James Rimington-Wilson, Esq., of Broomhead Hall, Yorkshire. In 1875

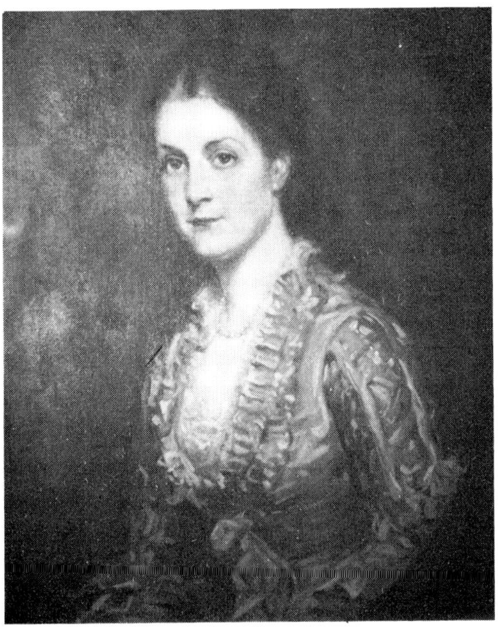

Mrs Moncrieff (1880)

she married Colonel Alexander Moncrieff (q.v.) and had seven children, all of whom the artist (a close family friend) painted when small, and again as young adults. Mrs. Moncrieff became Lady Moncrieff in the year her painting was exhibited at the RA.

Colonel Alexander Moncrieff, C.B., F.R.S.

Prov: Untraced
Exh. RSA, 1881 (110)

Duncan Bowden-Smith, grandson of the sitter, owns a copy, by Spink, of the original.

Colonel Alexander Moncrieff (1829–1906) was the eldest son of Captain Moncrieff of Culfargie, Perthshire. He was greatly interested in both science and art. He served in the Crimea with the Royal Artillery, and afterwards commanded the 35th Brigade, Scottish Division. He was best known for inventing the Moncrieff system of mounting heavy ordnance, and was knighted in 1880 for his invention of the Moncrieff Disappearing Gun Carriage, which is thought to have played a large part in military successes in the Crimean War. Colonel Moncrieff was on intimate terms with many distinguished men in the world of art and science, but also enjoyed the life of a country gentleman at his home, Bandirran, Perthshire. In 1875 he married Harriet-Mary Rimington-Wilson, (q.v.) and they had seven children. (q.v.)

Portrait of a Lady

Prov: Untraced
Exh. L, 1881 (52); RSA, 1882 (66)

Waiting

Prov: Untraced
Exh. L, 1881 (1345) £25

Andrew Ramsay, Esq., LL.D., F.R.S.

31½ × 27½ (80 × 70 cms)
Prov: 1933 presented by Mr. Ramsay to the Geological Survey, Burlington House, Piccadilly.
Exh. RA, 1881 (332); RSA, 1882 (138)

Sir Andrew Crombie Ramsay (1814–1891) Director-General of the Geological Survey (1871–1881) was born and educated in Glasgow. He became a Fellow of the Royal Society 1862, and was President of the Geological Society 1862–4. As a geologist his heart was in the physical side of the subject, and he was absorbed by the history and origins of the natural features of a district. He was simple and modest, with a boyish exuberance of spirits. Delighting in the open air, he was an excellent walker. The painting may commemorate his retirement from the post of Director-General of the Geological Survey in 1881, on which occasion he was knighted.

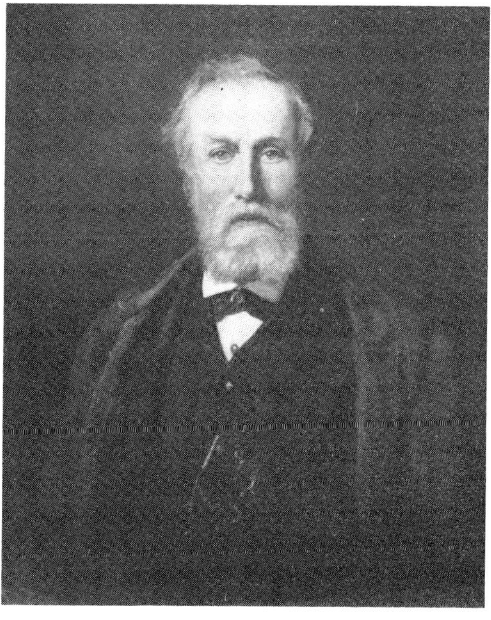

Andrew Ramsay, Esq., LL.D., F.R.S. (1881)

Mrs. George Gibbs, and her Sons Stanley and Antony

Prov: Untraced
Exh. RA, 1881 (547)

Mrs. Henry Lubbock

Prov: Untraced
Exh. RA, 1881 (1398)

Mrs. Williams

Prov: In 1964 belonged to R. E. Wear, Esq., of Biggin Hill, Kent.

A photograph of this painting is in the National Portrait Gallery Library.

Half-length. The sitter wears a mob cap with bow on her dark hair. Her dress has an embroidered edge to the neck and sleeves. She holds a piece of lace or embroidery in her left hand.

It is presumed Mrs. Williams was the mother of Edith Williams, q.v. below.

Edith, Daughter of Mrs. S. Williams

Prov: In 1964 belonged to R. E. Wear Esq., of Biggin Hill, Kent.

A photograph of this painting is in the National Portrait Gallery Library.

Half-length. The sitter is seated, and wears a low-necked dress with frilled neckline and frilled sleeves. She holds a book in her right hand.

The sitter was the daughter of Samuel Williams, of Shirley, Tunbridge Wells, Sussex. In 1882 she married Sir Arthur Sackville Trevor Griffith Boscawen, M.P. for Tunbridge Wells, so this was probably an engagement portrait. Lady Boscawen died in 1919, and her husband later re-married.

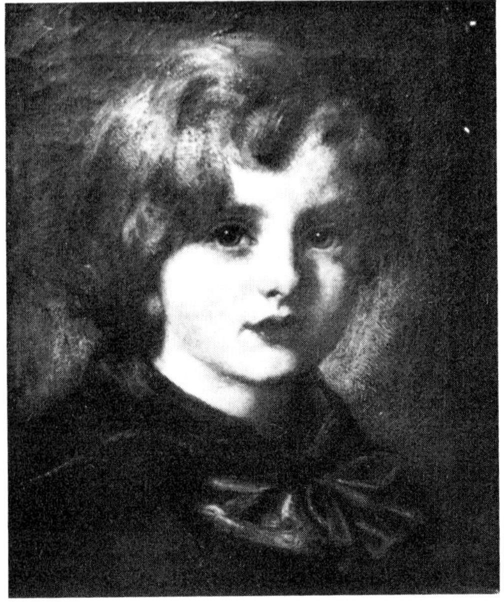

Johnnie (1881)

'Johnnie'

14 × 12½ (35.5 × 32 cms) Signed
Prov: Peter Audley-Miller, Antiques, Oxford; Mrs. Savage.
Exh. G, 1881 (130)

It is believed that the sitter is the artist's third son, John, born 1874.

'Johnnie'

Pastel. 17 × 14 (43.2 × 35.7 cms) Painted *c.* 1881
Prov: Sitter to his daughter, Diana Bray

This was the same sitter, it is thought, as in the portrait above.

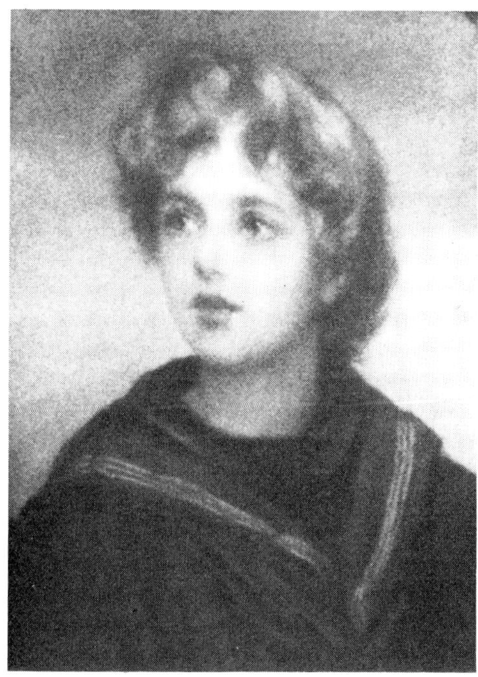

Johnnie (c.1881)

'Florrie'

Prov: Untraced
Exh. RSA, 1881 (94)

Florrie was the daughter of J. R. Findlay, Esq., of Edinburgh.

Mrs. Walter Salmond

Prov: Untraced
Exh. RA, 1882 (89); L, 1882 (653)

W. Compton Smith, Esq.

Prov: Untraced
Exh. RA, 1882 (177)

See also Essie, daughter of W. Compton Smith, 1874.

R. G. Palmer, Esq.

Prov: Untraced
Exh. RA, 1882 (246)

Mary, Daughter of Lord Aveland

Prov: Untraced
Exh. RA, 1882 (334)

Mary Adelaide (1878–1960) was Lord Aveland's youngest daughter. She married, 1903, the 14th Earl of Dalhousie, and her sons John and Simon became the 15th and 16th Earls of Dalhousie respectively.

Noticed in the year's *Academy Notes*.

Dulciana, Ethel and Jeannette Wood

Prov: Untraced
Exh. RA, 1882 (788)

These were the three daughters of C. L. Wood, Esq.

Industry

Prov: Untraced
Exh. M, 1882 (701) £105; RBA, 1883 (98) £63

Indolence

23½ × 19½ (59.7 × 49.5 cms)
Prov: Sold by the artist Christie's May 16, 1907 (lot 188) bt. Amor, 10 gns
Exh. L, 1882 (537) £105; G, 1883 (129)

Interrogated

Prov: Untraced
Exh. IPOC (1st Exh.) 1882 (294)

Beggar Girl

15 × 12 (38.2 × 30.6 cms) Unsigned, but on the back of the stretcher the original exhibition label is inscribed 'J. Hanson Walker, 16 Vicarage Gate'.
Prov: Auctioned Bearnes & Waycotts, Torquay, March 20, 1985 (£480); Sotheby's July 24, 1985 (lot 227/R) (£600), bt. Mrs. Mowbray.
Exh. IPOC (1st Exh.) 1882 (781). (Plate p. 70)

Dorothy, Daughter of Viscount Hood

17 × 12½ (43.3 × 32 cms) Signed
Prov: Sitter to her nephew, Alexander, 7th Viscount Hood.
Exh. G, 1882 (1); RP, 1895 (67)

Dorothy was the youngest daughter of the 5th Viscount Hood. She never married, but became the family historian, writing *The Admirals Hood*, and *Looking Back on London* – a city about which she was very knowledgeable. Dorothy's father, Francis Wheler Hood was in the Grenadier Guards, and was a Conservative member of the House of Lords. Her mother was the daughter of A. W. Ward, Esq. (Plate p. 69)

Jessie Lawrence

60 × 36 (152.5 × 91.5 cms) *c* 1882
Prov: By descent to G. S. Barstow, Esq., great grandson of both sitter and artist!

Jessie Lawrence, born September 29, 1852 was the daughter of George Lawrence of Monmouthshire. She married her cousin, Alfred Tristram Lawrence, in 1875. He later became Judge of the High Court, and 1920–21 Lord Chief Justice, being created Lord Trevethin. There were five children of the marriage. Her son Geoffrey, (Lord Oaksey) presided over the Nuremberg trials. Jessie Lawrence is remembered as creating a warm, affectionate atmosphere around her. (Plate p. 73)

Lord Mure

Prov: Untraced
Exh. GI, 1883 (106)

Lord Mure was a Judge of the Court of Session, Edinburgh. He died 1891.

The Late Colonel Mure, M.P.

Prov: Untraced
Exh. GI, 1883 (235)

Colonel Mure (1830–80) after serving in the army and seeing action in the Crimea, was elected Liberal M.P. for Renfrew, 1873, like many of his ancestors before him. In 1859 he married Constance Wyndham, youngest daughter of the 1st Baron Leconfield.

Maud-Isobel, Daughter of Colonel Sir Alexander Moncrieff

Cut down to 30 × 25 (76.6 × 63.5 cms)
Prov: Duncan Bowden-Smith, Esq., nephew of the sitter. Present whereabouts unknown.
Exh. G, 1883 (44); RSA, 1886 (695)

Maud-Isobel (1877–1948) was the eldest daughter of Colonel Sir Alexander and Lady Moncrieff. She married the Rev. Van Cooten.

The Sunbeam

Prov: Untraced
Exh. RA 1883 (277); L, (34) £400; M, 1885 (as 'Sunbeams') (428) £350; GI, 1903 (293) £157.10s.

The Hon. Ashley Eden

71 × 59 (127 × 150 cms)
Prov: The Bengal Chamber of Commerce and Industry, Calcutta.
Exh. RA 1883 (390)

The Hon. Ashley Eden, (1831–1887) Lt. Governor of Bengal 1877–1882, was the third son of the 3rd Lord Auckland, Bishop of Bath and Wells. In 1852 he became an Assistant Magistrate in India. Though impartial, he was outspoken, and his contempt for the conventional often led to criticism. Criticism also followed him when he was sent as special envoy first to Sikkim, and afterwards Bhutan, (1861–4) where circumstances forced him to sign a treaty that appeared too favourable to that country. As Secretary to the Governor, 1862–71 he showed a marked capacity for business, and he was a popular and successful Lt. Governor. He effected reforms in finance, indigo farming and the administration of hospitals and schools. He encouraged the cultivation of cinchona as a substitute for quinine, and the development of the railway system. (Plate p. 72)

General Sir George Willis, K.C.B., at Kassassin, Sept. 9th, 1882

Prov: Untraced
Exh. RA 1883 (679); L, 1883 (275)

This was a second portrait painted by the artist of General Sir George Willis. (See also 1879). This portrait was mentioned in the *Academy Notes* for 1883.

Spring

Prov: Untraced
Exh. M, 1883 (185) £100

Portrait of Jolliffe

Prov: Untraced
Exh. RBA, 1883 (350)

Jolliffe was the artist's fourth son, born 1877. See Walker family tree.

Portrait of a Boy

Prov: Untraced
Exh. RBA, 1883 (95) £35

'He Comes, He Cometh Not'

Prov: Untraced
Exh. RBA, 1883 (185)

Elsie

Watercolour
Prov: Untraced
Exh. D, 1883 (121)

This was probably the artist's third daughter Elsie, born 1876. See Walker family tree.

'Over the Hills and Far Away'

Pastel. 23½ × 20 (59.7 × 51 cms)
Prov: Sold by the artist at Christie's, April 22, 1901 (lot 44) bt. Morgan, 10 gns.
Exh. RBA, 1883 (288), Glasgow International Exhibition, 1888 (597) £55

Sly Boots

Prov: Untraced
Exh. G, 1884 (65)

Bessie

Prov: Untraced
Exh. G, 1884 (109)

Bessie was the daughter of the Rev. Philpot-Graham.

Mrs. Duncan McClaren

Prov: Untraced
Exh. RA, 1884 (631)

This portrait was of Priscilla, daughter of Jacob Bright of Rochdale who was Mr. McClaren's third wife: he had been twice widowed previously. Duncan McClaren, (born 1800), was Liberal M.P. for Edinburgh, and Provost of that City 1851–4.

Young Nimrod

Prov: Untraced
Exh. IPOC, 1884 (612)

Gracie

Prov: Untraced
Exh. RBA, 1884 (174)

Cecil, Son of Walter Severn, Esq.

Prov: Untraced
Exh. D, 1884 (216)

Walter Severn (1830–1904) was a watercolourist, designer and landscape painter. He was a founder member of the Dudley Art Gallery, London where he exhibited nearly all his work: he later became its President. In 1884 Walker was on the Council for the gallery. There were thirty-seven Council Members, among them Ruskin, whose niece Severn had married. A family memoir by Walker's son Jolliffe records that his father painted Severn's son Cecil and daughter Helen Christian in oil, in exchange for a watercolour Severn had given him. Unfortunately the Very Rev. Dean Wild, (son of Helen Christian Severn) (q.v.) has no recollection of ever seeing either portrait.

Helen Christian, Daughter of Walter Severn, Esq.

Prov: Untraced
Exh. D, 1884 (275)

Helen Christian was the sister of Cecil Severn. (q.v.)

Dorothy Walker

19½ × 13½ (48.5 × 34.5 cms)
Prov: The sitter; Wyon Stansfeld, her son.
Exh. G, 1884 (166); L, 1885 (151)

Dorothy Walker was the artist's fourth daughter, born 1882. This portrait was copied by the artist, and exhibited in 1886 as *The Age of Happiness*. See Walker family tree. (Plate p. 82)

Theresa Helena Whitaker

Prov: Philippa Savery, daughter of the sitter; Anne Packham, her niece. Painted *c.* 1884

This portrait is damaged, and therefore has not been measured. Theresa Helena (1866–1955) was the artist's youngest sister-in-law. (See also 1870).

Dorothy Walker

Gouache. 13¼ × 9½ (33.6 × 23.5 cms)
Prov: Professor Tony Stansfeld, son of the sitter.
Exh. L, 1885 (151)

Dorothy Walker was born 1882. See Walker family tree. (Plate p. 68)

Portrait of a Child

Prov: Untraced
Exh. IPOC, 1885 (615)

Alaric-Rimington Moncrieff

17 × 14 (43.2 × 35.6 cms) Inscribed on the reverse 'Alaric Rimington 3rd son of Col. Alexander Moncrieff, CB., FRS., (of Culfargie). Born in London 21st March 1880. Painted by J. Hanson Walker, Nov. 1885'.

See also 1906.

Kitty, Daughter of W. W. Ouless, R.A.

Prov: Sitter; destroyed by bombing, World War II, 1939–45
Exh. G, 1885 (259)

Kitty's father, W. W. Ouless (1848–1933) was a friend of the artist. Born in Jersey, he attended the R. A. Schools 1865–9, and became a highly successful portraitist. Catherine 'Kitty' (1879–1960) was the eldest of his three daughters, and became an artist herself. She never married.

Head of a Girl

16¼ × 12½ (41.2 × 31.7 cms)
Prov: Painting of the same title and measurements sold at Sotheby's, April 3, 1977 (lot 148) bt. Gustant, £75

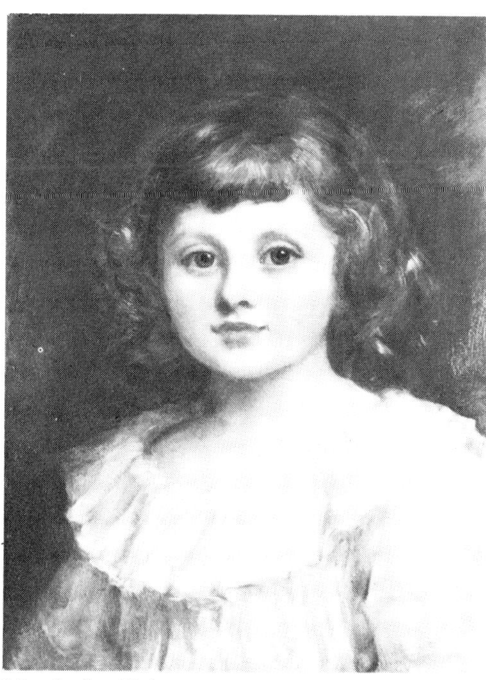

Head of a Girl

'Free as the Air'

27 × 24 (68.6 × 61 cms) Signed.
Prov: Bt. E. J. Gregory-Carlton, Esq. at mid 1960's auction held by Messrs. Parker, Cheam, Surrey.
Exh. L, 1885 (361) £105; Glasgow International Exhibition 1888 (617) £55. (Colour Plate 6)

'The Age of Happiness'

17 × 14 (43.2 × 35.7 cms) Signed
Prov: By descent to Mrs. Jane Feather, grand-daughter of the sitter.
Exh. IPOC, 1886 (559); L, 1887 (120) £52.10s; L, 1891 (31) £30

This is a portrait of the artist's fourth daughter Dorothy, born 1882. It appears to be a copy of his earlier portrait of her, exhibited 1885 (q.v.) It is believed the artist took *The Age of Happiness* with him to America in 1886 as a sample of his work, and that he made other copies of the same painting. (Plate p. 82)

Pets

Cut down to 30 × 22 (76.2 × 56 cms)
Prov: The sitter; James Stansfeld, her grandson.
Exh. RA, 1886 (612); M, 1886 (660) £130

The subject of this picture is the artist's fourth daughter, Dorothy, born 1882. See Walker family tree.

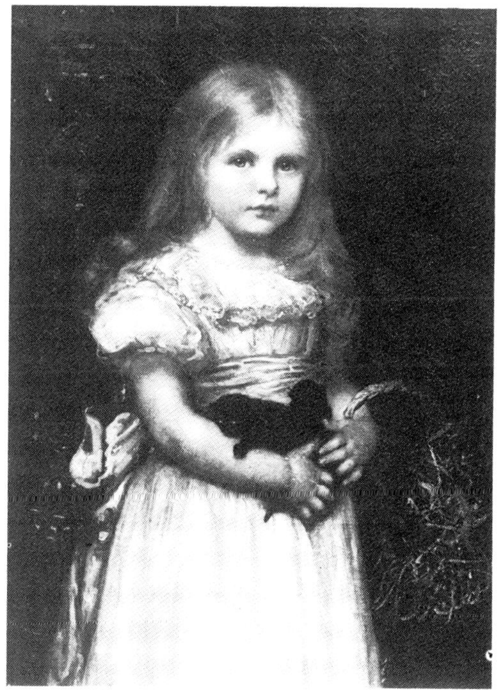

Pets (Dorothy Walker) 1886.

Dorothy

12 × 10 (30.5 × 25.5 cms)
Prov: James Stansfeld, Esq., the sitter's grandson.
Exh. RBA, 1887 (232)

The sitter, (as in the portrait above) is the artist's fourth daughter, Dorothy. On the back of the painting is inscribed 'Painted 1886. For dear Dorothy, a birthday present from her father, October 26th, 1922.' See Walker family tree.

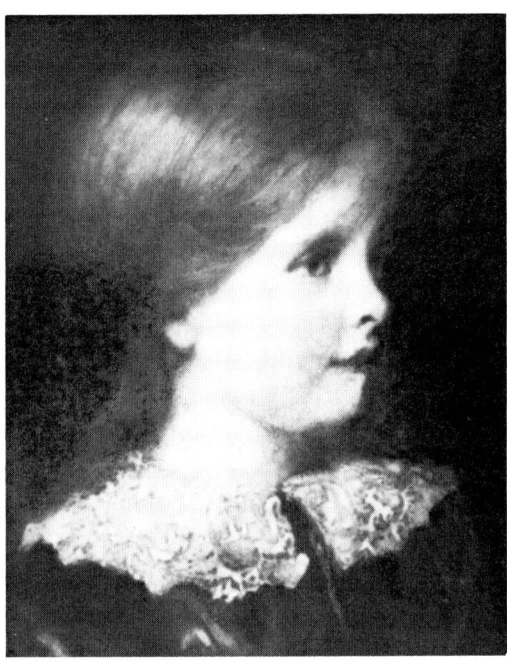

Dorothy (1886)

Sweet Sixteen

Prov: Untraced
Exh. IPOC, 1886 (807)

Arthur Luckock

Prov: Untraced
Exh. RA, 1886 (417)

The Rev. Herbert Mortimer Luckock, the sitter's father, was Canon of Ely, 1874–5 and Principal of Ely Theological College. He was the author of several books, including *Tables of Stone* and *Studies in the History of the Prayer Book*.

Mrs. Edouard Majolier

Prov: Untraced
Exh. RA, 1886 (280); L, 1886 (931)

Susan Majolier was one of several Hennessey sisters, one of whom was the mother of Anton Dolin the dancer, and another the wife of Paul, Lord Methuen, of Corsham Court. Mme Majolier, whose husband was French, lived in France. Every time she had a baby she came to England so that if a son was born he would not be liable for National Service in the French army. Some five times she crossed the Channel in all weathers and had a daughter: the sixth time she remained at home, and had a son!

A Willing Captive

Prov: Untraced
Exh. RA, 1886 (1014); L, 1886 (1075) £150; AAG, 1887 (441); M, 1891 (31) £80

A Field Flower

Prov: Untraced
Exh. G, 1886 (248)

A Country Lass

Prov: Untraced
Exh. RBA, 1886 (18) £50

His First Offence

Prov: Untraced
Exh. RBA, 1886 (171)

A Beggar Boy

Prov: Untraced
Exh. RBA, 1886 (329) £25 10s.

May Walker

Prov: Untraced
Exh. M, 1886 (915)

May, born 1872, was the artist's second daughter. See Walker family tree.

Gerard-Alexander Moncrieff

Cut down to 30 × 25 (76.6 × 63.5 cms)
Prov: The sitter to his nephew, Duncan Bowden-Smith, Esq.
Exh. RSA 1886 (90)

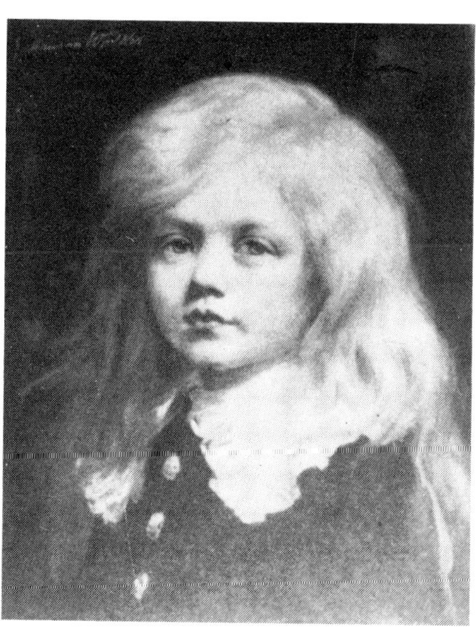

Gerard-Alexander Moncrieff (1886)

Gerard-Alexander (1878–1950) was the second son of Colonel Sir Alexander Moncrieff, (q.v.) He died, unmarried, in Madeira. He was painted again by the artist in 1906.

Evelyn Ouless

Prov: Untraced
Exh. RA, 1886 (953)

Evelyn Ursula Ouless (1881–1963) was the second of the three daughters of the portraitist W. W. Ouless, R.A. She remained unmarried. (See Kitty Ouless 1885, and Margaret, 1905).

May Walker

Oval
Prov: Untraced
Exh. RA, 1887 (952)

Only a photograph still in the possession of Mrs. Palmer exists of this painting of the artist's second daughter, born 1872. See Walker family tree.

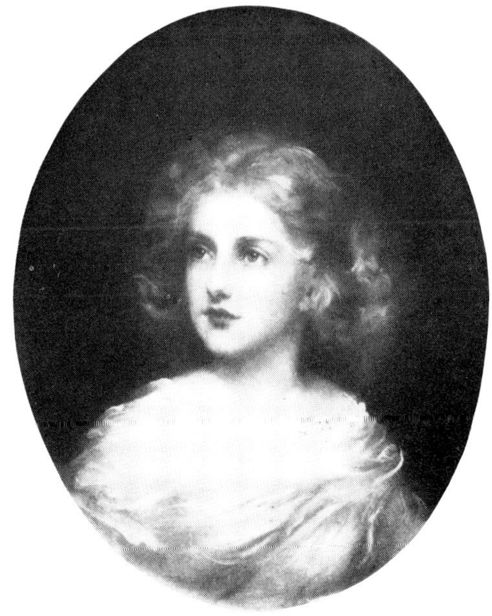

May Walker (1887)

Mrs. Wood of Freeland

Prov: Untraced
Exh. RA, 1887 (169)

'Saint-Like'

Prov: Untraced
Exh. L, 1887 (1015)

'A Sweet Singer'

15 × 12 (38.2 × 30.5 cms)
Prov: By family descent to Mrs. Burt, niece of the sitter
Exh. IPOC, 1887 (527)

Jolliffe Walker, born 1877, was the artist's fourth son. See Walker family tree.

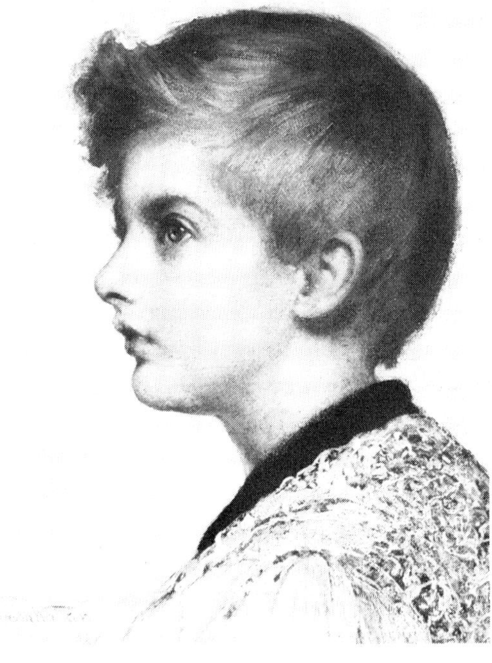

A Sweet Singer (1887)

Isabel, Countess of March and Kinrara

80½ × 51½ (217 × 141 cms) Painted between 1882 and 1887.
Prov: Caryl Craven, Esq., sitter's brother; Lady Helen Gordon-Lennox, sitter's daughter; her son, the Duke of Northumberland.

Inscribed on the frame: 'Isabel (née Craven) 2nd wife of the 6th Earl of March & Kinrara born April 28th, 1865, died November 20, 1887'.

Isabel was the daughter of the Hon. William Craven. She married the eldest son of the Duke of Richmond and Lennox in 1882 following the death of his first wife, (Amy May Ricardo) in 1879. When the subject died aged twenty-two she left two baby daughters; the eldest became Lady Muriel Beckwith and the youngest the Duchess of Northumberland. The Earl of March & Kinrara became the 7th Duke of Richmond & Lennox in 1903. He was M.P. for West Sussex from 1869, and an ADC to Queen Victoria, Edward VII and George V. (Colour Plate 7)

'A Rehearsal'

53 × 84 (134.5 × 214 cms)
Prov: Sold by the artist at Christie's March 30, 1901 (lot 77) bt. Romer £50 8s.
Exh. RA, 1888 (501); L, 1890 (89) (as 'The Rehearsal') £420

There appear to have been two versions painted of this picture, which depicted a portrait group of children.

A Portrait

Prov: Untraced
Exh. M, 1888 (357)

Head of a Child

Prov: Untraced
Exh. IPOC, 1889; L, 1891 (as Child's Head) (181) £35

Head and shoulders. The sitter wears a cream shirt with large frilled collar. In a letter written to Walker, who was in America, dated February 12, 1887 Leighton wrote; 'Please remember me to the Marquands and your friends the Osborns'. This was the Osborns' small son.

Mrs. Ernest Myers

Prov: Untraced
Exh. RA, 1889 (747)

Portrait of Maud

17¼ × 14½ (44.5 × 37 cms)
Prov: The sitter to her daughter, Mrs. Pamela Smith
Exh. RA, 1891 (1041); RP, 1892 (146); M, 1893 (156)

Maud, born 1887 was the youngest of the Hanson Walker children. See Walker family tree. (Plate p. 83)

Frances and Mary Langton

Prov: Untraced
Exh. RA, 1890 (344)

Frances and Mary were the daughters of William Gore Langton. Frances Aline Gore Langton (1883–1951) married Brigadier General John Harington, C.B., D.S.O. Alice Mary (1881–1961) married Commander Hubert Gore Langton, D.S.O., R.N. See also *Mrs. Langton* 1891.

'Fairfield'

17½ × 14⅜ (44.5 × 36.5 cms) Signed. Painted 1890
Prov: In possession of the sitter's widow, Mrs. Fairfield Osborn.
Exh. National Academy of design, N.Y. 1895 (325), loan exhibition of portraits for the benefit of St. John's Guild and the Orthopaedic Hospital.

Mrs. Charles Holland

Prov: Untraced
Exh. RA, 1890 (649)

'Sis' Walker

Prov: Untraced
Exh. RA, 1890 (1138)

Marion Walker 'Sissie' (born 1870) was the artist's eldest daughter. See Walker family tree.

The Hon. Thomas Agar-Robartes

36 × 29 (91.5 × 73.5 cms) Painted 1890–95
Prov: Bequeathed by Lord Robartes with the contents of Lanhydrock House to the National Trust, 1966.

The frame is inscribed with the names of sitter and artist.

The Hon. Thomas Agar-Robartes (1880–1917) was killed in action in the First World War, in 1917. He was the eldest son of the Hon. Thomas Charles Reginald Agar-Robartes, 6th Viscount Clifden. He had a twin sister, the Hon. Everilda, who lived at Lanhydrock until her death in 1969. (Plate p. 86)

The Hon. Gerald Agar-Robartes

26 × 22 (66 × 56 cms) Painted *c.* 1890
Prov: Bequeathed by Lord Robartes with the contents of Lanhydrock House to the National Trust, 1966

The frame is inscribed with the names of sitter and artist.

The Hon. Gerald Agar-Robartes (1883–1966) was the second son of the Hon. Thomas Agar-Robartes, 6th Viscount Clifden. He succeeded to the title on the death of his father in 1930, his elder brother (q.v.) having been killed in action. It was he who bequeathed Lanhydrock to the National Trust in 1966. (Plate p. 87)

May Walker

Prov: Untraced
Exh. RA, 1891 (112); L, 1893 (172)

Mrs. Palmer, the sitter's daughter has a photograph of this portrait, which shows the artist's second daughter May, (b. 1872) wearing a fur cloak trimmed with hearts over her long dress. It was recorded that she was just going to a fancy dress ball in this when her father, struck by her appearance, asked her to pose for him, and she never got to the ball!

Mrs. William Younger

Prov: Untraced
Exh. RA, 1891 (118)

Helen Younger was the daughter of Colonel R. Gunter. In 1888 she married William Younger, Conservative Member of Parliament for Stamford, Lincs. They lived at Melton Mowbray and Auchen Castle, Moffat.

Mrs. Langton

Prov: Untraced
Exh. RA, 1891 (699)

It is presumed this was a portrait of the mother of Frances and Mary Langton, see 1890.

Maud Walker

10 × 7 (25.5 × 17.8 cms) Painted *c.* 1891
Prov: Robin Smith, the sitter's grandson.

Profile, head and shoulders.
Maud Walker (born 1877) was the artist's youngest child. See Walker family tree.

Mrs. Whidborne

Prov: Untraced
Exh. RA, 1892 (178); RP, 1895 (89)

Queen of Hearts

Prov: Untraced
Exh. L, 1892 (1032) £85

View near Bath

Prov: Untraced
Exh. L, 1892 (1159)

Hero

39 × 29 (99.2 × 73.7 cms)
Prov: Sold by the artist at Christie's March 30, 1901 (lot 75) bt. Shepherd £21
Exh. M, 1892 (639) £84

Miss Helen Seely

56 × 33 (142.5 × 84 cms)
Prov: By descent to Mr. Van Hamm Wilshire, Conn., U.S.A.; sitter's grandson.
Exh. Cincinnati Art Museum, 1892 (397); Cincinnati Art Museum 1896; Cincinnati Art Museum 1905 (687)

Helen Seely, (1879–1914) was the third daughter of Dr. Seely of Cincinnati. In 1907 she married Joseph Wilshire, who worked for the Fleischmann Company of Cincinnati, of which he eventually became President. Helen had one son, Joseph White III, the present owner's father.

Elsie Walker

55 × 36 (139.7 × 91.5 cms) Painted *c.* 1892
Prov: By descent to Mrs. Olivia Stewart-Smith, grand-daughter of the sitter.

Elsie, born 1876, was the artist's third daughter: see Walker family tree. (Colour Plate 8)

Mrs. Frank St. Clair Grimwood

61 × 38 (185 × 96.5 cms) Signed. Painted 1891
Prov: Sold C. G. Sloan & Co., U.S.A., Nov. 3, 1984 (lot 1081) bt. Benjamin Hastings (U.S.A.)
Exh. RA 1892 (976); M, 1892 (379)

Ethel Grimwood, (born October 4, 1867) was the daughter of Charles Brabazon Moore, an Indian Judge. She married 1887 Frank St. Clair Grimwood, whose death at the massacre of Manipur, 24th March 1891 is commemorated in the ante-chapel of Merton College, of which he was a post-master. Mrs. Grimwood's account of the massacre *My Three Years in Manipur* was published in 1891. That year she received the Royal Red Cross personally from Queen Victoria at Windsor. The citation read 'in recognition of her devotion to the wounded under the most trying circumstances, during the attack on the Residency at Manipur'. (See *The Times*, June 8 1891). On June 30, 1895 Mrs. Grimwood was re-married to Mr. Andrew Cornwall Miller, (born 1866) a paper mill owner of Carshalton, Surrey.

The medal worn by Mrs. Grimwood has been identified as the Royal Red Cross and not the 'V.C.': therefore the Royal Academy wrongly described the painting as 'Mrs. Frank St. Clair Grimwood 'dressed in black and wearing the V.C.'

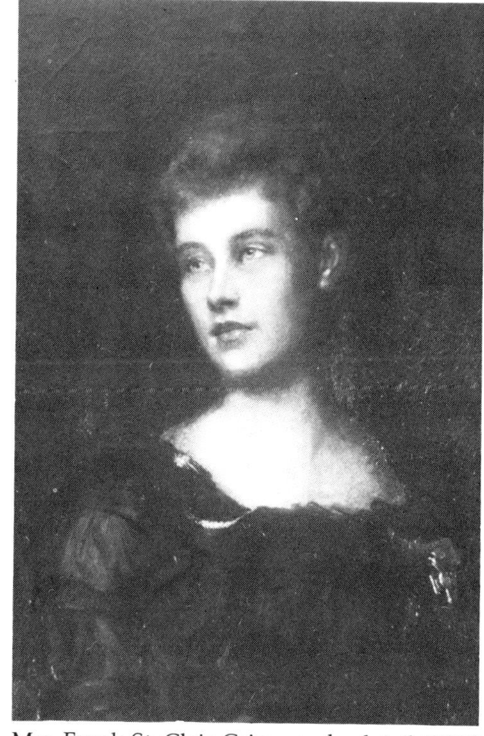

Mrs. Frank St. Clair Grimwood – detail (1891)

Mrs. Sydney Pitt

Prov: Untraced
Exh. RA 1893 (32)

Marion 'Sissie' Pitt was the artist's eldest daughter, born 1870. See Walker family tree.

Elaine

Prov: Untraced
Exh. M, 1893 (30)

Dorothy Walker

20 × 16 (51 × 40.7 cms)
Prov: The sitter to Mrs. Burt, her daughter
Exh. RP, 1893 (73)

The sitter was the artist's fourth daughter, Dorothy, born 1882.

Churton Walker

Prov: Untraced
Exh. RP, 1893 (121)

Churton was the artist's fifth son, born 1879; see Walker family tree.

The Trysting Place

35½ × 28 (90.2 × 71.2 cms)
Prov: Sold by the artist at Christie's, June 4, 1898 (lot 83) bt. Agnew £29.8s.

May Walker

27½ × 23½ (70 × 59.7 cms) Signed
Prov: The sitter to her daughter, Mrs. George Palmer.
Exh. RA, 1894 (533)

May was the artist's second daughter, born 1872: see Walker family tree. (Colour Plate 9)

Mrs. Eleanor Duer Wilson

Prov: Untraced
Exh. 'Portraits of Women' loan exhibition, National Academy of Design, New York, November 1894 (350). Exhibition for the benefit of St. John's Guild and the Orthopaedic Hospital. Lent by Mrs. W. H. Osborn.

Roger-Murray Moncrieff

Approx 12 × 12 (30.5 × 30.5 cms) Painted *c.* 1894
Prov: The sitter to his nephew, Duncan Bowden-Smith, Esq.

Roger-Murray, (1885–1956) was the fifth child of Colonel Sir Alexander Moncrieff. He did not marry, and died at Bandirran, Perthshire. See also entry for 1906.

Elsie Walker

Cut down to 24½ × 20 (62.5 × 51 cms)
Signed. Painted 1894–6
Prov: The sitter to her son, Breynton Mills: Mrs Breynton Mills, his widow

Elsie was the artist's third daughter, born 1876: see Walker family tree.

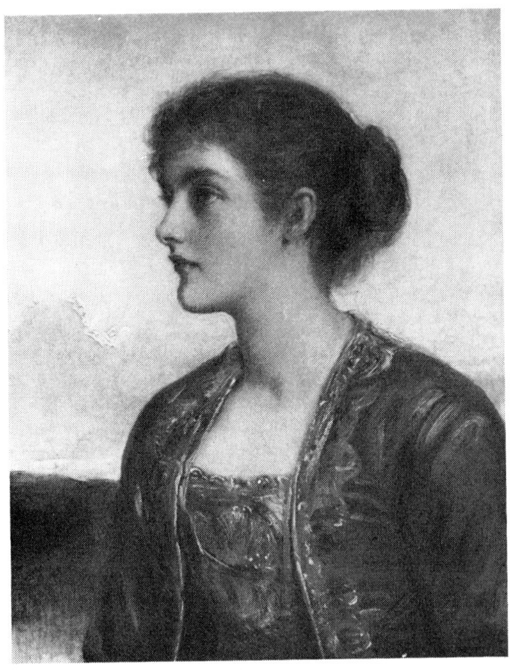

Elsie Walker, (c.1895)

Mrs. John Hanson Walker

Prov: Untraced
Exh. RA, 1894 (298)

This portrait of the artist's wife may have been painted to celebrate their silver wedding anniversary, January 8th, 1892.

Portrait of a Lady

Prov: Untraced
Exh. RA, 1895 (851)

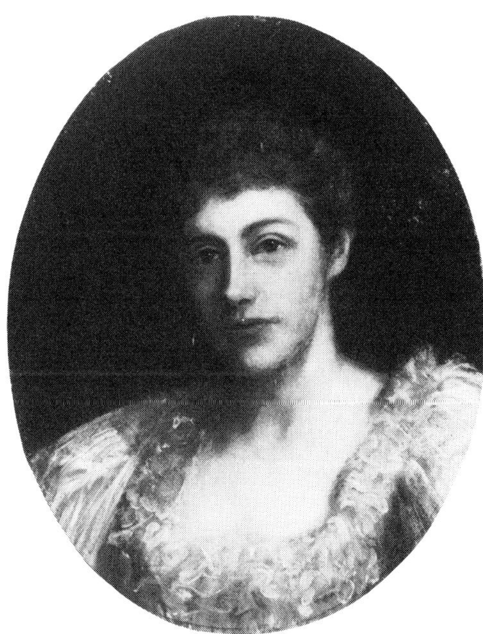

Elsie Walker (1895)

Elsie Walker

Oval: cut down to head and shoulders.
Originally signed.

Prov: By descent to Mrs. Olivia Stewart-Smith, grand-daughter of the sitter.
Exh. RA, 1895 (778)

It is believed that this was the portrait of the artist's third daughter Elsie, (born 1876) which caught the eye of Robert Mills when it was exhibited at the Royal Academy. He sought an introduction to the Walker family, and married Elsie at St. George's Hanover Square on July 6, 1898.

Lady Mary Foley

Prov: Untraced
Exh. RA, 1895 (791)

This was a presentation portrait. Lady Mary Foley (1822–1897) was born Mary Charlotte Howard, eldest daughter of the 13th Duke of Norfolk. As a young woman she was one of Queen Victoria's twelve bridesmaids. She married, 1849, Thomas Henry, 4th Baron Foley, who was a Captain in the Hon. Corps of Gentlemen-at-Arms.

Mrs. John Trotter

Prov: Untraced
Exh. RA, 1896 (496)

Mrs. John Trotter was the mother of Mrs. Francis Augustus Bevan (q.v. below)

Mrs. Francis Augustus Bevan

Prov: Untraced
Exh. RA, 1897 (1027)

Mrs. Bevan was Marion, daughter of John Trotter, Esq., (q.v. Mrs. John Trotter 1896). She became Mr. Bevan's third wife in 1875, and there were three daughters and one son of the marriage. Mr. Bevan (1840–1919) was Chairman of Barclays Bank for over twenty years, and also Chairman of the Committee of London Clearing Banks. He was married firstly to Elizabeth Marianne (1840–63), third daughter of Lord Charles Russell, and secondly to Constance (1841–72) youngest daughter of Sir John Weir Hogg.

The Late Lord de Tabley

50 × 39½ (127.2 × 100.5 cms) Signed

Prov: Tabley House, Cheshire. (University of Manchester)
Exh. RA, 1897 (304)

It is reasonably certain that this posthumous portrait of Lord de Tabley, (1835–95) was painted for his sister, Eleanor Lady Leighton. John Byrne Leicester, 3rd and last Baron de Tabley was the eldest son of George Warren, the 2nd Baron. As a child he lived in Italy and Germany. He became a good minor poet, first publishing his poems under the pseudonym 'George Preston'. He was also a skilled numismatist. Colour Plate 10

Pomona

Prov: Untraced
Exh. L, 1897 (Autumn Exh.) (424) £150

Sea Echoes

Prov: Untraced
Exh. L, 1897 (Autumn Exh.) (121)

Duncan-Campbell Moncrieff

17 × 14 (43.5 × 35.5 cms) s. & d. 1898
Prov: The sitter to his nephew, Duncan Bowden-Smith, Esq.

Duncan-Campbell, (1890–1979) was the youngest of the seven children of Colonel Sir Alexander Moncrieff. (q.v.) He did not marry, and died at Hemley, Suffolk. He was painted by the artist in 1906. Plate 101

Maud Walker

34 × 27 (86.5 × 68.5 cms) Signed
Prov: By descent to Robin Smith, the sitter's grandson.
Exh. RA, 1898 (556)

Three-quarter length. Maud is dressed as Juliet, with a cream satin dress, large lace collar and cuffs and red bows on the sleeves. She wears a skull cap on her long auburn hair. She is seated, and holds a book in her left hand. Maud was the artist's youngest child, born 1887. See Walker family tree.

Annabel Lee

Prov: Sold by the artist, Christie's December 12, 1898 (lot 114) £15.15s.

Princess Elizabeth, Carisbrooke, 1647

Prov: Untraced
Exh. RA, 1898 (908); L, (Autumn Exh.) 1900 (192) £84; AAG, 1904 (558)

Sylvia

23½ × 19½ (56 × 45.5 cms)
Prov: Sold by Mrs. Hichens, Christie's (London) June 23, 1924 (lot 48) bt. Brearley (£8.15.6d); sold Parke Bernet Galleries, N.Y., May 18, 1945 ($80)
Exh. B, 1899 (408) £31.10s.

Head and shoulders. Auburn-haired girl wearing a white organdy mob cap and a green gown. Background of sky.

Hope Delayed

Prov: Untraced
Exh. B, 1899 (140) £63

'Sisters'

58 × 78 (147.2 × 198.4 cms) s. & d. 1899
Prov: Mrs. Elsie Mills (née Walker); Giles Mills, her son; Mme Marianne Mills, his widow.
Exh. RA, 1899 (124); L, 1899 (Autumn Exh.) 1014; M, 1900 (126) £630

This painting shows the artist's three eldest daughters, all of whom had been recently married. Mrs. Mills (Elsie his third daughter, who sits on a stool) had been married to Robert Mills in 1898. Mrs. Romer, (May, the second daughter to the left) had married Frank Romer in 1895 and Mrs. Pitt (the eldest daughter, Sissie) had married Sydney Pitt in 1888.

A family story relates that the seventeenth century Japanese screen in the painting had been used as background when painting a sitter in San Francisco. Walker was so attracted by it that he asked if he might have it in lieu of his fee, and was granted this request!

This painting has always been known in the family as *The Three Graces* (after Reynolds). (Plate p. 94)

Sweet Auburn

Prov: Untraced
Exh. IPOC, 1899 (28) £25

Constance Walker

Oval. 23½ × 20 (59.5 × 50.7 cms) Painted 1899.
Prov: Miss Marjorie Walker, daughter of the sitter

Head and shoulders. The sitter wears a black lace dress mounted over red material. Her dark hair is piled behind her head and she wears a fur round her shoulders and a pearl necklace.

Constance Walker (née Leake) was the wife of the artist's eldest son, Frederick. She died young, in 1901 (the same year as her husband) leaving two baby daughters, Marjorie and Dorothy. See 1905 and 1912.

'A Shy Sitter'

24 × 36 (61 × 91 cms) Signed, and inscribed with title on the reverse.
Prov: Sold Sotheby's June 11, 1986 (lot 125) bt. Richard Green. £7,000.
Exh. M, 1899 (175) £52.10
(Plate p. 97)

Beatrice

Prov: Untraced
Exh. NG, 1899 (157); L, 1899 (1142) £105

The Corsair's Bride

Prov: Untraced
Exh. M, 1899 (175) £52 10s.

Miss Mary Colley

60 × 36 (152.2 × 91.5 cms) s. & d. 1899
Prov: By family descent to Miss Wellesley-Colley, niece of the sitter; sold by her to Roy Wilcox, Esq., Bath.
Exh. RA, 1899 (150)

Mary was the second child of Philip Wellesley-Colley, Esq. She never married, but pursued a career as a skilled horsewoman. (Colour Plate 12)

Miss Bessie Colley

60 × 36 (152.2 × 91.5 cms) s. & d. 1899
Prov: By family descent to Miss Wellesley-Colley, niece of the sitter; sold by her to Roy Wilcox, Esq., Bath.
Exh. RA, 1899 (157)

Bessie was the fourth child of Philip Wellesley-Colley, Esq. She married the third son of Sir Acquin Martin and had three children, a son and two daughters. The Martin family, (of Bombay and Calcutta) had made a fortune from engineering and jute. (Colour Plate 11)

Kate Romer

24 × 20 (61 × 51 cms)
Prov: by descent to Mrs. E. M. Ascherson, daughter-in-law of the sitter

Head and shoulders. Sitter wears a white off-the-shoulder dress and her dark hair is swept up on top of her head.

Kate Romer (a sister of Frank Romer, the artist's son-in-law) died in 1901 aged twenty one, giving birth to her son, Stephen Ascherson. She was a keen musician, and a founder-member of the children's orchestra.

Study of a Young Girl

Oval. 29 × 23 (73.7 × 58.5 cms)
Prov: Sold by Mr. Fischof, Fischof Blakeslee Sale, Chickering Hall, New York, March 9/10 1900 (lot 42) bt. G. L. Morrison, $550.

Head and shoulders. Young woman with red/brown hair, white low-cut dress, and full sleeves. Dark brown background.

Wareham

10 × 8 (25.5 × 20.5 cms) Dated 1900
Prov: By descent to James Stansfeld, Esq., the artist's great grandson.

This is a small sketch of a group of trees.

An English Rose

Prov: Untraced
Exh. B, 1900 (376)

Full title of painting: 'An English Rose, as sweet as English air can make her'. (Tennyson)

Companions

Prov: Untraced
Exh. B, 1900 (60) AAG, 1901 (190)

The Baron de Ferrieres

Oval. 21¾ × 17½ (55.1 × 44.5 cms)
Prov: Presented to the Cheltenham Art Gallery in 1900 by a group of Subscribers.

This painting commemorated the fact that Baron de Ferrieres (1823–1908) had presented Cheltenham with a gift of £1,000 towards the building of a Public Art Gallery, together with 43 paintings, (mainly of the Dutch and Belgian school). The gallery was opened on October 26, 1899. The portrait, given to the gallery by personal friends and others as a token of their regard for the Baron, hangs over the entrance door of the room named after him.

Charles Conrad du Bois, Baron de Ferrieres, the son of Baron du Bois of Belgium, took the name de Ferrieres through his mother, who was of Huguenot ancestry. De Ferrieres was a trained engineer, but never practised. In 1851 he married an heiress, Miss Sheepshanks of Bray, Berkshire (whose father gave the Sheepshanks Collection to the nation). The paintings presented to Cheltenham were inherited by the Baron from his father, an art connoisseur. The Baron stood as Liberal M.P. for Cheltenham 1880–85, and was also Mayor of that city for many years. (Plate p. 99)

Pamela

21½ × 17½ (54 × 44 cms)
Prov: Sold by the artist Christie's July 16, 1915 (lot 81) bt. Hale 4½ gns.
Exh. AAG, 1900 (523); AAG 1906 (554)

Love's Indolence

Prov: Untraced
Exh. L, 1900 (Autumn Exh.) (65) £73

Mrs. Davson

65½ × 41½ (84.5 × 105.5 cms) s. & d. 1900
Prov: Sold at 'The Perfect Touch' Chicago 1978, bt. Mr. Davison, of Rockford, Illinois.

It is thought this may be a portrait of Anne Davson (née Miller) of Perth, Scotland (1849–1920) who was the wife of Henry Katz Davson (1820–1909) knighted in 1903 for his services in the West Indies. A photograph taken of Mrs. Davson when she was presented at Court *c.* 1867 shows her wearing an identical necklace and pendant to those in this portrait. The Davsons had four sons, of whom Sir Edward became a baronet and Sir Ivan was knighted.

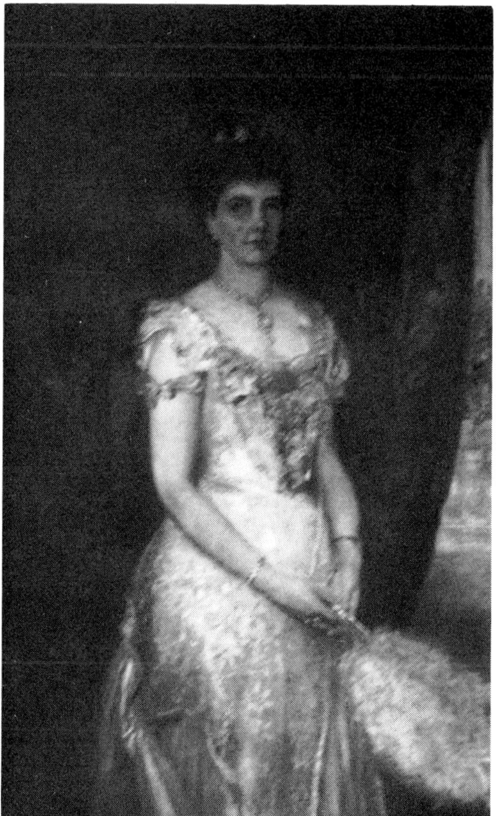

Mrs Davson (1900)

Herbert Spencer

46 × 37½ (117 × 95.5 cms)
Prov: Bequeathed to the City of Derby Art Gallery by Mr. Spencer, 1908
Exh. City of Derby A.G. 1920 (exhibition of loan and permanent collection pictures).

This is a copy of Herbert Spencer's portrait by J. B. Burgess, painted in 1872 and bequeathed by the sitter to the National Portrait Gallery 1904. (Cat. No.1358). The measurements are the same as the original.

Herbert Spencer seems to have been in two minds as to whether to employ Walker to copy his portrait, and whether to use Burgess's portrait of 1872 or Herkomer's, painted 1898. Two letters (in the possession of James Stansfeld, the artist's great grandson) written from Brighton in October 1900 and January 1901 indicate this. In the second letter he settled with Walker to make the copy of the Burgess portrait for 60 gns.

Herbert Spencer (1820–1903) gave up his early training as an engineer to devote himself to philosophical study and writing. He was the founder of evolutionary philosophy. Spencer has been diversely judged: Carlyle called him 'the most immeasurable ass in Christendom'!

Elsie, Daughter of Sydney Pitt, Esq.

Prov: Untraced
Exh. RP, 1901 (116)

Elsie was the artist's grand-daughter, born 1897.

Mrs. McCorquodale

36 × 28 (91.5 × 71.2 cms) s. & d. 1901
Prov: Sold at 'The Perfect Touch', Chicago, 1978 (lot 1447) bt. Mr. Davison of Rockford, I11. $385.00

It is thought that this is the portrait of Mrs. A. C. McCorquodale, and may have once been the property of her niece, Mrs. Herbert Sotheby, who died in the 1970's. (See *A Portrait of Marjorie* below).

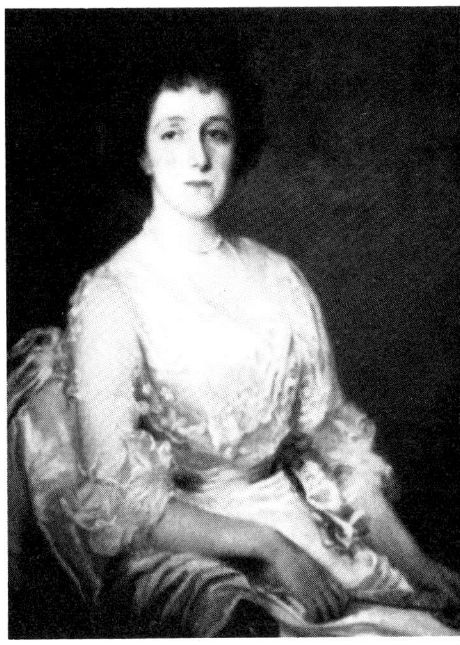

Mrs. McCorquodale, (1901)

A Portrait of Marjorie

36½ × 28 (92.8 × 71.7 cms) s. & d. 1901 on the reverse
Prov: Sold from the estate of Jane Erdmann Whitney, Christie's, New York, 1986 (lot 180); $1,400 bt. Nicholas Mills, England (gt. grandson of the artist).

Marjorie, (*c.* 1890–*c.* 1926) was the only daughter of Mr. and Mrs. Alec McCorquodale. She married her first husband during World War I but he was killed three weeks later. She was remarried to Henry Sotheby of Ecton Hall, nr. Northampton, but neither marriage had any issue. On her death she bequeathed everything to Raine Spencer, her niece. (Plate p. 103)

Springtime

Prov: Untraced
Exh. B, 1901 (9) £42

C. J. Cater Scott

44 × 34 (111.7 × 86.5 cms) s. & d. 1901
Prov: Sold Sotheby's May 23, 1973 (lot 197) bt. R. Edmonson.

The National Portrait Gallery Library hold a photograph of this portrait.

Maid of Athens

Prov: Untraced
Exh. M, 1901 (224)

Wayfarers

35 × 27 (89 × 68.7 cms)
Prov: Sent by the artist for sale Christie's March 30, 1901 (lot 34) but failed to reach the reserve of 22 gns.

Dr. C. D. F. Phillips

Prov: Untraced
Exh. RA 1902 (753)

Subject was Charles Douglas Ferguson Phillips of 10 Henrietta Street, Cavendish Square, London; surgeon, trained in Aberdeen and Edinburgh and registered 1859.

A Sunbeam

Prov: Untraced
Exh. GI, 1902 (293)

The Pride of the Village

Prov: Untraced
Exh. L, 1902 (1230) £42

'Ideal Head'

Prov: Sold Arthur Furber sale, Fifth Avenue Galleries, New York March 12/13, 1903 ($300).

'Unnamed Lady'

26 × 22 (66.2 × 56 cms) s. & d. 1903
Prov: Mrs. C. E. D. Wilson, Coventry; sold by Messrs. Lowery & Partners, March 21, 1985; bt. Mr. Robert Horne

It has, unfortunately, been impossible to trace the identity of this sitter. (Plate p. 104)

Betty Frances Grace Romer

20 × 16 (51 × 40.5 cms) Signed
Prov: Michael Macdonald, sitter's second son.

This portrait of the artist's grand-daughter, Betty Romer (1897–1940) was painted when she was six. Betty married (1919) John Henry Lloyd Macdonald, and had four children, John Alistair, David Hugh Ross (Michael), Betty Celestina (Sally) and Frank Gerald Somerled (Garry).

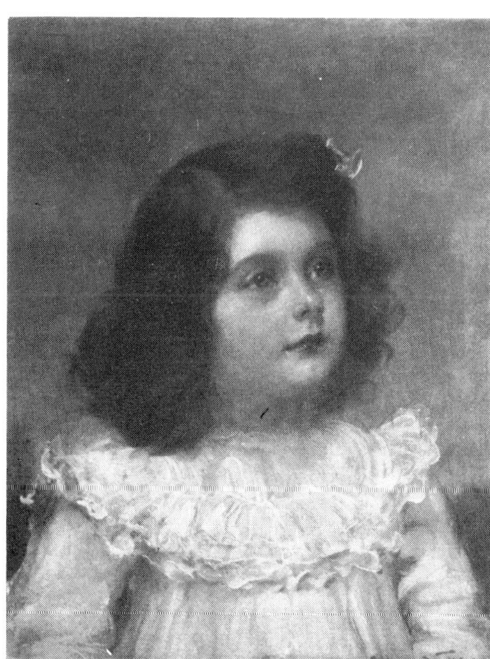

Betty Romer, 1903.

Mrs. Macdonald joined the John Lewis Partnership in 1938 and rose quickly in it. In October 1939 she became Branch Manager of their shop in Southsea. When she died aged 43 the John Lewis House Magazine published her obituary, in which they spoke of her indomitable courage, energy, sense of humour and competence in business.

Amoretta

Prov: Untraced
Exh. AAG, 1904 (558)

Head of a Girl in a White Dress

16½ × 13½ (42.1 × 34.5 cms)
Prov: Sold by Hughes, Christie's June 18, 1904, (lot 154); bt. Loeffler £32.11s.; sold Loeffler, Christie's November 23, 1923 (lot 155); bt. Good & Fox, 11 gns.

Young Girl

22 × 18 (56 × 45 cms)
Prov: Sold by Edward Brandus, Fifth Avenue Galleries, New York March 9/10/11 1900 (lot 41) bt. S. W. Weast, $170

Mrs. James Stansfeld and Sister

55½ × 38 (141 × 96.5 cms) s. & d. 1904
Prov: Mrs. Lidderdale (the 'sister') to her grandson, Robin Smith
Exh. GI, 1906 (341)

This portrait of the artist's fourth daughter, Dorothy and youngest daughter, Maud (later Mrs. Lidderdale) was probably painted to celebrate Dorothy's engagement to James Stansfeld. (Plate p. 106)

An English Maiden

22 × 18 (56 × 45 cms)
Prov: Sold Mr. Blakeslee, (Dowdeswell & Dowdeswell and Blakeslee Collections), Mendelssohn Hall, New York, April 7/8 1904 (lot 83) bt. Louis Bamberger $110

Catalogue description: 'The life-size head and shoulders of an auburn-haired young English girl with the delicate complexion and translucent skin which is often found with hair of this colour. With her head slightly inclined toward the right shoulder she looks straight at the spectator with calm eyes and a sweet and modest expression. She wears a low-cut white dress, with a diaphanous white scarf or wrap thrown over her shoulders and the background represents the interior of a forest.' (Messrs. Dowdeswell of London had decided to discontinue their branch in New York, and Mr. Blakeslee was also reducing his stock of imported paintings).

The White Rose

22 × 18 (56 × 45 cms) Signed.
Prov: Sold Mr. Blakeslee, (Dowdeswell & Dowdeswell and Blakeslee Collections), Mendelssohn Hall, New York, April 7/8 1904 (lot 2) bt. R. C. Vose $150

Catalogue description: 'A sweet-faced young lady, her head gracefully poised in profile with a mass of wavy auburn hair brushed over her ears and gathered in a large knot behind, has fastened a white rose to her dress over her left breast and the pale yellow petals contrast with the soft white of her dress and the refined flesh colour of her bosom. The head is in relief against a mass of foliage in the background, below which is seen a distant landscape.'

Lady in White

22 × 18 (56 × 45 cms)
Prov: Sold by Mr. Eugene Fischof of Paris, Fifth Avenue Galleries, New York Jan 12/13, 1905 (lot 30) bt. Street & Smith, $140

Sylvia

22 × 18 (56 × 45 cms)
Prov: Sold by Mr. Eugene Fishof of Paris at Fifth Ave. Galleries, New York, Jan 12/13, 1905 (lot 114) bt. D.G. Reid $450.

An English Beauty

22 × 18 (56 × 45 cms)
Prov: Sold by Mr. Eugene Fishof of Paris at Fifth Ave. Galleries, New York, Jan 12/13, 1905 (lot 135) bt. Trautman $320.

What appears to have been another version of this painting was sold by Mrs. Fischof at the Fifth Ave. Galleries Feb 22/23 1907 (lot 77) bt. Edward C. Hoyt. $290

Sheer Indolence

Prov: Untraced
Exh. M, 1905 (10) £35

Margaret, Daughter of W. W. Ouless, Esq., R.A.

44 × 36 (114.5 × 91.6 cms)
Prov: The sitter to her daughter, Mrs. Brian Pomeroy (née Lucy Hayne)
Exh. L, (Autumn Exh.) 1905 (243)

Margaret Olivia Ouless (1883–1967) was the third daughter of Walter Ouless, R.A. She was married to Robert Hayne. (Plate p. 105)

Dorothy Walker

18½ × 13¾ (47 × 45 cms) Painted *c.* 1905
Prov: The sitter to her sister, Miss Marjorie Walker.

Head and shoulders. The subject wears a cream dress with large frilled collar, which is crossed in front. She has dark shoulder-length hair, parted in the middle.

Dorothy Walker (Bubbles) 1899–1939 was the second daughter of the artist's eldest son, Frederick. She never married (see also Marjorie Walker, 1912)

John Kenelm Wingfield Digby M.P.

43 × 33 (109.3 × 84 cms) Painted *c.* 1906
Prov: Mr. Simon Wingfield Digby, the sitter's grandson, Sherborne Castle.

Three-quarter length, the sitter is shown seated in a chair, wearing a shooting suit with white collar and blue tie.

It is thought that this posthumous portrait of Mr. Wingfield-Digby (1860–1905) was painted *c.* 1906. He was a Member of Parliament for the Yeovil Division of Somerset and later North Dorset, which he won, as a Conservative, from the Liberals. He held his seat for fifteen years, and on his death the Conservatives lost it!

Pasithae

Prov: Untraced
Exh. L, 1906 (938) £40; GI, 1907 (619) £40

Title of painting continues – 'the youngest grace, Pasithae the Divine'.

Nancy Romer

Prov: Untraced
Exh. RA 1906 (724); GI, 1907 (38)

Nancy (1900–1913) was the daughter of Frank and May Romer, and therefore the artist's grand-daughter.

May-Gladys Moncrieff

Oval.
Prov: The sitter; destroyed by bombing at 21 Kensington Park Gardens, 1939–45

May-Gladys, (1889–1973) was the sixth of the seven children of Colonel Sir Alexander and Lady Moncrieff, and this portrait was painted in 1906. She married Mr. Edward Bowden-Smith, in 1915, and had one son, Duncan. (Plate p. 100)

Malcolm-Matthew Moncrieff

30 × 30 approx. (cut down from full-length)
Prov: The sitter to his nephew, Duncan Bowden-Smith, Esq.

Malcolm-Matthew (1876–1970) was the eldest son of Colonel Sir Alexander Moncrieff. He married Perrin, the grand-daughter of Sir John Millais and emigrated to New Zealand. This portrait was painted *c.* 1906.

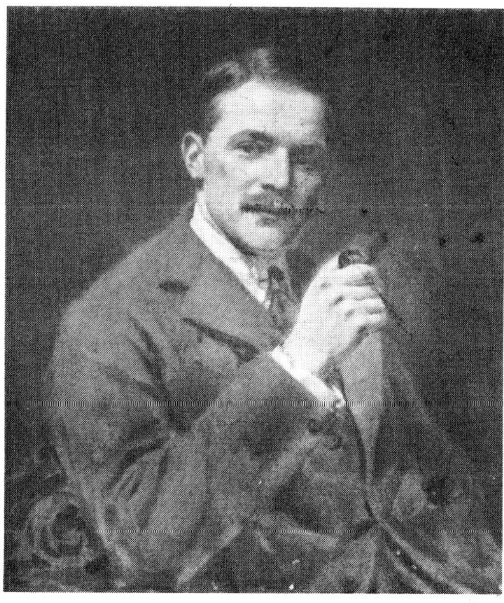

Malcolm-Matthew Moncrieff (1906)

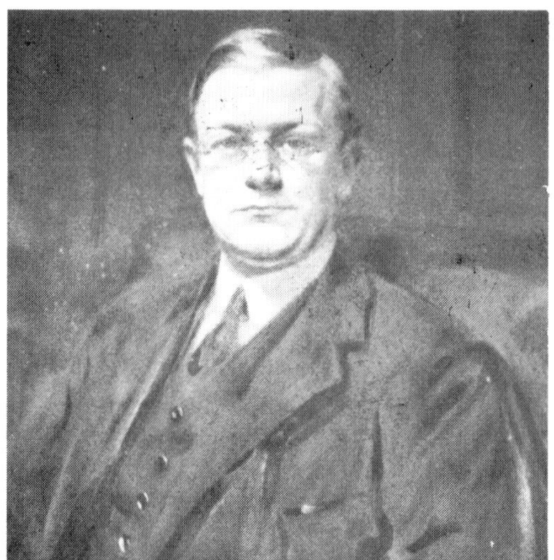

Gerard-Alexander Moncrieff

30 × 30 approx. (cut down from full-length) Painted *c.* 1906
Prov: The sitter to his nephew, Duncan Bowden-Smith Esq.

Gerard-Alexander (1878–1950) was the second son of Colonel Sir Alexander Moncrief (See also 1886).

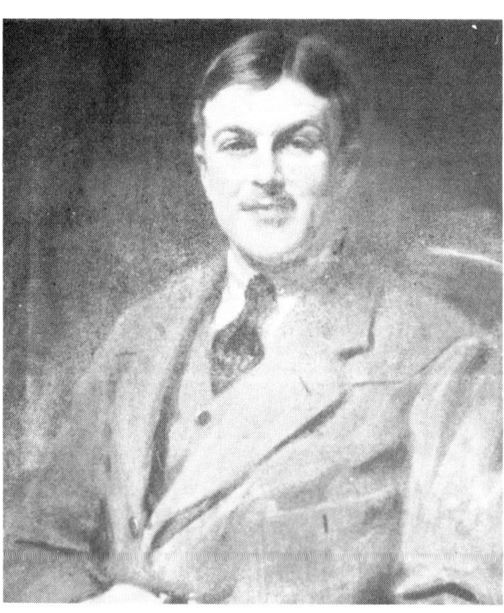

Duncan-Campbell Moncrieff (1906)

Duncan-Campbell Moncrieff

30 × 30 approx. (cut down from full-length) Painted *c* 1906
Prov: The sitter to his nephew, Duncan Bowden-Smith, Esq.

Duncan-Campbell (1890–1979) was the youngest of the seven children of Colonel Sir Alexander Moncrieff. (see also 1898).

Giles Mills

17 × 13½ (43 × 35 cms) s. & d. 1907. Inscribed on the reverse 'Presented to Elsie Mills on her birthday, Jan. 1 by her father and mother 1907'
Prov: Elsie Mills; Giles Mills her son; Marianne Mills, his widow.

Giles Mills (1905–1985) was the artist's grandson.

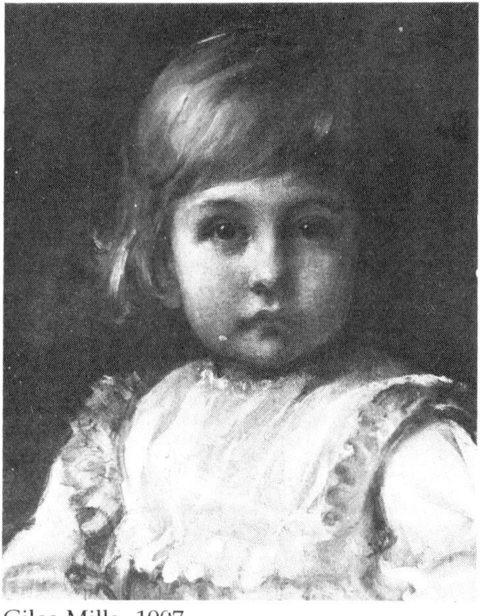

Giles Mills, 1907.

Sunset in the River Puddle, Cavey, Dorset

Prov: Untraced
Exh. AAG, 1906 (541)

Lucille

18 × 22 (45.7 × 56 cms)
Prov: Sold from collection late William T. Hamilton and Mrs. Hewlett Sands of Brooklyn, New York, Fifth Ave. Galleries, N.Y., April 18/19/20, 1906 (214) bt. E. Hughes $250.

Study of a Head

22½ × 18¼ (57.2 × 46.3 cms)
Prov: Sold by Mr. Eugene Fischoff of Paris at the Waldorf-Astoria, New York, Feb. 23/4 1906 (lot 59) bt. A. B. Smith $210.

Miss Maud Hanson Walker

38 × 30 (96.5 × 76.3 cms)
Prov: The sitter to Mrs. Pamela Smith, her daughter
Exh. RA, 1907 (126); M, 1907 (64); GI, 1908 (556); AAG 1909 (362)

Maud was the artist's youngest child; see Walker family tree.

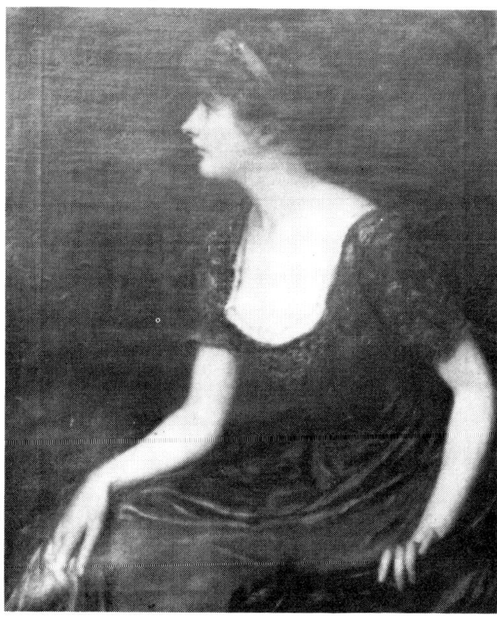

Miss Maud Hanson Walker (1907)

Breynton and Jack, Sons of Robert Mills, Esq.

30½ × 25½ (77.5 × 65 cms) s. & d. 1907
Prov: Breynton Mills, the sitter, to his daughter, Belinda Morse.
Exh. RA, 1907 (749)

Breynton, (left) (1900–1974) and Jack (1902–27) were the artist's grandsons. Breynton started his career in the army, but gave it up on his father's death to be a stockbroker. He rejoined the army at the outbreak of war, serving in N. Africa and Italy and winning the M.C. After the war he ran the family textile works in Rouen. On retirement he returned to England, where he continued his interest in horse racing. John Yarnton Mills (Jack) served in World War I in HMS Ajax. Later he volunteered to join the Naval Air Arm, and died in a flying accident, unmarried, in 1927 off Malta. (Plate p. 108)

Mill Stream, Wareham, Dorset

Prov: Untraced
Exh. M, 1907 (150) £21; Leeds City AG Spring Exh. 1908 (440); Cheltenham Municipal Gallery, 1908.

Camille

Prov: Untraced
Exh. AAG, 1907 (165)

Chloe

Prov: Untraced
Exh. AAG, 1907, (198)

Doris

21½ × 17½ (54.5 × 44.5 cms)
Prov: Sent for sale by the artist at Christie's, May 16, 1907 but failed to reach reserve of £7 7s.

Red Paeonies

17½ × 13½ (44.5 × 34.5 cms)
Prov: Sold Christie's July 30, 1915 (lot 75) bt. Wallis £1 10s.
Exh. M, 1908 (84) £12 12s.

Parthenia

Pastel. 24 × 20 (61 × 51 cms)
Prov: Sold by the artist Christie's March 30, 1912 (lot 85) bt. Leafe £4.4s.
Exh. L, 1908 (Autumn Exh.) (441) £26.5s; AAG, 1910 (484)

Meditation

22 × 15 (56 × 38 cms)
Prov: Sale of Leroy Steward, A. D. Hewitt and Mrs. Dempster Hamlen at Fifth Ave. Art Galleries April 1/2 1909 (lot 49) bt. G. C. Heimerdinger $200 *American Art Annual*: (the *NY Times* quotes $560).

Happy Childhood

Prov: Untraced
Exh. GI, 1909 (221), L, (Autumn Exh.) 1909 (997)

Kitty

Prov: Untraced
Exh. GI, 1909 (478)

Child's Head

Prov: Untraced
Exh. GI, 1909 (635)

Bianca

Prov: Untraced
Exh. AAG, 1909 (124)

Juliet

Prov: Untraced
Exh. AAG, 1909 (153)

Portrait of a Lady

Prov: Untraced
Exh. RA 1909 (237)

A Portrait: Maud Walker

36 × 28 (91.5 × 71.3 cms) Signed
Prov: The sitter: Mrs. Pamela Smith, her daughter.
Exh. RA 1910 (736); GI, 1911 (820)

Maud Walker was the artist's youngest child; see Walker family tree.

Mrs. Crichton-Stuart

26 × 22 (66.2 × 56 cms) s. & d. 1910
Prov: By descent to the sitter's grandson, Mr. P. J. Crichton-Stuart.
Exh. RA 1911 (719)

Helen Katherine Crichton-Stuart (1874–1948) was the daughter of the Hon. J.C. Phillipo, M.D. of Jamaica. She married firstly, the Hon. Arthur St. Aubyn, who died 1897, (the only son of the marriage becoming the 3rd Lord St. Levan). She married secondly, 1904 Patrick James Crichton-Stuart, (q.v.) by whom she had a son and a daughter. (Plate p. 110)

Patrick James Crichton-Stuart

26 × 22 (66.2 × 56 cms) s. & d. 1910
Prov: By descent to the sitter's grandson, Mr. P. J. Crichton-Stuart

Patrick James Crichton-Stuart (1868–1935) whose father was M.P. for Llandaff, was in the Grenadier Guards when young. In 1904 he married the widow of the Hon. Arthur St. Aubyn. (q.v.) (Plate p. 111)

Robert Mills

24 × 19 (61.2 × 48.5 cms)
Prov: By descent to Mrs. Olivia Stewart-Smith, the grand-daughter of the sitter and the great grand-daughter of the artist.

Painted *c.* 1910. In 1909 Robert Henry Davis Mills (1853–1921) had retired from the textile works he had started near Rouen, France and was living at Steventon Manor, Hampshire where he bred race-horses, becoming a well-known figure on the turf both in England and France. He was High Sheriff of the County of Southampton 1916–17. (Colour Plate 13)

Phyllis

Prov: Untraced
Exh. GI, 1910 (569) £30; RHA, 1911 (70) £31.10s.

Marion

Prov: Untraced
Exh. AAG, 1910 (224)

A Brigand's Wife

Prov: Untraced
Exh. AAG, 1911 (249)

Ivan

16½ × 12 (42 × 30.5 cms)
Prov: John Hanson Walker; Diana Bray, his daughter
Exh. AAG, 1911 (301)

Ivan was a grandson of the artist. His father, who shared the same name as Hanson Walker, was also a painter and sculptor.

A Portrait

Prov: Untraced
Exh. GI, 1911 (165)

Marjorie Walker

17 × 13½ (43.2 × 34.2 cms) Painted *c.*1912
Prov: Miss Marjorie Walker, the sitter

Profile, head and shoulder.

The subject is Marjorie Hanson Walker (born 1897) the eldest daughter of the artist's eldest son, Frederick. Like her sister Dorothy (see 1905) she was brought up by her uncle, the Rev. Aubrey Leake of Bishop Auckland, co. Durham, both her parents having died when she was four. See Walker family tree.

Sweet Simplicity

23½ × 17½ (59.7 × 44 cms)
Prov: Sold by the artist Christie's March 11, 1912 (lot 130) bt. Huggins, £15 15s.

Kathleen Mavourneen

23½ × 19½ (60.3 × 49.7 cms)
Prov: Sold by the artist Christie's, March 30, 1912 (lot 86) bt. Yewlett, 9 gns.

Artemis

16½ × 13½ (42 × 34.2 cms)
Prov: Sold by the artist Christie's, March 11, 1912 (lot 131) bt. Agnew £15 15s.

Girl Feeding Pigeons

Prov: Untraced
Exh. City of Derby A.G. (Autumn Exhibition of Modern Art, 1912) £105

John Savery

22 × 18 (56 × 45.8 cms) s. & d. 1913
Prov: John Savery; Mrs. Savery, the sitter's widow.

Head and shoulders. Sitter has long, curling hair.

John Blythe Loveday Savery (1907–1977) was the son of Mrs. Hanson Walker's youngest sister, Nell.

A Portrait

Prov: Untraced
Exh. L, 1913 (1125)

A Mountain Lass

Prov: Untraced
Exh. L, 1913 (Autumn Exh.) (987) £12 12s.

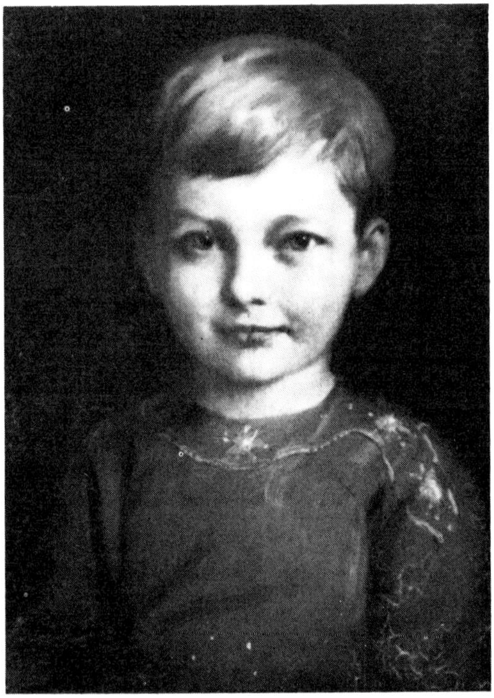

Portrait of Wyon Stansfeld (1913)

Portrait of Wyon Stansfeld

15 × 11¼ (38.3 × 28.5 cms)
Prov: The sitter; James Stansfeld, his son.
Exh. RA 1913 (656)

A Quiet Interval

26 × 21½ (66.2 × 54.7 cms)
Prov: Sold by the artist, Christie's November 24, 1924 (lot 26) for the benefit of the Artist's Benevolent Institution. Bt. Grose £2 2s.
Exh. AAG, 1913 (66)

Mrs. Meakins

Prov: Untraced
Exh. RA 1914 (259)

'She is pretty to walk with, witty to talk with, and pleasant to think on'

Prov: Untraced
Exh. AAG, 1914 (181)

'Fresh as a Flower just blown'

Prov: Untraced
Exh. AAG, 1914 (278)

A Portrait

Prov: Untraced
Exh. AAG, 1914 (355)

Anthony (Tony) Stansfeld

15 × 12 (38 × 30.5 cms) Painted *c.* 1914
Prov: The sitter; Jane Feather, his niece.

Anthony Ralph Woolridge Stansfeld, born 1913; grandson of the artist. Writes under the name Dane Chandos, and is a Professor of Art at Mercer University, Macon, Georgia.

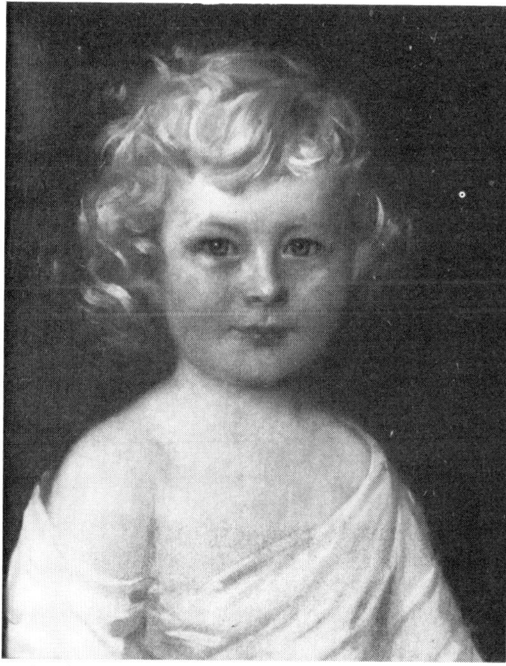

Anthony Stansfeld (1914)

Audrey

24 × 20 (61 × 51 cms)
Prov: Sold Christie's July 16, 1915 bt. Sanger £3.3s.; sold Parke-Bernet, New York, March 5, 1942 by the French Gallery, London, bt. Patterson

Head and shoulders of a girl with long auburn hair falling below her shoulders, wearing a white bodice.

Elsie Pitt

20 × 16 (51 × 40.6 cms) s. & d. 1915
Prov: The sitter, (Mrs. Woolner)

Elsie, grand-daughter of the artist, (born 1897) was married in 1923 to Christopher Woolner, a grandson of Thomas Woolner, the pre-Raphaelite sculptor. She later used the name Anne rather than Elsie. (Plate p. 114)

Diana Mills

14 × 12 (35.7 × 30.5 cms) s. & d. 1915
Prov: The sitter; Mrs. Olivia Stewart-Smith, her daughter.

Diana Mills, (born June, 1914) a grand-daughter of the artist, married John Barstow on October 24, 1934. (Plate p. 109)

Granville Mills

24 × 20 (61 × 51 cms) Dated 1915
Prov: The sitter; Yarnton Mills, Esq., his son.

William Robert Granville Mills (1858–1916) was the son of the Rev. William Yarnton Mills, of Miserden, Glos and Maria Hurst, of Horsham Park. He was an engineer in India, and married Cordelia Roberts, by whom he had five children.

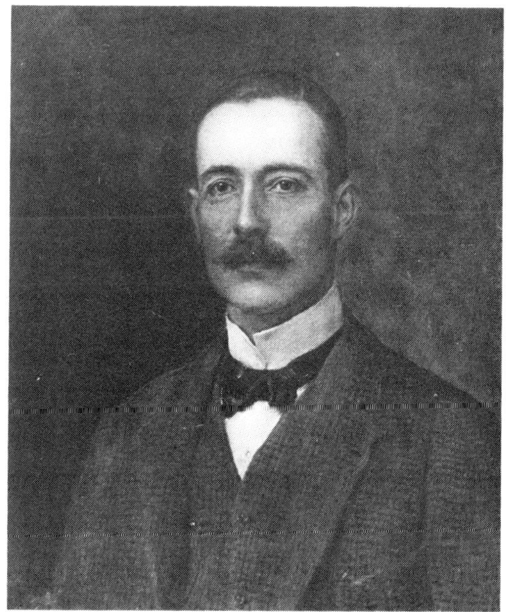

Granville Mills (1915)

Elizabeth Stansfeld

16 × 12 (41 × 30.5 cms) Painted 1916
Prov: The sitter; Mrs. Jane Feather, her daughter.

Elizabeth Stansfeld, (born June 1905) a grand-daughter of the artist, married Kenneth Burt, in 1936. This portrait was painted 1916.

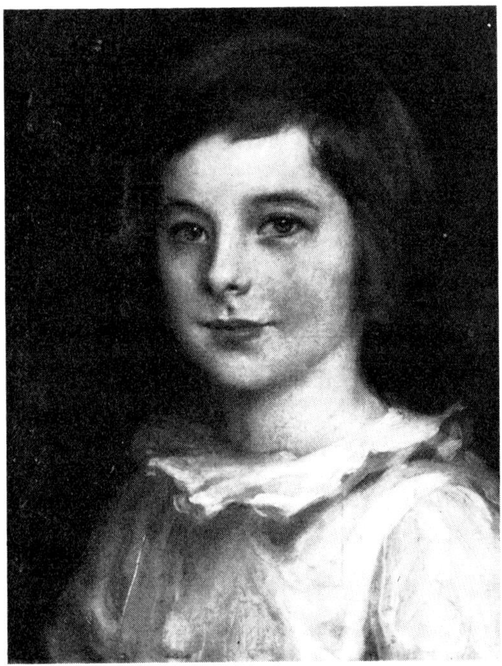

Elizabeth Stansfeld (1916)

Mrs. John Hanson Walker

Prov: Untraced
Exh. RA 1917 (466)

W. R. G. Mills

20 × 20 (51 × 51 cms)
Prov: Yarnton Mills, Esq.; brother of the sitter.

This is a posthumous portait of William Robert Granville Mills (Billy) 1897–1917, who was killed in action, Ypres Salient, February 1917 aged 19. Billy Mills was the son of Granville Mills (q.v. 1915) and his wife Cordelia. He was a scholar of Winchester College (1911–15) and elected to the Senior Classical Scholarship at Christ Church, Oxford in 1915. He was given a Commission in the Royal Field Artillery in February 1916. (Plate p. 117)

Susan Romer

15 × 13 (38.2 × 33 cms) s. & d. 1917
Prov: The sitter (Mrs. Palmer)

Susan, the painter's grand-daughter, born May 23, 1908 was eleven at the time this portrait was painted. She married George Palmer on December 20, 1935.

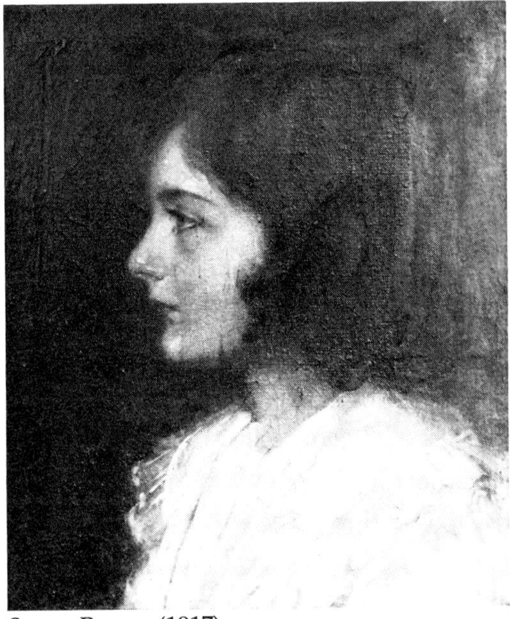

Susan Romer (1917)

Captain E. G. Davidson, M.C.

44 × 34 (111.7 × 86.5 cms)
Prov: Mrs. Scott (sitter's mother); Breynton Mills, her nephew; Mrs. Breynton Mills

This is a posthumous portrait of Captain 'Ted' Davidson, and was painted from a photograph. 'Ted' Davidson was the only surviving child of Constance (Mills) and Alfred Davidson, her first husband. Captain Davidson entered the 19th Hussars from Sandhurst, and won his M.C. in the retreat from Mons. He was several times mentioned in despatches. He was killed in April 1918. (Plate p. 116)

The Rev. Aubrey Leake

21¼ × 17¾ (51.3 × 45.2 cms) Painted *c* 1918
Prov: The sitter; Miss Marjorie Walker, his niece.

Head and shoulders. The sitter wears clerical dress.

The Rev. Aubrey Leake was the brother-in-law of Frederick Walker, the artist's eldest son. When Frederick and his wife died, he brought up their two daughters, Marjorie and Dorothy.

Ursula Reiss

Prov: Untraced
Exh. RA 1918 (490)

Ursula was the daughter of Charles Reiss and his wife Esmé MacEwan. They lived in Chester Square. Charles Reiss was born 1880, therefore Ursula was a young girl at the time she was painted.

Tony Stansfeld

16 × 13½ (40.7 × 34.3 cms) Painted *c.* 1919
Prov: The sitter

Tony Stansfeld is the artist's grandson. (See 1914). (Plate p. 115)

Diana Mills

31 × 25½ (78.7 × 64.7 cms) Painted 1919
Prov: The sitter; Mrs. Olivia Stewart-Smith, her daughter.

This is a portrait of the artist's grand-daughter, born 1914 (see also 1915). (Colour Plate 14)

Sissie Pitt

Pastel. 26 × 22 (66.2 × 56 cms) Painted *c.* 1920
Prov: By descent to Mrs. Bowdler, grand-daughter of the sitter.

Marion Pitt, (née Walker) was the artist's eldest daughter, born 1870. See Walker family tree. (Plate p. 118)

Duncan Simonds

Pastel. 15 × 12 (38.2 × 30.5 cms) Painted 1921
Prov: Sitter to his brother, Kenneth Simonds, Esq.

Duncan Simonds was born June 1, 1917 and is a grandson of Mrs. John Hill (see 1879).

Mrs. Matilda Hurst

26 × 22 (66.2 × 56 cms) s. & d. 1921
Prov: By descent to Robert Hurst, great-grandson of the sitter.

Matilda Jane Hurst (1836–1926) was the daughter of James Scott, a London solicitor. Her husband, Robert Hurst of Horsham Park, whom she married in 1859 was a member of the Middle Temple, and sat as Liberal M.P. for Horsham 1865–74, when the seat was abolished. Mrs. Hurst was an accomplished hostess, and had five children. Her second son Reginald ran his estate in Gloucestershire after distinguishing himself in the 1914–1918 war, and her third son, Sir Cecil Hurst was President of the Court of International Justice at the Hague (1929–1939). Her eldest son

Robert ('Bob') died young of T.B. and her two daughters remained unmarried. (Plate p. 119)

Mrs. Lidderdale

26 × 22 (66 × 56 cms) s. & d. 1922 Canvas inscribed on the reverse 'a present to dear Maud from her father and mother on her birthday, May 19th, 1922.'

Half-length, showing the subject in profile and wearing her hair piled on her head. Green dress with v-neck.

Maud, (who later in life preferred the name 'Jill') was the painter's youngest daughter, born 1887. See Walker family tree.

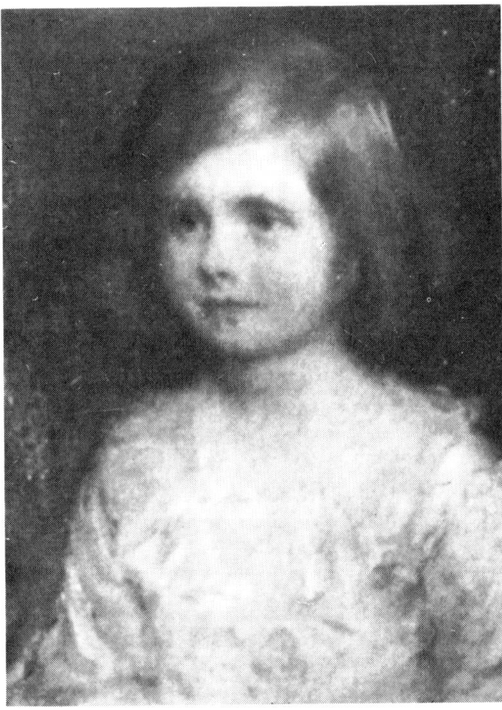

Pamela Lidderdale (1922)

Pamela Lidderdale

15 × 12 (38.3 × 30.5 cms) Painted 1922. Canvas inscribed on the reverse, 'painted by John Hanson Walker'.

Prov: The sitter (Mrs. Pamela Smith)

This portrait is of the artist's grand-daughter, born December, 1917. See 'Mrs Lidderdale' 1922.

Mrs. John Hanson Walker

S. & d. 1923
Prov: Untraced

Only a photograph (in the possession of Mrs. Pamela Smith) exists of this portrait. (Plate p. 113)

Philippa Savery

22 × 18 (56 × 45.8 cms) s. & d. 1924
Prov: The sitter; Mrs. Anne Packham, her niece.

Miss Savery is the daughter of Nell, Fanny Hanson Walker's youngest sister. A resident of Bath, for many years she kept an antique shop there, in Abbey Street. She was about 15 when this portrait was painted. (Plate p. 121)

Un-dated Paintings

The Green Dress

21½ × 17½ (54.5 × 44.5 cms)
Prov: Sold by the artist Christie's November 24, 1924 (lot 26) for the benefit of the Artists General Benevolent Institution. Bt. Grose £2.2s.

The Red Sash

21½ ×17½ (54.5 × 44.5 cms)
Prov: Sold by the artist Christie's November 24, 1924 (lot 27) for the benefit of the Artists General Benevolent Institution. Bt. Moore £3.3s.

NOTES

Chapter 1.

1. Mrs Russell Barrington, *Life, Letters and Work of Frederick Leighton* 1906 Vol. I p. 251
2. Alice Corkran, *Lord Leighton* 1904 p. 40
3. Edgcumbe Staley, *Lord Leighton of Stretton* 1906 p. 189
4. Staley, *Leighton* p. 189
5. Corkran, *Leighton* p. 40
6. Barrington, *Leighton* Vol. II p. 62
7. Tate Gallery: *Illustrated Catalogue of Acquisitions 1978–80* (Tate Gallery Publications, London 1981)
8. Barrington, *Leighton* Vol. II p. 66
9. Stephen Jones, *National Art Collection Fund Review 1985* p. 95
10. Barrington, *Leighton* Vol. II p. 88
11. Barrington, *Leighton* Vol. II p. 87
12. Barrington, *Leighton* Vol. II p. 85
13. Corkran, *Leighton* p. 40
14. Barrington, *Leighton* Vol. II p. 56

Chapter 2.

15. W. S. Spanton, *An Art Student and his teachers in the Sixties* 1927 p. 15
16. W. P. Frith, *Autobiography and Reminiscences* 1888 p. 56
17. Barrington, *Leighton* Vol. I p. 269
18. Barrington, *Leighton* Vol. I p. 272
19. Taken from Lady Enfield's *Diaries of Henry Greville* 1883
20. Barrington, *Leighton* Vol. I p. 270
21. Spanton, *An Art Student* p. 24
22. Estella Canziani, *Round About Three Palace Green* 1939 p. 20
23. Spanton, *An Art Student* p. 50
24. Canziani, *Three Palace Green* p. 70
25. Spanton, *An Art Student* p. 45
26. Canziani, *Three Palace Green* p. 70
27. Canziani, *Three Palace Green* p. 21
28. Staley, *Leighton* p. 189
29. Corkran, *Leighton* p. 46
30. Barrington, *Leighton* Vol. I p. 270
31. Barrington, *Leighton* Vol. I p. 270
32. Barrington, *Leighton* Vol. I p. 274
33. Barrington, *Leighton* Vol. II p. 42

Chapter 3.

34. Corkran, *Leighton* p. 41
35. Barrington, *Leighton* Vol. I p. 270

36. Barrington, *Leighton* Vol. I p. 271
37. Barrington, *Leighton* Vol. I p. 272
38. Barrington, *Leighton* Vol. I p. 272
39. Barrington, *Leighton* Vol. I p. 269
40. *Survey of London*, Vol. XXXVII (North Kensington) 1973 p. 140
41. Letter in the possession of Mrs. Pamela Smith
42. Esmé Gordon, *The Royal Scottish Academy 1826–76* 1976 p. 79
43. *The Letters of Charles Dickens* (Pilgrim Edition Vol. III p. 4) quoted by permission of the Oxford University Press
44. Frith, *Autobiography* p. 458
45. *Art Union* Vol. 7 (1845) p. 48
46. *Art Journal* (1860) p. 214
47. *Art Journal* (1857) pp. 62–3
48. Barrington, *Leighton* Vol. I p. 271
49. Barrington, *Leighton* Vol. I p. 271
50. Barrington, *Leighton* Vol. I p. 273

Chapter 4.

51. Corkran, *Leighton* p. 42
52. Barrington, *Leighton* Vol. I p. 273
53. Information kindly supplied by Hugh Marles, from his draft catalogue entry for the forthcoming *Tate Gallery Collection*.
54. Previously unpublished letter written to Mrs. Russell Barrington by John Hanson Walker, by kind permission of Leighton House
55. Spanton, *an Art Student* p. 39
56. Canziani, *Three Palace Green* p. 30
57. Information taken from Christopher Wood's *Olympian Dreamers* 1983
58. Letter in possession of Kensington and Chelsea Public Library, (no. 12460) not previously published.
59. Taken from the unpublished memoirs of the artist's son, Jolliffe Walker.
60. Barrington, *Leighton* Vol. I p. 273
61. Letter in the possession of Mr. James Stansfeld, not previously published.
62. Barrington, *Leighton* Vol. I p. 274
63. Barrington, *Leighton* Vol. I p. 274
64. Barrington, *Leighton* Vol. I p. 274
65. Letter in the possession of Mr. James Stansfeld, not previously published.
66. Barrington, *Leighton* Vol. I p. 275
67. *Art Journal* (1881) p. 193
68. *Times* Review of the Royal Academy May 4, 1872
69. L. & R. Ormond, *Lord Leighton* 1975 p. 18
70. David Piper, *The English Face* 1957 p. 310
71. Letter, previously unpublished, in the possession of Mr. J. Stansfeld.
72. Information taken from William Gaunt's *The Impressionists* 1970
73. *Survey of London* Vol. XLII 1986 p. 248

Chapter 5.

74. By kind permission of the Chetham Library, Manchester
75. By kind permission of the Chetham Library, Manchester
76. By kind permission of the Chetham Library, Manchester
77. Letter, previously unpublished, in the possession of Mr. J. Stansfeld

78. *Art Journal* (1877) p. 246
79. Barrington, *Leighton* Vol. I p. 276
80. Taken from M. H. Spielman, *Millais and his Works* 1898
81. J. G. Millais, *Life and Letters of Sir John Everett Millais* 1899 Vol. II p. 189
82. Millais, *Life of Millais* Vol. II p. 189
83. *Times* Review of the Royal Academy May 4, 1878
84. *Magazine of Art* (1878) p. 136
85. *Athenaeum* (1878) p. 575
86. *Magazine of Art* (1878) p. 136
87. *Society Portraits 1850–1939* (1985) Colnaghi Exhibition catalogue p. 46
88. *Times* Obituary for Tom Taylor, July 13, 1880
89. *Times* Review of the Royal Academy May 8, 1879
90. *Art Journal* (1879) p. 128
91. Information from two sources: Simon Wilson's Tate Gallery lecture on the Pre-Raphaelite Rebellion given 1984 and Christopher Wood's *Olympian Dreamers*
92. *Times* Review of the Royal Academy, May 3, 1880

Chapter 6.

93. From the unpublished Memoirs of Jolliffe Walker
94. Barrington, *Leighton* Vol. II p. 6
95. Mary Gladstone, *Diaries and Letters* (1930) p. 242–3
96. Canziani, *Three Palace Green* p. 59
97. *Survey of London* Vol. XXXVII p. 140
98. Information from three sources: *Survey of London* Vol. XXXVII; Ormond, *Leighton*; and Canziani, *Three Palace Green*
99. *Strand Magazine* (1896) Vol. IV p. 126
100. Information taken from Canziani, *Three Palace Green* p. 85
101. Barrington, *Leighton* Vol. I p. 276
102. Barrington, *Leighton* Vol. I p. 43
103. Information taken from *Chambers Encyclopaedia* 1895
104. Simon Wilson, *British Art from Holbein to the Present Day* 1979 p. 112
105. John Ruskin, *Fors Clavigera* 1878
106. Ormond, *Leighton* p. 85
107. Royal Archives RAPP Vic l/3 23, by kind permission of H.M. the Queen
108. Barrington, *Leighton* Vol. II p. 267
109. Barrington, *Leighton* Vol. II p. 268
110. Canziani, *Three Palace Green* p. 30
111. Ormond, *Leighton* p. 119
112. *Who Was Who* 1897

Chapter 7.

113. David Franks, *The New York Directory* 1886/7
114. Edith Wharton, *A Backward Glance* 1972 p. 21
115. *History of the Carnegie Mansion* Cooper-Hewitt Museum, New York
116. Barrington, *Leighton* Vol. I p. 277
117. *National Cyclopaedia of American Biography* 1898 Vol. VIII p. 390
118. *Dictionary of American Biography* Vol. XXI Supplement I, 1944
119. Information given by the Cincinnati Historical Society
120. *Arts and Decoration* (U.S.A.) Vol. 35 June 1931 pp. 18–21

Chapter 8.

121. Information taken from Ormond, *Leighton* and Jeremy Maas, *Victorian Painters* 1978
122. Wilson, *British Art* p. 115
123. Ormond, *Leighton* p. 106
124. Piper, *The English Face* p. 302
125. Letter quoted by kind permission of Westminster City Libraries Archive Dept. (Ref. WCL 365)
126. Information taken from Mary Bennett's *Catalogue of the Millais Exhibition*, Walker Art Gallery, Liverpool 1967
127. Ethel Grimwood, *My three years in Manipur* 1891
128. *Art Journal* (1892) p. 188
129. Information kindly supplied by Hugh Marles, who wrote the draft catalogue entry for the forthcoming *Tate Gallery Collection*
130. Taken from two sources: Ormond, *Leighton* p. 144 and Barrington, *Leighton* Vol. II p. 334
131. Taken from various sources, mainly Barrington, *Leighton*; William Gaunt, *Victorian Olympus* 1952; and Ormond, *Leighton*
132. Corkran, *Leighton* p. 41
133. *Magazine of Art* (1899) p. 534
134. *Art Journal* (1897) p. 58
135. Letter quoted by kind permission of the Royal Academy (Ref. LEI 1/44)
136. Mary Bennett, *Catalogue of Millais Exhibition* Liverpool 1967
137. *Art Journal* (1896) p. 319
138. *Art Journal* (1897) p. 320
139. Information taken from Wilson, *British Art*
140. Information taken from Ormond, *Leighton*
141. Piper, *The English Face* p. 294
142. Taken from J. Maas, *Victorian Painters*
143. Taken from F. Huggett, *Victorian England as Seen by Punch* 1978

Chapter 9.

144. Marghanita Laski in *Edwardian England* (ed. Nowell-Smith) 1964
145. *Chambers Encyclopaedia* 1895
146. Letters, previously unpublished, by kind permission of J. Stansfeld
147. Card, previously unpublished, by kind permission of J. Stansfeld.
148. Wilfred Blunt, *Guide to the Watts Gallery* 1980
149. Canziani, *Three Palace Green* p. 43
150. Information from Christie's sales records, Lloyds Bank Plc and John Russell in *Edwardian England*
151. Canziani, *Three Palace Green* p. 59
152. Christie's sales catalogues and Lloyds Bank Plc.
153. Millais, *Life and Letters of Sir J. E. Millais* Vol. II p. 120
154. Letters, previously unpublished, by kind permission of Leighton House
155. Piper, *The English Face* p. 329
156. Spanton, *An Art Student* p. 59.

BIBLIOGRAPHY

ANON, *Sketch of the Official Career of Sir Ashley Eden*, Kelly Prosono Dey, Calcutta, 1877
BARRINGTON, Mrs. Russell, *Life Letters and Work of Frederic Leighton*, 2 vols, George Allen, London, 1906
CANZIANI, Estella, *Round About Three Palace Green*, Methuen, London, 1939
CORKRAN, Alice, *Lord Leighton*, Methuen, London, 1904
ENFIELD, Viscountess, *Leaves from the Diary of Henry Greville*, Smith Elder, London 1883
FRITH, W. P., *Autobiography and Reminiscences*, Richard Bentley, London, 1888
GAUNT, William, *The Impressionists*, Thames & Hudson, London, 1970
GAUNT, William, *Victorian Olympus*, Jonathan Cape, London, 1952
GORDON, Esmé, *The Royal Scottish Academy 1826–76*, Skilton, Edinburgh, 1976
GRIMWOOD, Ethel St. Clair, *My three years in Manipur*, Richard Bailey, London, 1891
HILLIER, Bevis, *The Style of the Century 1900–1980*, The Herbert Press, London, 1982
HOUSE, M; STOREY, G; TILLOTSON, K, *The Letters of Charles Dickens*, (Pilgrim Edition) Clarendon Press, Oxford, 1974
HUGGETT, Frank, *Victorian England as Seen by Punch*, Sidgewick & Jackson, London, 1978
HUTCHISON, Sidney, *History of the Royal Academy 1768–1968*, Chapman & Hall, London, 1968
LAVER, James, *A Concise History of Costume*, Thames & Hudson, London, 1969
MAAS, Jeremy, *Victorian Painters*, Barrie & Jenkins, London, 1978
MALLALIEU, H. L., *Dictionary of British Water Colour Artists up to 1920*, Antique Collectors Club, Woodbridge, Suffolk, 1976
MILLAIS, J. G., *Life & Letters of Sir John Everett Millais*, (2 vols), Methuen, London, 1899
NOWELL-SMITH, Simon, *Edwardian England*, Oxford University Press, 1964
ORMOND, L. & R., *Lord Leighton*, Yale University Press, New Haven and London, 1975
PERUGINI, M. E., *Victorian Days & Ways*, Jarrolds, Norwich, 1932
PIPER, David, *The English Face*, Thames & Hudson, London, 1957
RHYS, Ernest, *Lord Leighton, His Life and Work*, Bell, London, 1895
SPANTON, W.S., *An Art Student and his Teachers in the Sixties*, Robert Scott, London, 1927
SPIELMANN, M. H., *Millais and his Works*, William Blackwood & Sons, London, 1898
STALEY, Edgcumbe, *Lord Leighton of Stretton*, Walter Scott Publishing Co., London, 1906
WESTWATER, Martha, *The Wilson Sisters*, Ohio University Press, 1984
WHARTON, Edith, *A Backward Glance*, Constable, London, 1972
WILSON, Simon, *British Art from Holbein to the Present Day*, Tate Gallery & Bodley Head, London, 1979
WOOD, Christopher, *Olympian Dreamers*, Constable, London, 1983
WOOD, Christopher, *Victorian Panorama*, Faber, London, 1976
WOOD, Christopher, *Dictionary of Victorian Painters*, Antique Collectors Club, Woodbridge, Suffolk, 1978

GENERAL INDEX

References to illustrations are in bold. Entries relating to pictures and periodicals are in italics. All references to the works of John Hanson Walker are contained in the Index of Works.

INDEX OF WORKS

References to illustrations are in bold. Catalogue entries are in brackets. Illustrated catalogue entries carry brackets and an asterisk.